IMAGES
of America

ALBION AND NOBLE COUNTY

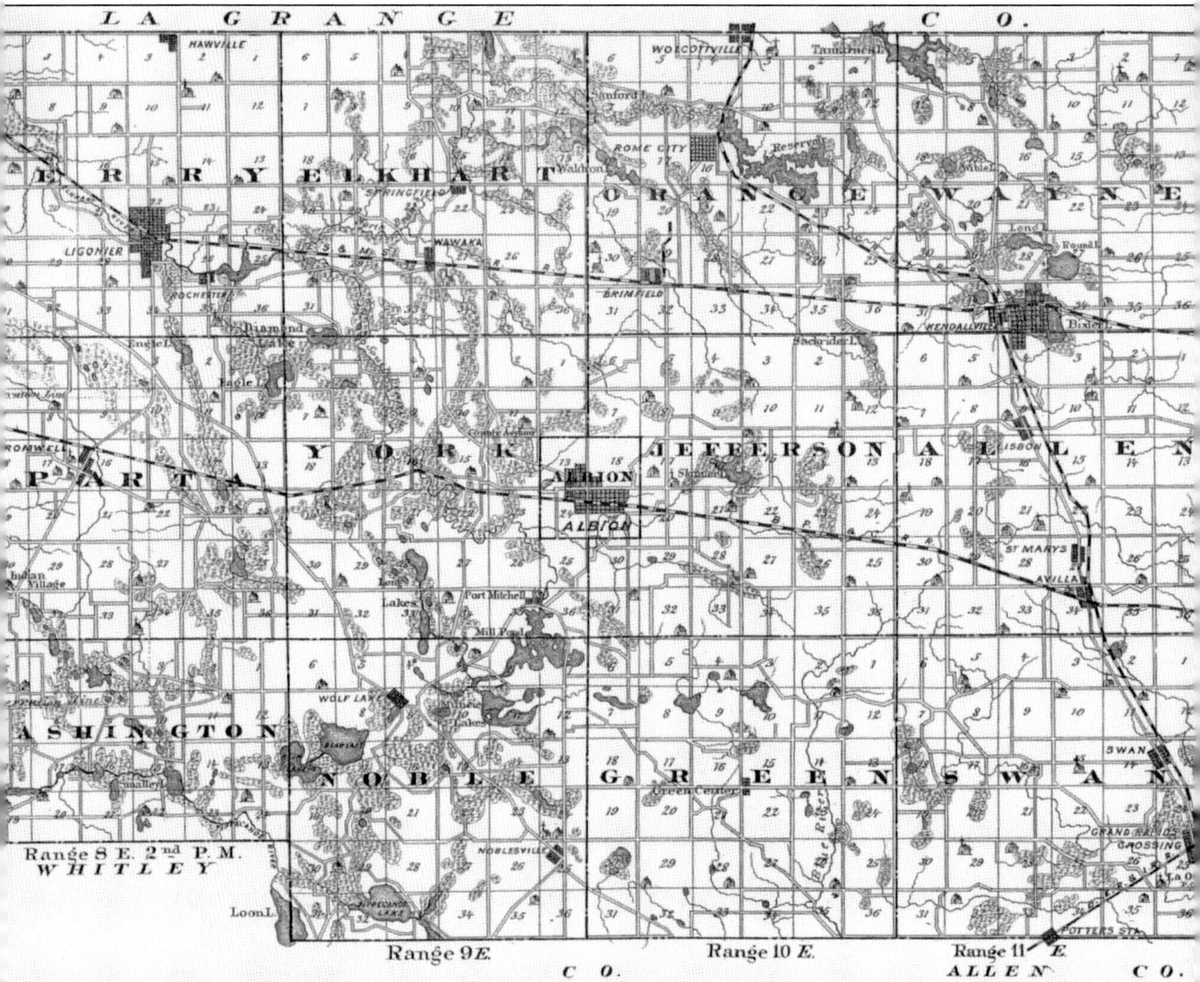

This 1876 map of Noble County shows the growth of early communities, roads, and railways, as well as the swamps and lakes that made travel so difficult. By then, Albion, in the center of the map, had earned the title of county seat. (Courtesy Noble County Historical Society.)

On the Cover: Kendallville firefighters pose with their horse-drawn apparatus around 1910. Kendallville, the only city in Noble County at the time, was protected by a pair of full-time firefighters, 17 volunteer firefighters, and two horses. Several other communities in Noble County boasted all-volunteer departments. (Courtesy Mike Mapes.)

IMAGES *of America*

ALBION AND NOBLE COUNTY

Mark R. Hunter and Emily Hunter

ARCADIA PUBLISHING

ISBN 978-1-4671-1451-6

Published by Arcadia Publishing
Charleston, South Carolina

Printed in the United States of America

Library of Congress Control Number: 2015933423

For all general information, please contact Arcadia Publishing:
Telephone 843-853-2070
Fax 843-853-0044
E-mail sales@arcadiapublishing.com
For customer service and orders:
Toll-Free 1-888-313-2665

Visit us on the Internet at www.arcadiapublishing.com

To the citizens of Albion and Noble County, especially those who share and preserve the local history of their homes and areas

Contents

Acknowledgments

A book such as this would not be possible without the assistance of people who care about, research, and preserve history. Special thanks go to the Noble County Historical Society and Old Jail Museum, the Stone's Trace Historical Museum, the Mid-America Windmill Museum, Noble County Genealogical Society, the Noble County Public Library, and the Ligonier Historical Society and Museum.

Many individuals have assisted along the way, and I apologize for anyone whom I might miss. They include, but are not limited to, the following: Noble County historian Sarah Knopp, Mike Mapes, Joy LeCount, Bill Shultz, Janet Sweeney, Tom Ryan, Lori Gagen, former Noble County librarian Linda Shultz, Albion town manager Beth Shellman, Judy Richter, Barry Mooney, Marcia Garrett, Ellen McBride, Helen Swanson, Lori Gagen, Tom Ryan, Carla Fiandt, and Vern Christlieb.

Special thanks also go to Maggie Bullwinkel and William Wallace of Arcadia Publishing, who must be particularly patient individuals.

Where noted, the images in this volume appear courtesy of the Noble County Historical Society (NCHS) and the Stone's Trace Historical Society (STHS). The Noble County Historical Society has a collection of historic artifacts, photographs, and documents that are kept at the Old Jail Museum, at 215 West Main Street in Albion. The Gothic Revival building was constructed in 1876 as the Noble County Jail, housing both inmates and the sheriff's family until a new jail was built in 1965. It and the 1888 Noble County Courthouse a block away are considered architectural gems in the center of Noble County.

INTRODUCTION

When Indiana was established in 1816, Noble County was forest and swampland, inhabited by Pottawatomie and Miami tribes. Receding glaciers had gouged out many of the area's lakes (called kettle lakes) and deposited rich soil as well as bogs of muck and peat. Noble County now has 117 lakes that were once connected by swamps that covered more than 10 percent of the land.

As part of an agreement with the local Native Americans, the federal government put up a brick residence/council house for Chief Wawaasaa, between 1816 and 1821. The building was destroyed by what was most likely a tornado. After the local tribes moved west, settlers repurposed the fallen bricks to use in constructing their home chimneys.

In April 1827, Joel Bristol and his family became the first recorded white settlers in Noble County. But they may not have been the first white people to see the area. Another settler later found a stone with an engraving that was carved by Andrew Clinton: "I was taken prisoner bey the Indians in 1776."

The area was part of Allen County, having previously been in regions attached to first Randolph County, then Knox County. On March 1, 1836, just eight years after the Bristols set up a way station along the Fort Wayne–Goshen Road, Noble County was officially organized. By then, the new population had already reached about 2,000.

Some say Noble County was named after Noah Noble, Indiana governor from 1831 to 1837. However, historical documents indicate that the name came from his brother James, who served as Indiana's first US senator from 1816 until he passed away in 1831.

Many settlers followed the Fort Wayne–Goshen Trail through the western part of the county. That would later become part of the first transcontinental road, the Lincoln Highway—the first national memorial to Abraham Lincoln. A 1919 Army convoy trip over that road inspired future president Dwight Eisenhower to champion a national interstate highway system.

With most of the population in the west, it made sense to place the county seat along the future Lincoln Highway. One of the three men appointed to settle the county seat's "permanent" fate was, as fate would have it, a commissioner named George Fate.

The location chosen was Sparta, in the west central part of Noble County. One citizen even allowed his home to be used as the first courthouse, but the seat of government did not stay there for long. In 1837, it was relocated to Augusta, about five miles straight east.

Citizens in Augusta, though small in numbers, were quite open to the idea. In fact, just as a Sparta resident offered up his home as a courthouse, an Augusta property owner actually built a courthouse on his own land and presented it to county officials in 1840. The first taxpayer-funded building was a primitive log jail. Over the next few years, Augusta developed, gaining two hotels, stores, mills, factories, and several attorneys. A fire destroyed the courthouse in early 1843. Although the remains of the original jail's cells remained as late as 1882, most of the surrounding land became the Augusta Hills Golf Course before being turned over for farmland.

Port Mitchell, less than three miles south of the county's center, fought for and got the designation of county seat in 1844. Thanks to a dam, the town had the advantage of waterpower and soon boomed with woolen mills, sawmills, and flouring mills. Government buildings were constructed, and Port Mitchell was to be the final move—until the state legislature decided two years later to give the people of Noble County a final vote.

A spirited debate resulted over where to place the Noble County seat, with speeches and even a campaign song composed as towns vied for the honor. The first election led to a runoff in 1846, and the final vote resulted in none of the existing towns winning. Instead, the county seat would go—this time permanently, for real—to "the Center."

The loss of the county seat, along with the collapse of a dam used to power mills, marked the end of Port Mitchell's business interests.

The new county seat took its name from the hometown of one of the commissioners appointed to name it: Albion, New York. Town records were moved there in September 1847, and in 1849 a jail was built. In 1859, arson consumed the courthouse and almost took the town with it. In 1876, the jail was replaced with a building that now houses the Noble County Old Jail Museum.

The population of the town was about 70 by 1848, and two years later it topped 250 (many of them county officials and lawyers). Since Albion was platted right at the border between two townships, one square mile was taken from each and given over to Albion Township, making that the smallest township in the United States.

Albion might have dominated as Noble County's major city, if not for the railroad. The Lake Shore & Michigan Southern Railroad was built through the northern third of Noble County in 1857, bringing sudden growth to communities like Kendallville, Brimfield, Wawaka, and Ligonier. Kendallville, at the junction of two railroad lines and the county's main road in the east, became the largest community in Noble County.

Kendallville's nearest competition, Lisbon, languished but became a station for the Underground Railroad that brought escaped slaves north. Augustus H. Whitford was the stationmaster and conductor in Lisbon.

Farther south, the Wesleyan church in LaOtto was also a station for the Underground Railroad, but that was not the only railroad to come through. While the town was founded as Simon's Corners in the 1830s, the name morphed into Simonsville. It changed again to Grand Rapids Crossing after two railroad lines (the Grand Rapids & Indiana and the Eel River) intersected there. It was not until 1875 that Noble County commissioners approved a new name: LaOtto.

Besides Kendallville, the only other city in Noble County is in the northwest corner: Ligonier is a historic Jewish community featuring one of the few surviving 19th-century synagogues in the country. By 1900, Ligonier had 300 Jewish residents and was called "Little Jerusalem," but that population later dwindled.

Railroads were more successful than the state's failed attempt in the 1830s to build a series of canals, but a dam built for the canal project created Sylvan Lake. Noble County's largest lake, the 669-acre body of water still exists decades later. In early years, the dam collapsed at least once, but was rebuilt and later reinforced.

Wildlife areas and vacation spots now dot Noble County, including the unique Black Pine Animal Sanctuary and the recreational jewel of Noble County, Chain O' Lakes State Park.

This visual history of Noble County and its seat of justice, Albion, cannot begin to cover every detail of close to two centuries of settlement and progress. Instead, this volume is meant to be a slice of life—an overview of the area's rich history.

One

Settlements and the Battle for a County Seat

Noble County is littered with former county seats that faded into small villages or vanished entirely. Many other communities that aspired to greatness became ghost towns. But getting and keeping the designation of county seat brought government buildings, officials, and, of course, lawyers. So townspeople fought for the honor, and—as a result—the seat of government has not always been at the center of the county or in its largest community.

Setting the first county seat in Sparta was a simple matter of population: almost everyone in early Noble County lived on the west side, along or near the Fort Wayne–Goshen Road. When the seat was moved three miles east to Augusta, it seemed Sparta would vanish. Then the railroad went through, and Sparta—now named Kimmell—became a major exporter of onions and other crops.

Only two miles from the center of the county, Augusta seemed to have a lock on the seat of justice. Then the courthouse burned, and Port Mitchell founders grabbed the chance to take the seat for themselves. Augusta vanished, with nothing to mark its passing except a historical marker and the Augusta Hills Golf Course, which now itself is gone.

Port Mitchell, about two miles *south* of the county's center, boasted plentiful waterpower and already had mills and a dam. It also got a courthouse, a separate building for other county offices, and a thriving business section. It seemed as if the town were set.

When the citizens got a chance to vote on the government's permanent home, democracy spoke. The election led to a runoff, and some say that the citizens of the former county seats divided their votes so that none of them won. Other communities had no better luck. Chosen instead was "the Center," where no town existed at all—just woods and hills. But that is where the government and its workers went, building a capitol from scratch. Despite efforts from other towns like Kendallville and Ligonier to get the seat moved again, it has remained in the geographical center of the county, Albion, ever since.

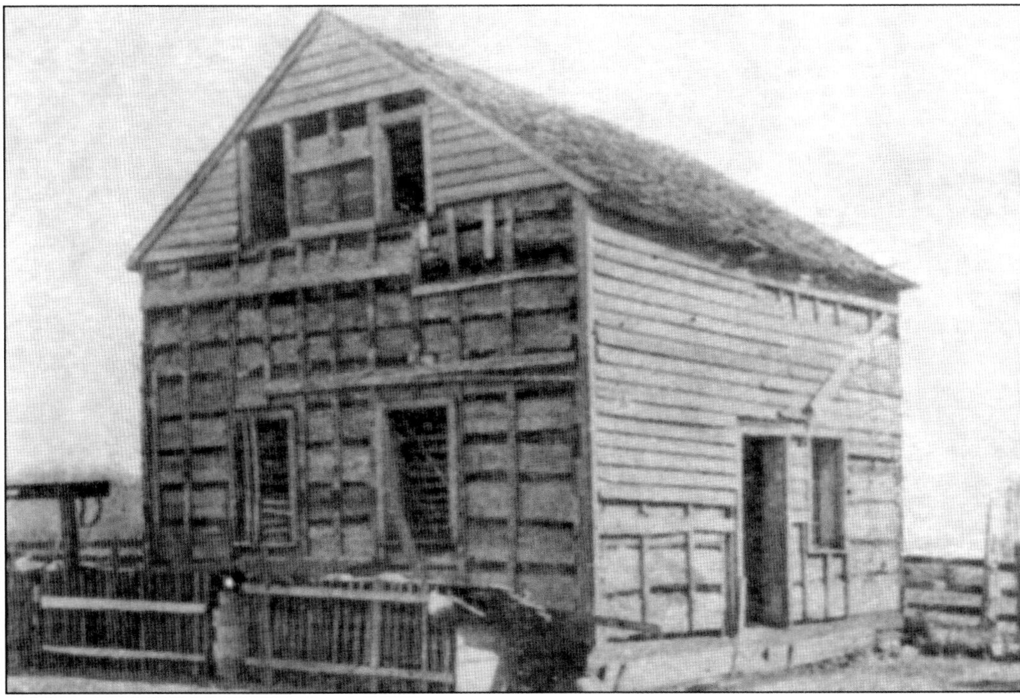

Noble County's first courthouse is engraved on an invitation to a 1908 reunion of Old Settlers of Noble County. It was built in Sparta in 1832—even though Sparta was not chosen as the first county seat until 1835. Three years after it was erected as Adam Engle's home, Judge Samuel C. Sample presided there over the county's first court. Sparta lost the county seat to Augusta in 1837. (NCHS.)

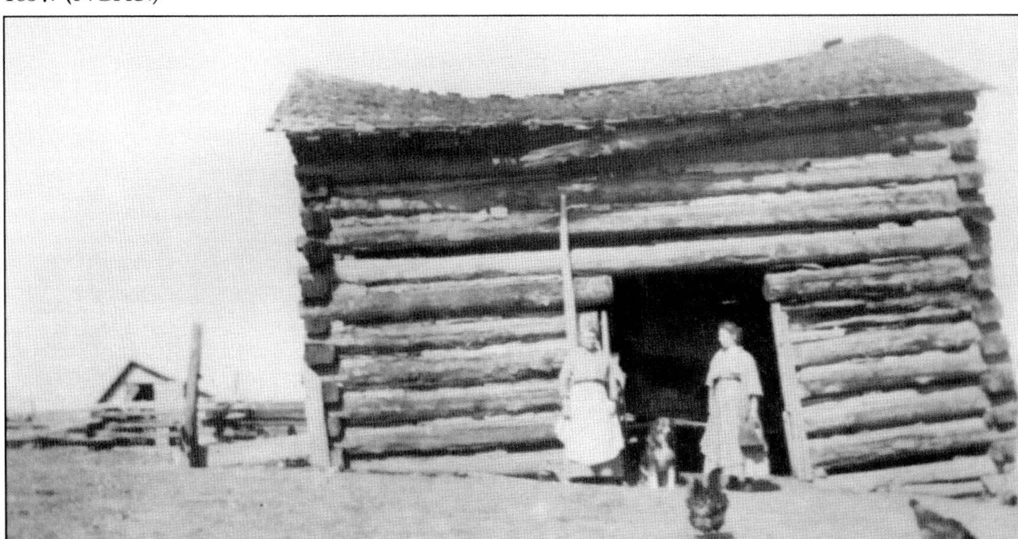

William Worman's descendants stand in front of the cabin that he built around 1855 near the future Swan, which was platted in 1870 in southeast Noble County. The wilderness in that area was broken by the construction of the Lima Plank Road, which brought some prosperity to towns like Swan. For a time, Worman co-owned a general merchandise store there with Jehu Bricker. (Courtesy Thomas W. Ryan.)

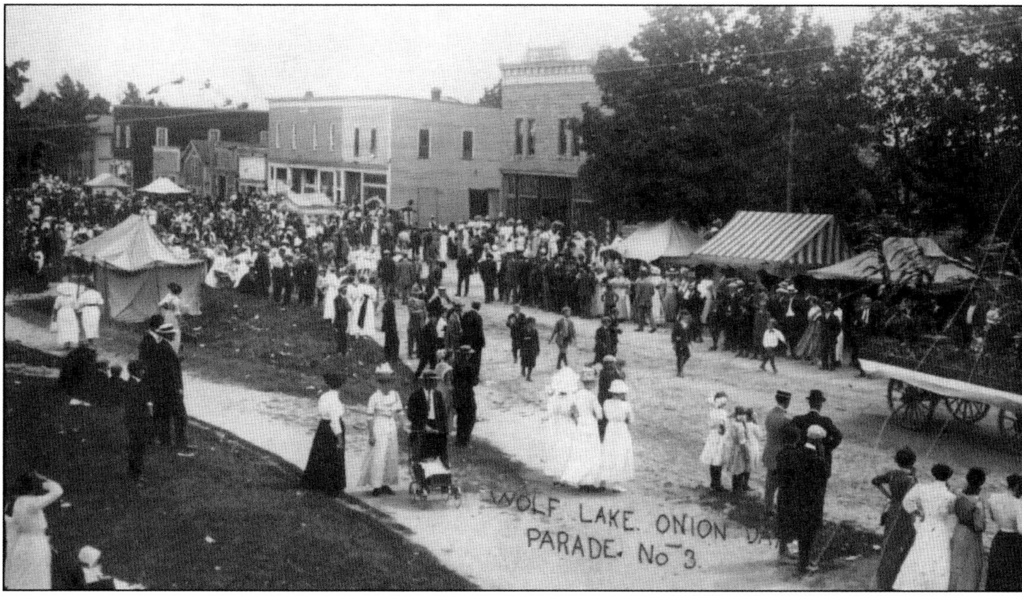

Crowds flood Wolf Lake in the early 1900s for Onion Days, an annual celebration made official in 1972. Located in southwest Noble County along what became the Lincoln Highway, Wolf Lake was founded in 1832 as Noble County's first town. The muck and black loam soil in the Wolf Lake area was ideal for growing onions, making the region one of the top onion producers in the Midwest. (NCHS.)

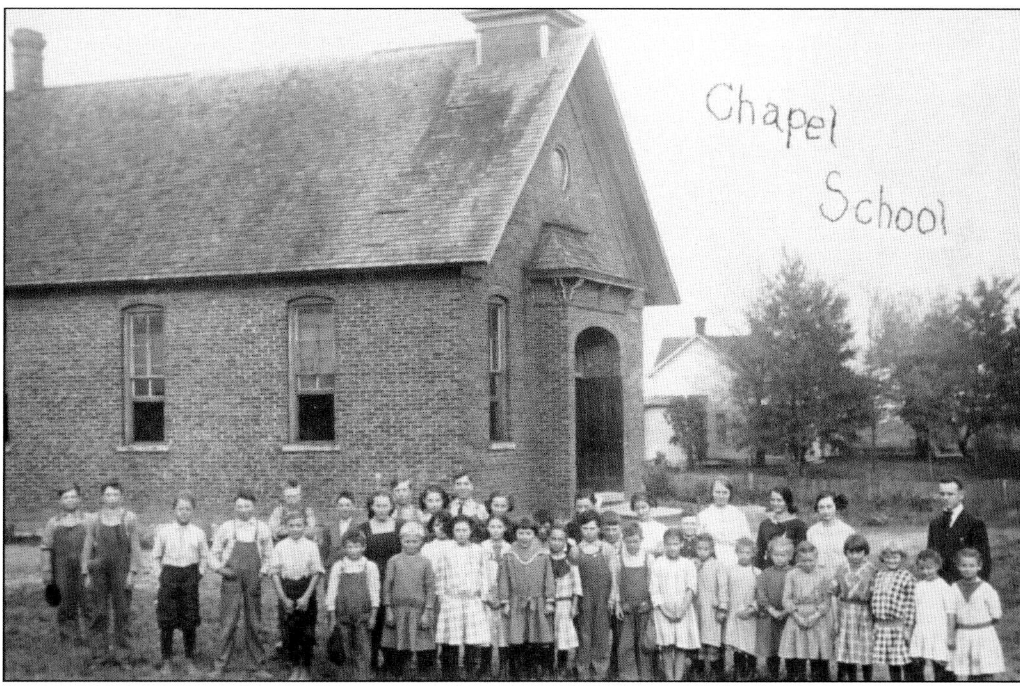

This early 1900s photograph shows students and their teacher at Chapel School, one of 11 one-room schools listed in Noble Township at around that time. The southwest Noble County Township was one of the first areas settled, and for a time had the center of population in the area. (NCHS.)

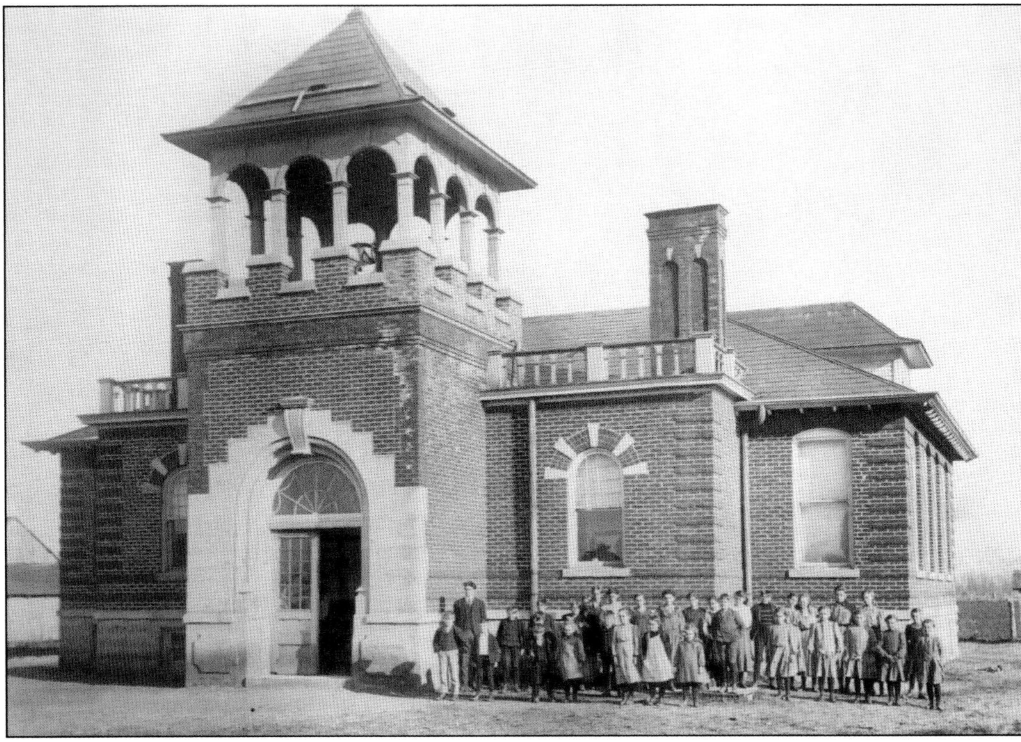

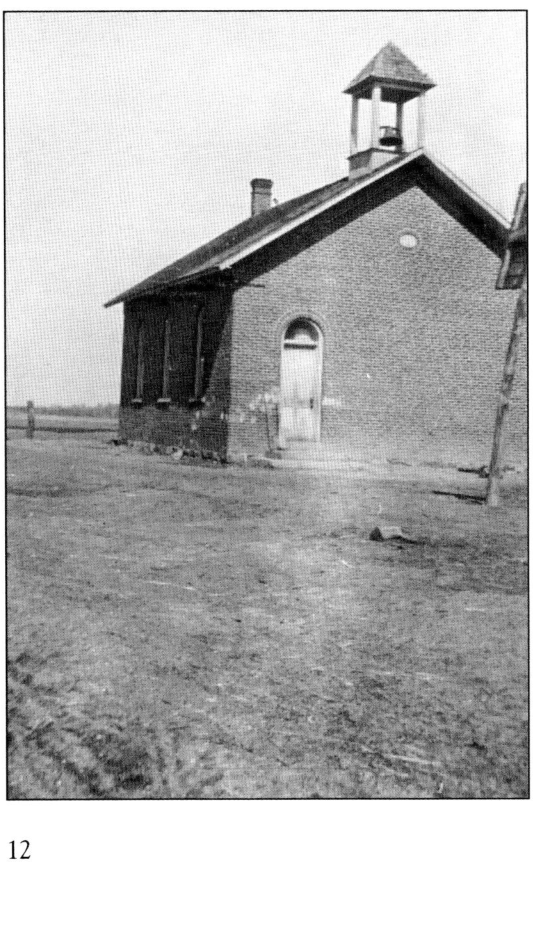

Students pose in 1911 at the school at Kimmell, formerly called Sparta. The town languished after the county seat was moved to Augusta in 1837. When the Baltimore & Ohio Railroad came through in 1876, it boomed again and for a time was the Midwest's greatest exporter of onions. The name was changed to Kimmell to honor the state representative who fought for the railroad to come through that area. (NCHS.)

The former York Center School was typical of one-room schoolhouses around Noble County, which were planned so schoolchildren did not have to walk far to reach their place of education. Most of these structures were made of brick, and over time they have been torn down or collapsed from age. A larger York Center School was later established, but it was also retired during consolidation. (NCHS.)

The second Noble County Courthouse in Albion had a relatively short life. After the first courthouse was destroyed by suspected arson on January 25, 1859, it was replaced by this brick building in 1861 at a cost of $11,000. But this structure soon proved to be too small, with total square footage about the same as today's Circuit and Superior 1 courtrooms. Twenty-six years later, it was torn down and replaced by the Romanesque Revival structure that stands today. In the photograph below, trees grow high around the building. During the demolition, government offices moved to the Albion Opera House across the street. (Both, NCHS.)

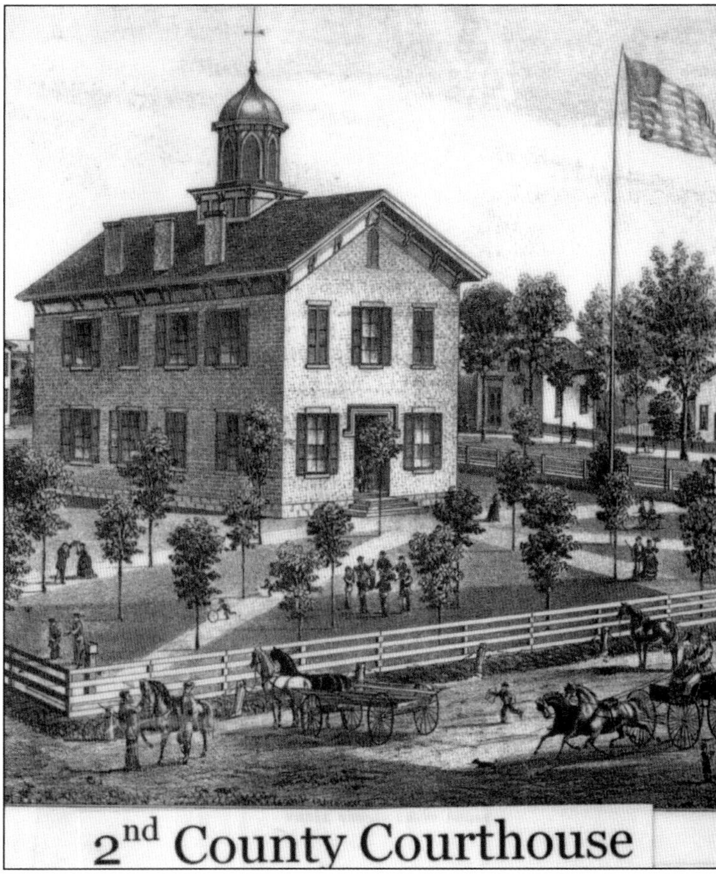

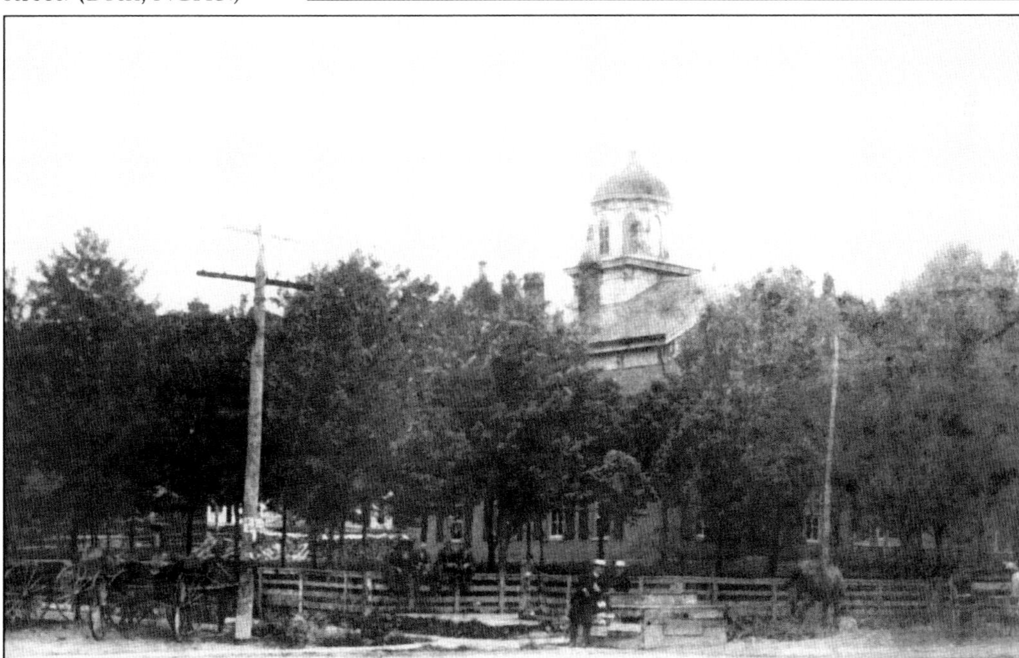

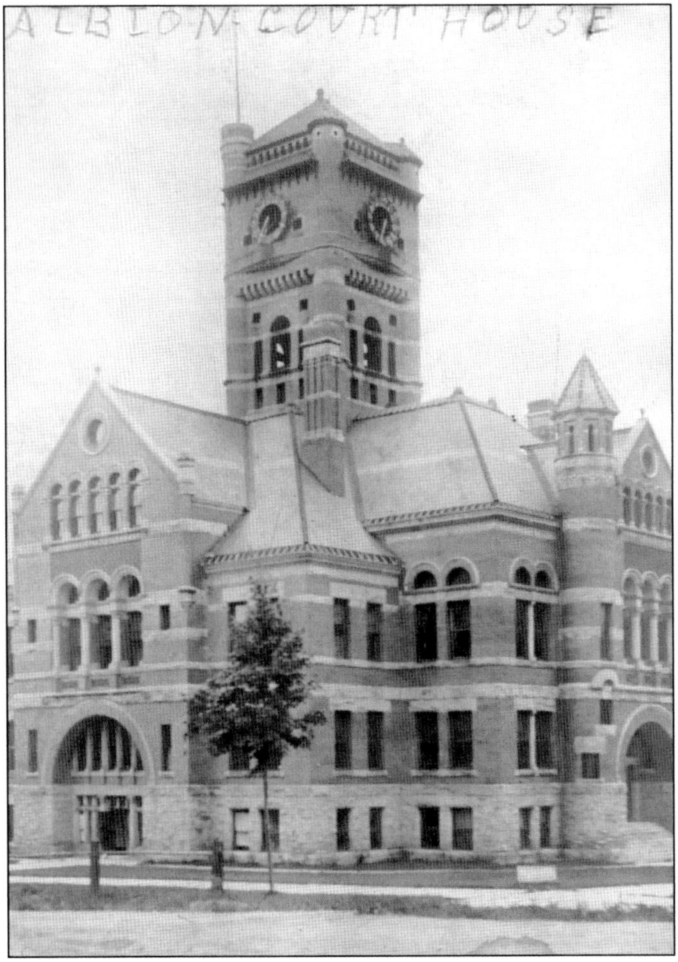

The sixth Noble County Courthouse, and the third on the same spot in Albion, was built in 1888. In 1981, it was listed in the National Register of Historic Places, as were several other Edward Oscar Fallis architectural designs around the Midwest. The cornerstone of the $114,062.41 Romanesque Revival structure was laid on May 29, 1888, and it was dedicated on October 15, 1889. (NCHS.)

An early south central Noble County structure is the backdrop for local residents. Pictured, from left to right, are Levi Jetmore of Churubusco and his unidentified wife, Jeff and Sarah Moon (Levi Jetmore's in-laws), the unidentified mother of Jeff Moon, unidentified, and an unidentified youth. The photograph was likely taken in 1844 along the Fort Wayne–Goshen Road, now US 33, which means the building may have been an inn. (NCHS.)

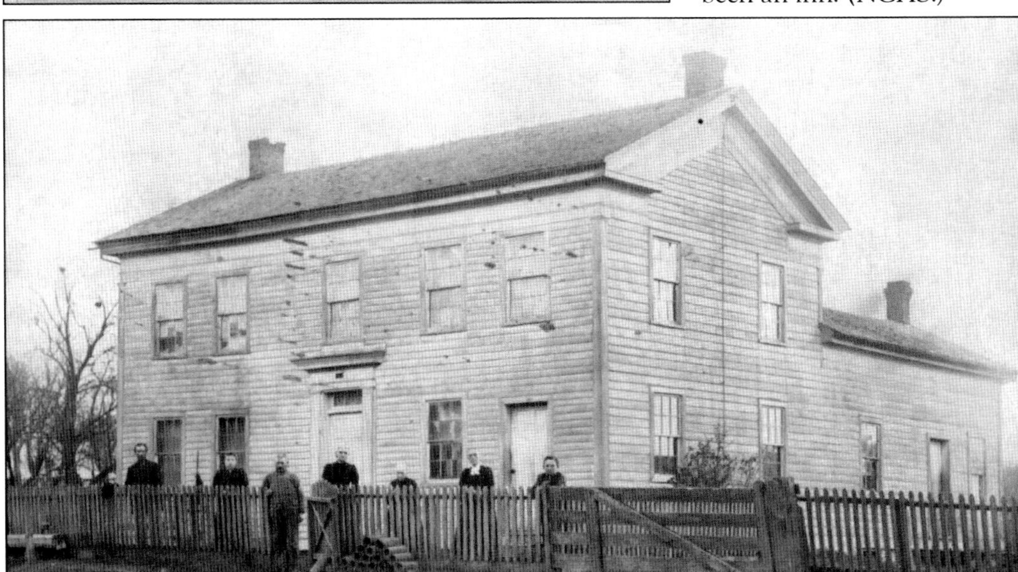

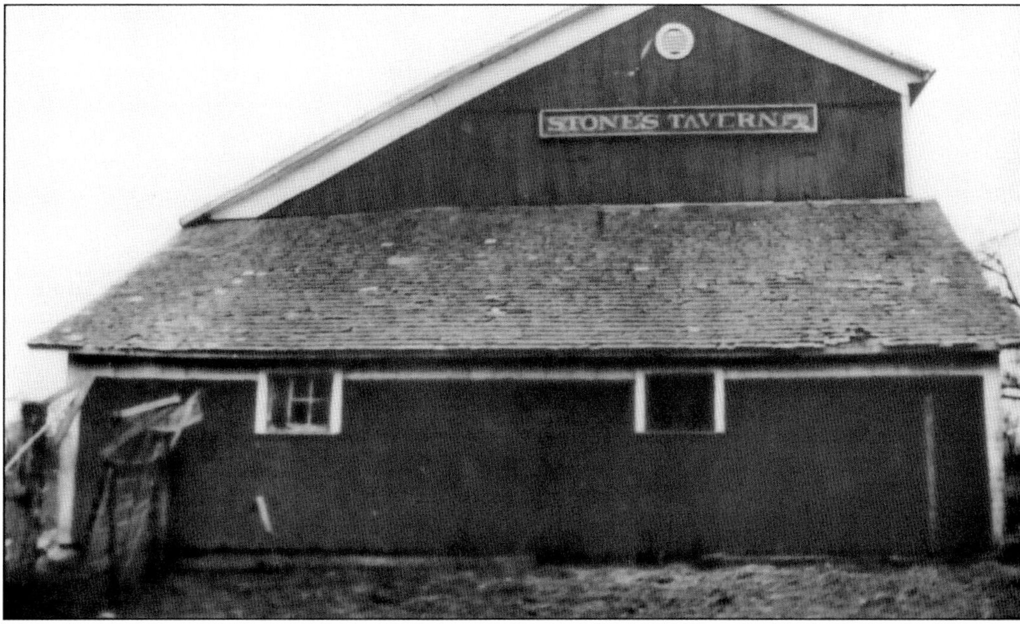

The above 1923 photograph is believed to be the oldest image of Stone's Tavern, opened by Richard Stone in 1839. Gen. "Mad" Anthony Wayne had directed the widening of an Indian trail into what is now US 33/Lincoln Highway, which brought increasing traffic to the area between Ligonier and Cromwell. Stone's Tavern became a busy landmark and was, among other things, a post office, stagecoach stop, and (in at least one memorable case) a jury room, as well as an inn. It was closed at about the time of the Civil War and then in 1964 was given to the Stone's Trace Historical Society. The photograph below was taken during remodeling. The newly renovated building was dedicated in 1966 and is now a national historic site where the annual Pioneer Festival is held. (Both, STHS.)

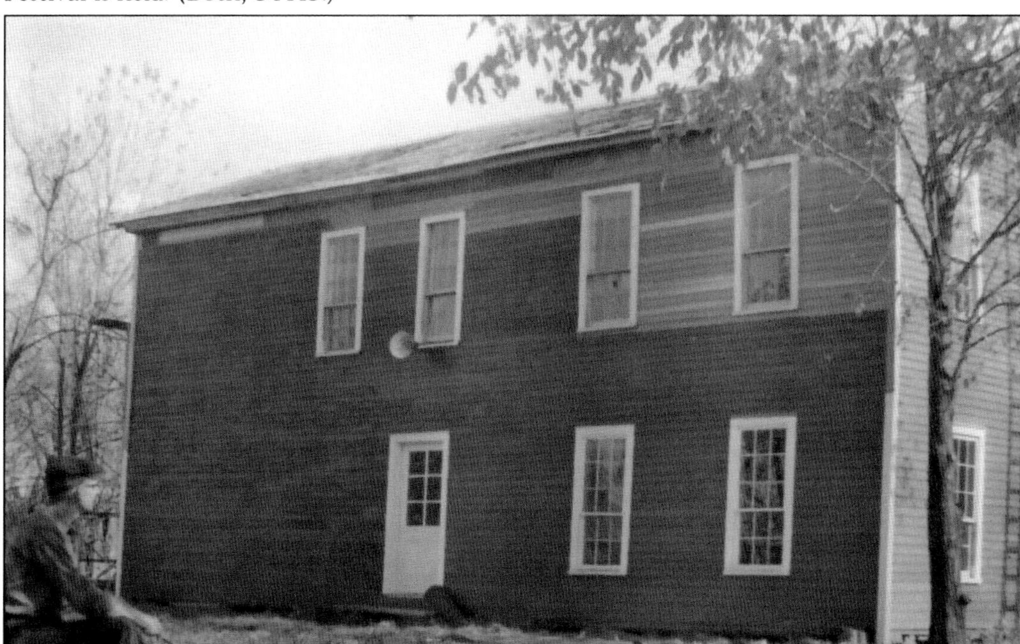

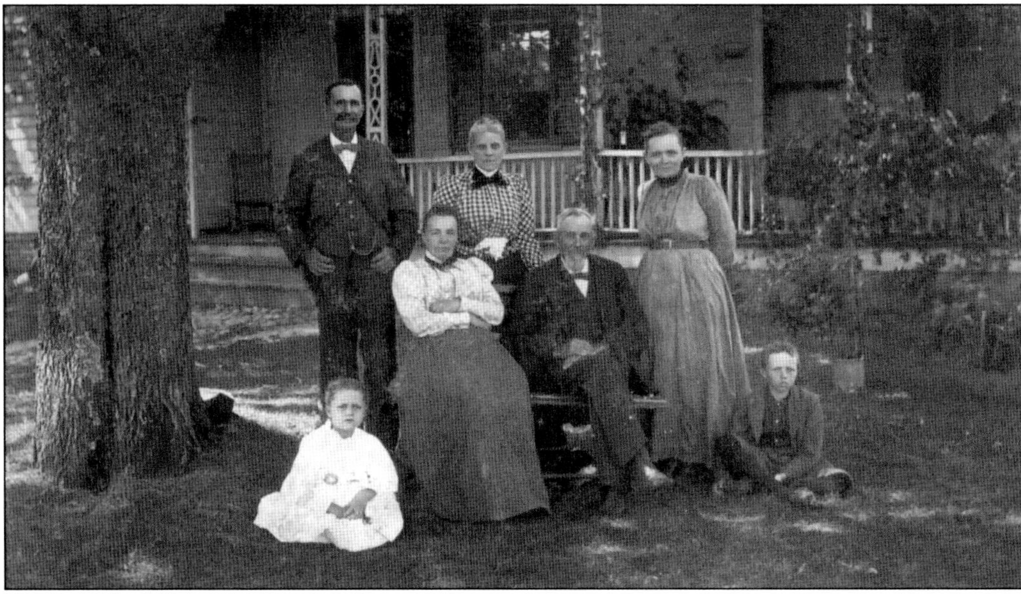

Brimfield was laid out in 1861 when William Bliss, a manufacturer of woolen goods in Rome City, purchased land three miles to the southwest and named it after his hometown of Brimfield, Massachusetts. Pictured here, the Bliss family includes, from left to right, (first row) Agnes McCarty, Emily Bliss, William Bliss, and Frank Bliss McCarty; (second row) Charlie Bliss, Nellie (Clock) Bliss, and Mary L. (Bliss) McCarty. (Courtesy Marcia Garrett.)

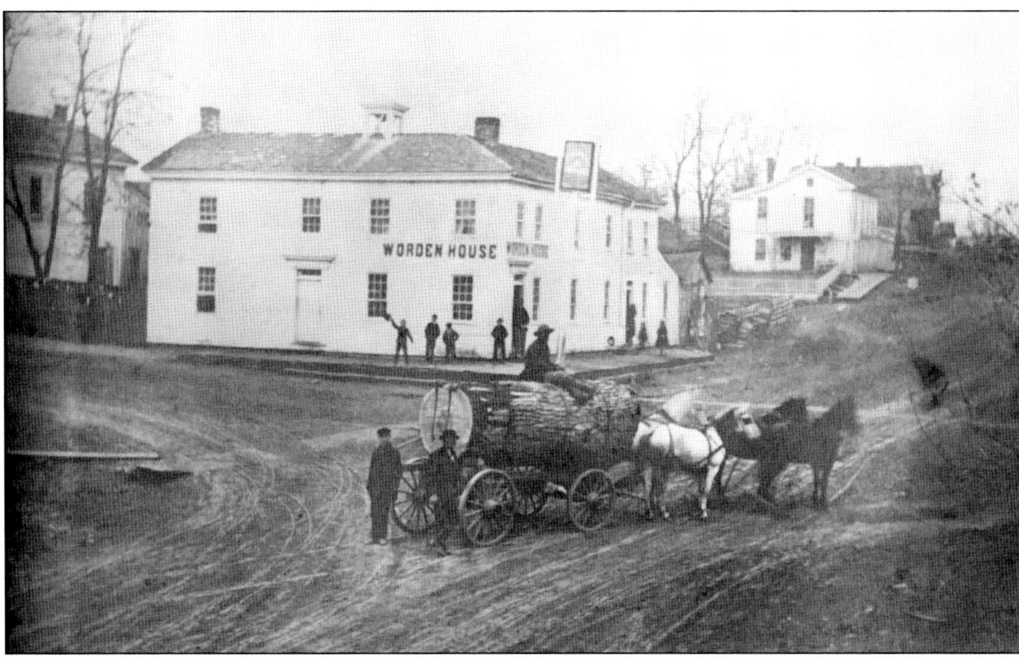

The area around Albion remained as heavily wooded hills for a time, but the forests were pushed back as the town grew. The size of the trees can be estimated by this log on its way to a lumber mill. The Worden House almost met an untimely end in 1859, when Albion's first courthouse burned in a fire that rained embers on the hotel. (Courtesy Beth Shellman.)

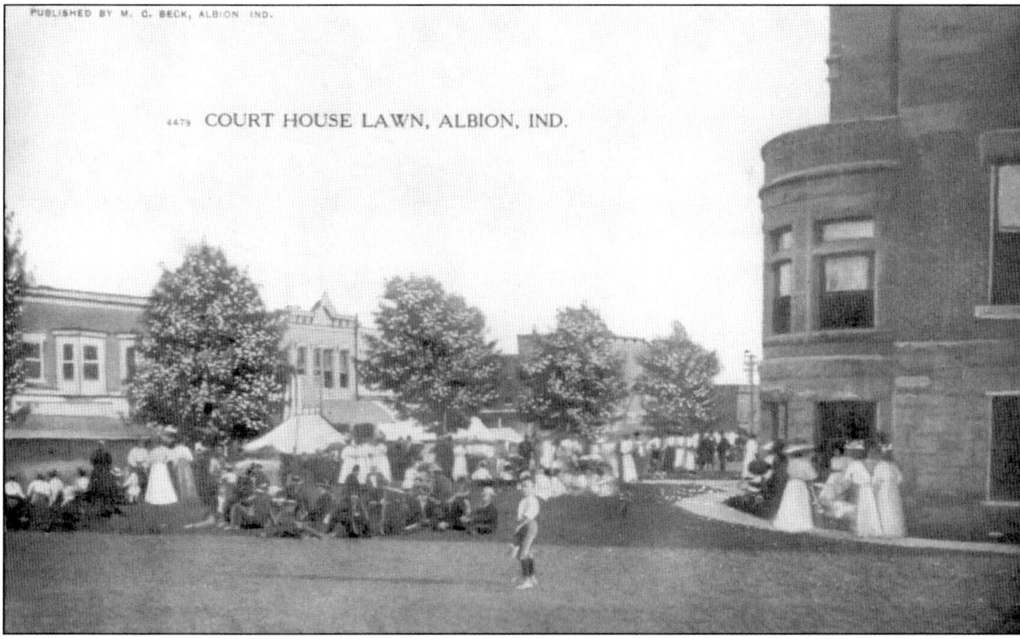

This photograph of a celebration on the Noble County Courthouse lawn was sold at the store of M.C. Beck, who was a popular druggist in Albion for many years. Beck's store was also described as a "news depot," with area newspapers being sold there. (Courtesy Vern Christlieb.)

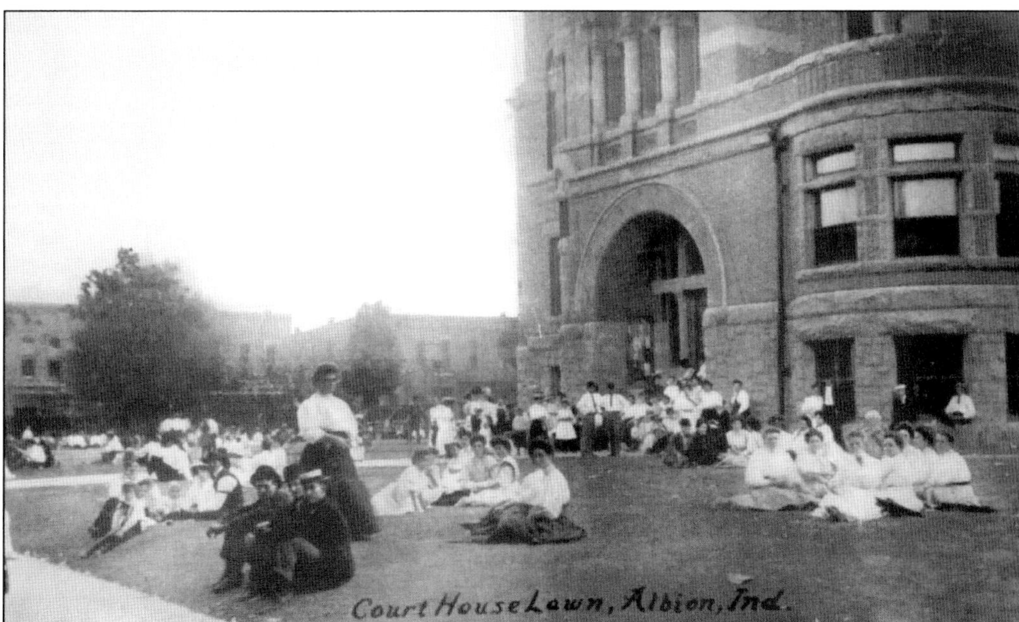

Albionites show off their finest fashions on the courthouse square. The 1888 structure is the third courthouse in Albion. The first was destroyed by arson, and the second was torn down after less than three decades. The most recent, designed by Edward Oscar Fallis of Toledo, Ohio, went up in 1888 and is now listed in the National Register of Historic Places. (NCHS.)

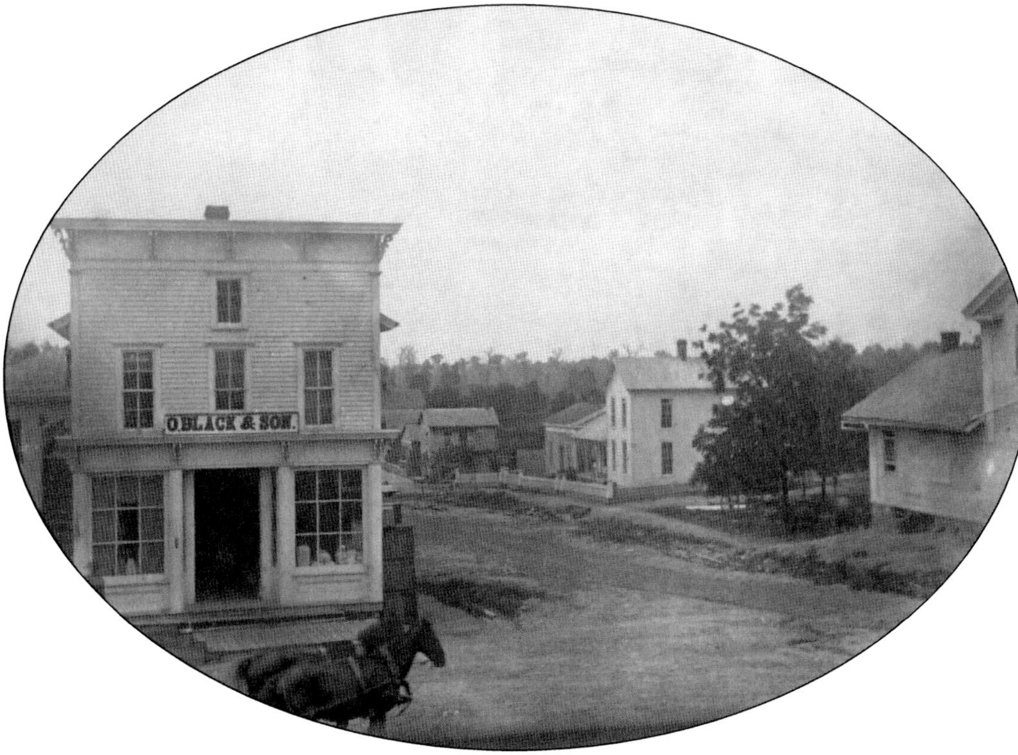

Owen Black Sr. came to Albion in 1856 and established a general merchandise store at the strategic intersection of Orange and Main Streets. That structure burned with the rest of the block in 1867, and fire leveled the above dry goods business in 1879. Within two weeks, Black began work on a new, fire-resistant, three-story brick building that has stood there since. (Courtesy Noble County historian Sarah Knopp.)

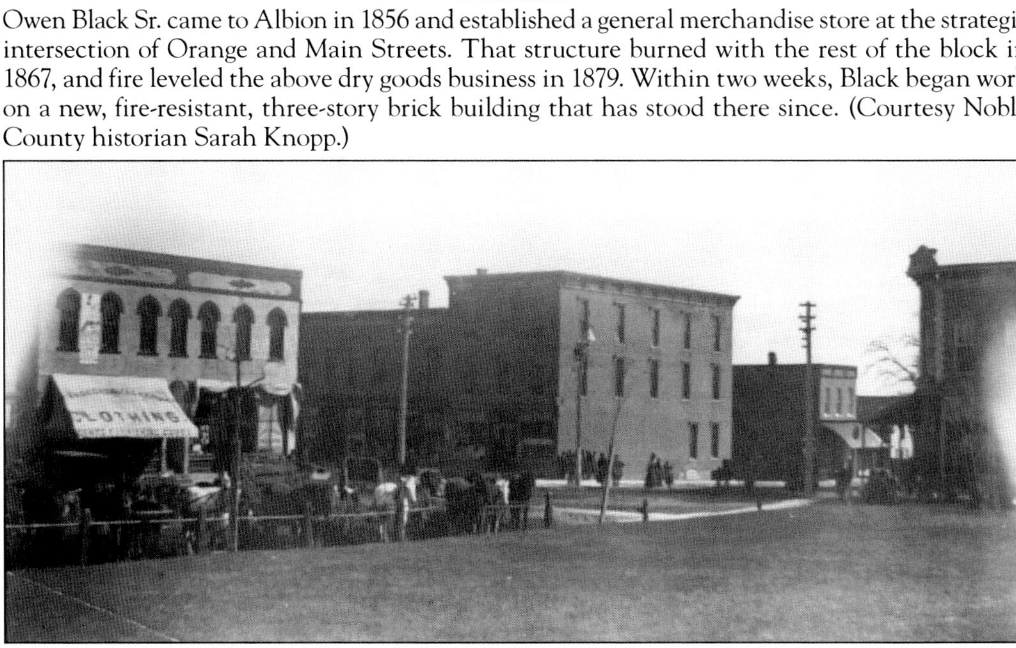

Horses and wagons line the east side of the courthouse square in 1906, while owners shop and socialize. Some Albion businesses around then included Mrs. Wilbur Marks's bakery, J.D. Black and Sons boots and shoes, Simon T. Ward's five-and-dime, P.A. Sunday's harness shop, W.H. Hart's Grocery, and M.C. Beck's drugstore. There were three doctors, a tailor, barbershop, cobbler, laundry, and Evans's and Alvord's "electrical theater." (NCHS.)

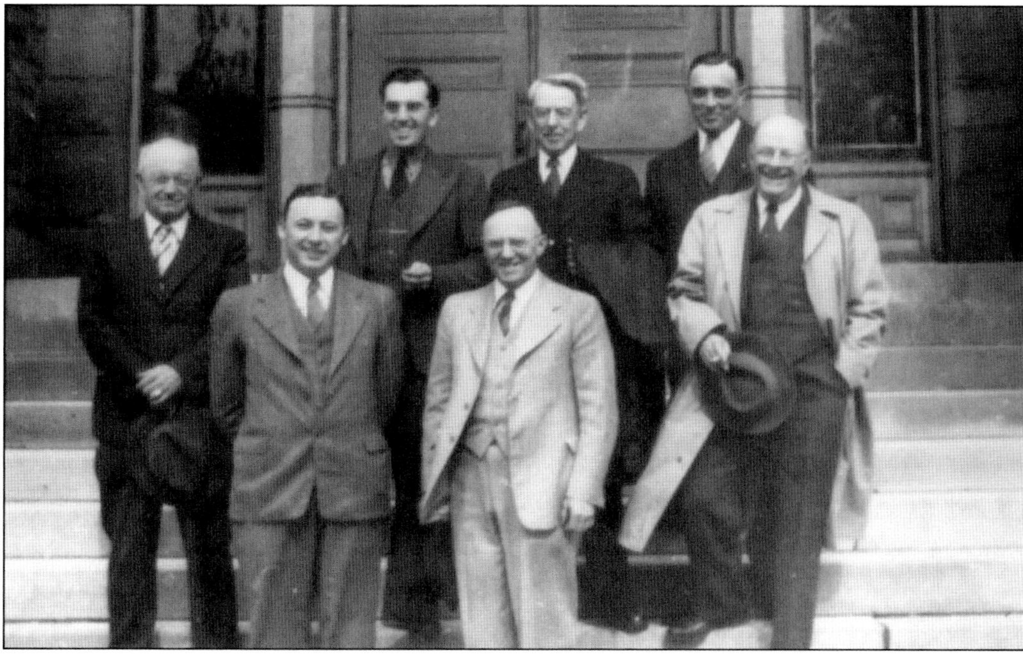

Noble County's elected officials gather in front of the courthouse in 1946. Pictured, from left to right, are (first row) Porter R. Black, clerk; and Walter Brown, treasurer; (second row) Forrest Parker, assessor; and Leland F. Frurip, auditor; (third row) Porter D. Crowell, prosecutor; Judge Fred L. Bodenhafer; and Donald M. Barcus, recorder. (NCHS.)

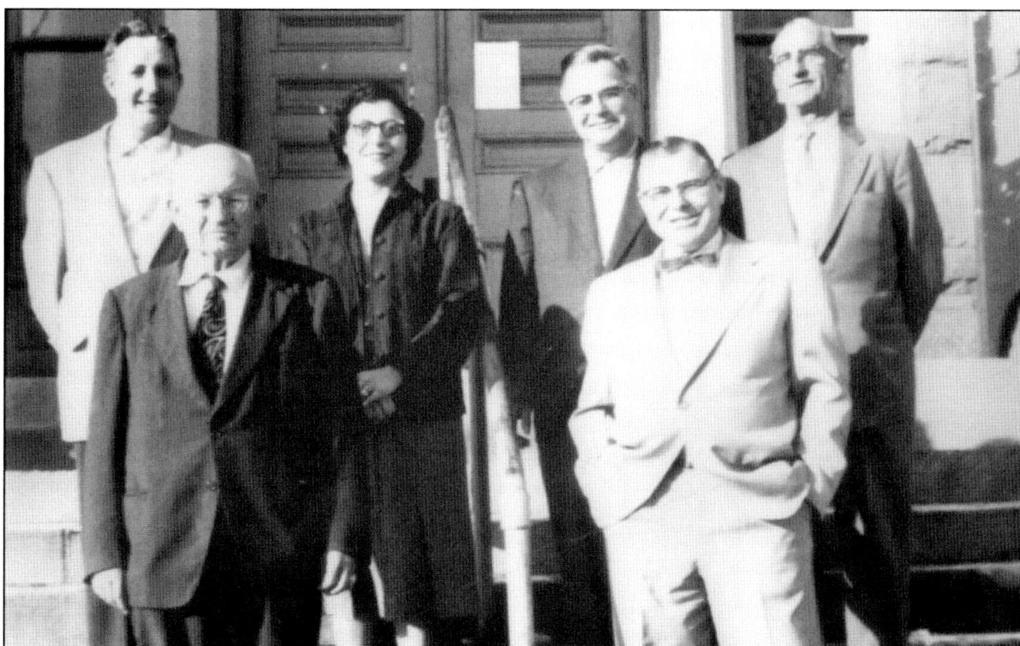

Noble County officials in 1954 include, (first row) Forrest Parker, assessor, and Paul C. Prickett, recorder; (second row) John Singleton Jr., auditor; Dode Frymier, clerk; Clayton Smith, treasurer; and Charles Haase, sheriff. (NCHS.)

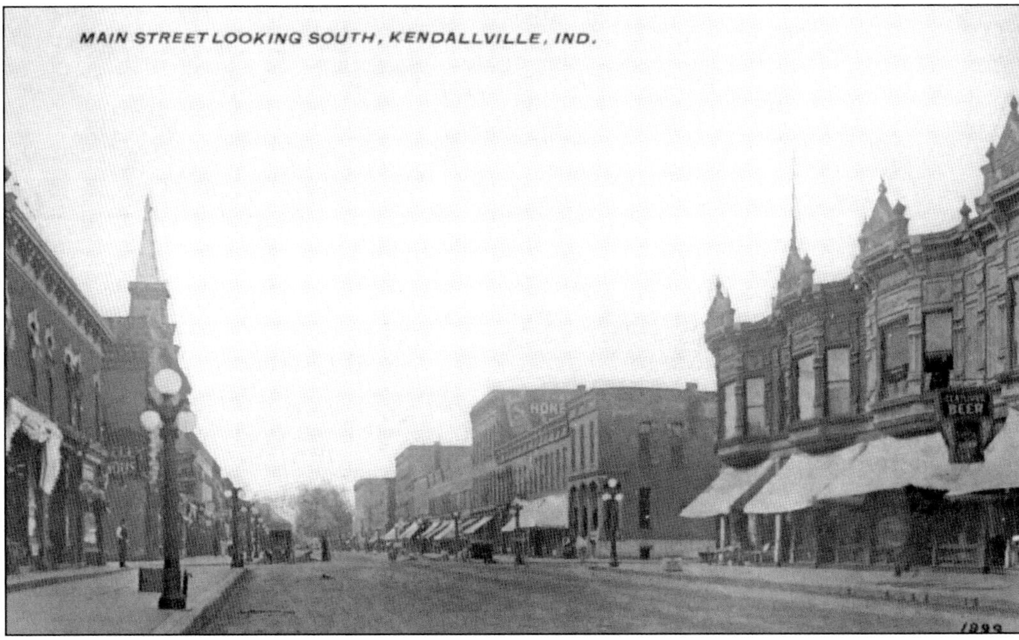

Kendallville's first occupant was David Bundle, who followed an Indian trail into Noble County and built a wigwam in early 1833. He was bought out by Frances Dingman, who constructed the first permanent home. The town was incorporated in 1863 and became a city in 1866 with the election of the first mayor, Tim Baker. By 2016, the population was approaching 10,000. (Courtesy Mike Mapes.)

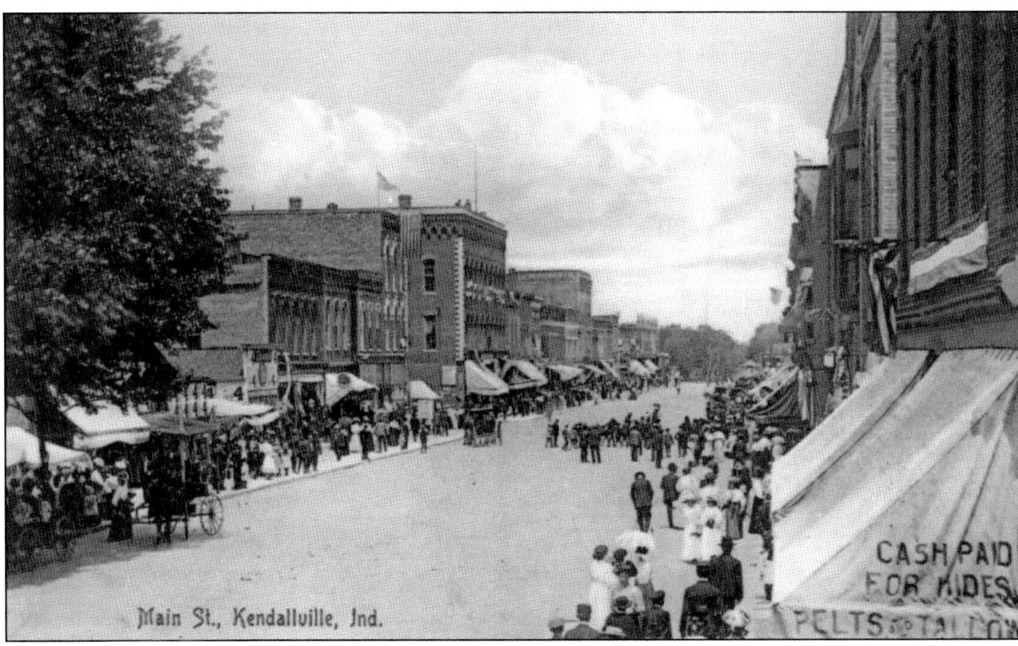

A postcard made in Germany shows a busy Kendallville downtown, probably during the fair in the late 1800s. Note the sign at bottom right, advertising for hides, pelts, and tallow. (Courtesy Mike Mapes.)

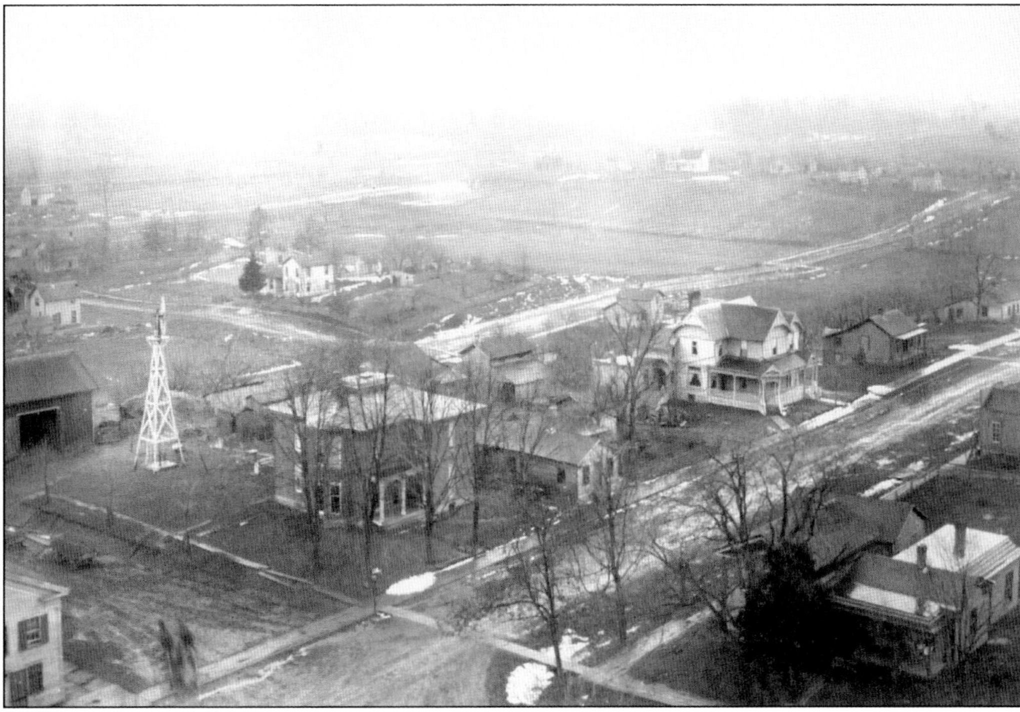

This c. 1892 courthouse tower photograph with a view looking southwest shows how little Albion there was in that direction. Noble County remains largely rural, with a population of less than 48,000. (Courtesy Noble County historian Sarah Knopp.)

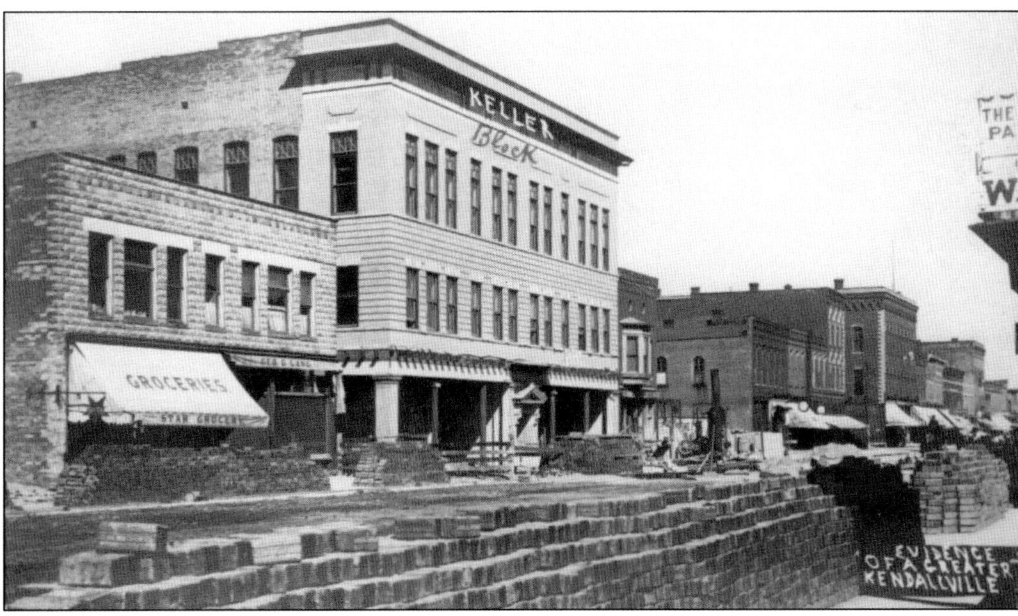

Stacks of bricks await the workers who will use them to pave Main Street in Kendallville. Bricks were often the first improvements to dirt streets, followed later by asphalt paving. (Courtesy Mike Mapes.)

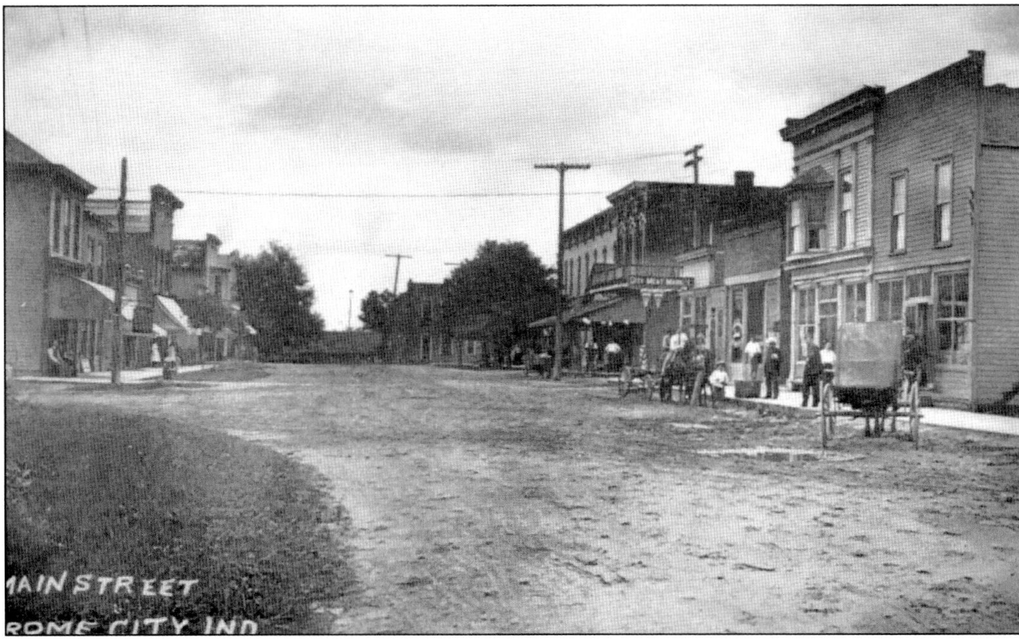

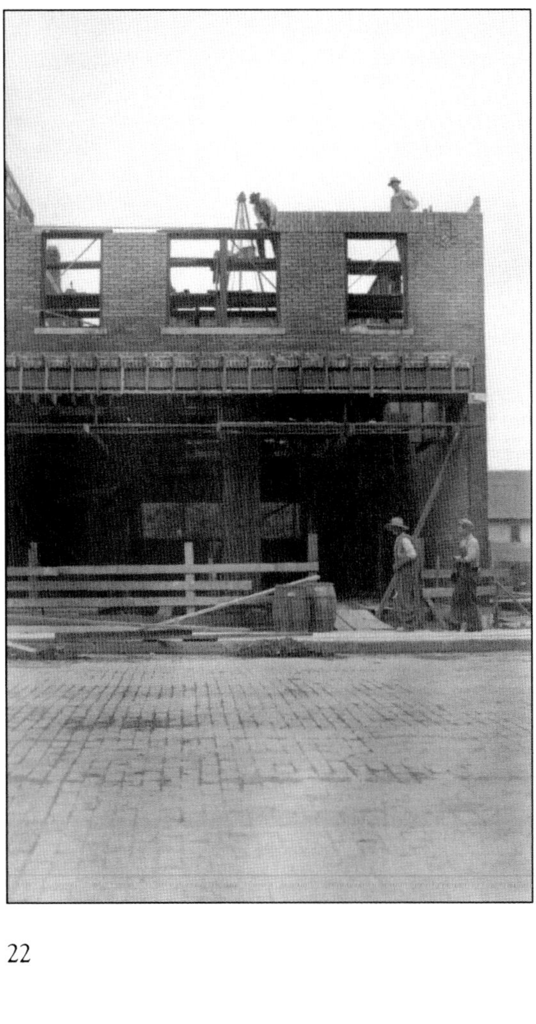

Rome City was laid out in 1839 by John Mather and Ebenezer Pierce, but Francis Aveline is credited for naming it. Aveline, a foreman on the Sylvan Lake dam project, tried to get his Irish and French laborers to get along and "do as did the Romans." The name stuck, but "City" was added by the post office, because another Indiana town was already called Rome. (Courtesy Mike Mapes.)

The Miller Building in Kendallville, pictured here under construction around 1911, still stands today. Dick Miller went into business with his brother-in-law Harry Gutelius to open a five-and-dime store. (Courtesy Mike Mapes.)

Two

Growing a County Seat from Scratch

When looking at images of individual buildings and towns in frontier areas, it is easy to forget how difficult it was to get from one to another. Not only did Albion rise from unpopulated wooded hills, but it had to do so with virtually no transportation system. Swamps were all around, and a peat bog 18 feet deep covered a subterranean lake just west of town. As the town straddled the dividing line between Jefferson and York Townships, just making the three-mile trip to vote became a chore. This resulted in the formation of Albion Township, which at two square miles became the smallest township in the United States.

Within that new township, as early as 1842, Isaac Brewer was believed to have built the first dwelling—on someone else's farm. The owner, Abel Barnum, allowed the squatter to stay there until after Albion was established in 1846. Roads were soon being cut to the county seat, including one that carried train passengers five miles from Brimfield to whatever county business they had.

The town was laid out by Samuel Hanna, William F. Engle, John L. White, Warren Chaffe, and James L. Worden, and many of those last names remained a part of the town from then on. By 1848, there were at least 70 people living in Albion, and two years later the population reached 250 as county workers and lawyers appeared. Still, it was not until 1874 that Albion was incorporated. That same year, the first sidewalk was built from the courthouse square to Albion's brand-new railroad depot.

Despite early growing pains and a series of fires, the designation as county seat and arrival of the railroad allowed Albion to prosper. Today, the town has several large industries, many small businesses, and a population of almost 2,400.

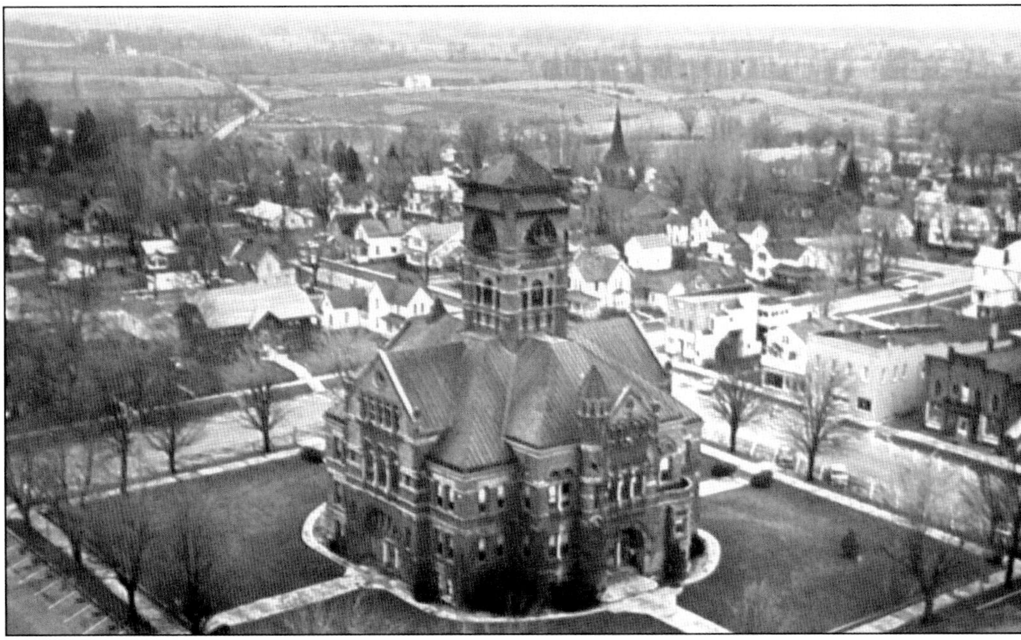

This early 1960s aerial view of Albion centers on the Noble County Courthouse, built near the center of the county in 1888. The town's Carnegie library stands across the street, center left. (NCHS.)

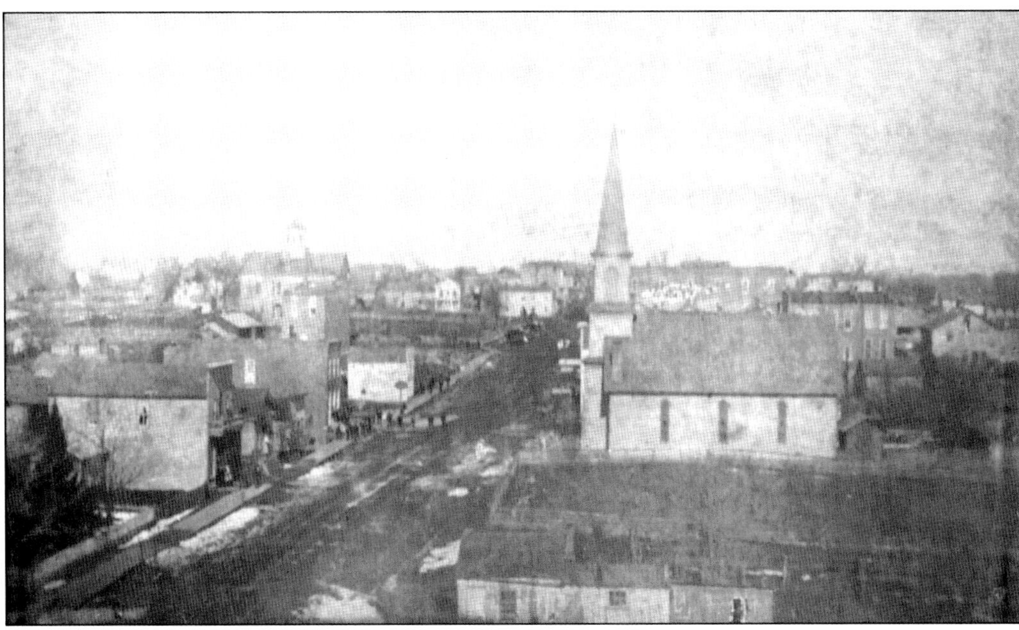

Albion's second courthouse and the South Orange Street Methodist Church are seen from the south in this 1878 photograph. Both buildings have since been torn down. (Courtesy Noble County historian Sarah Knopp.)

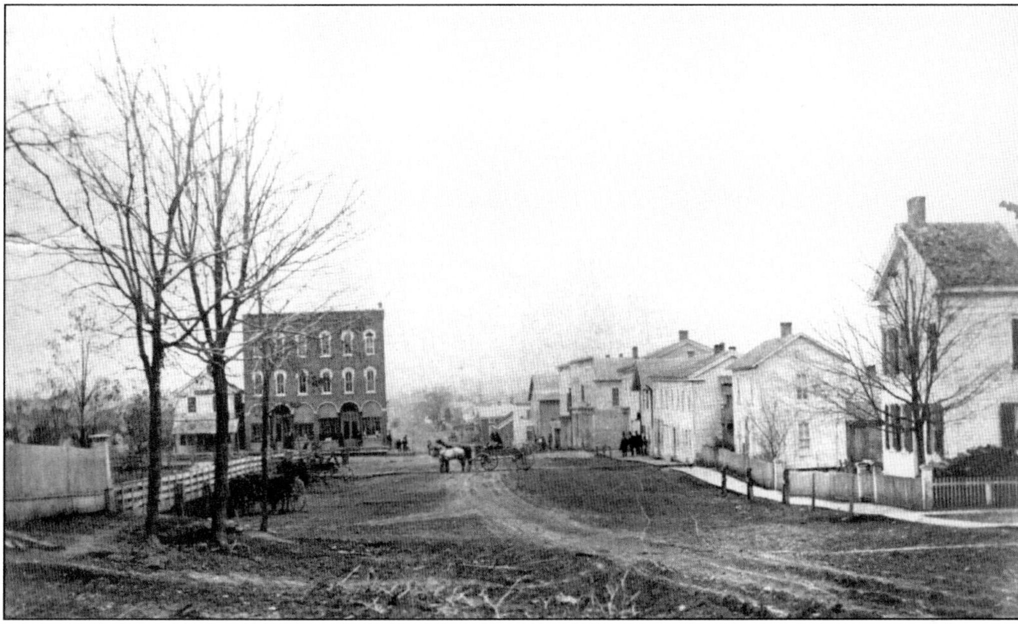

Every building visible in this 1870s photograph of downtown Albion was destroyed by a series of fires and replaced by brick buildings, with the exception of one at far right that later held a doctor's office. With a view looking east from Orange and York Streets, the photograph shows the geographic center of Noble County in the center, while the courthouse is off to the left. (Courtesy Noble County historian Sarah Knopp.)

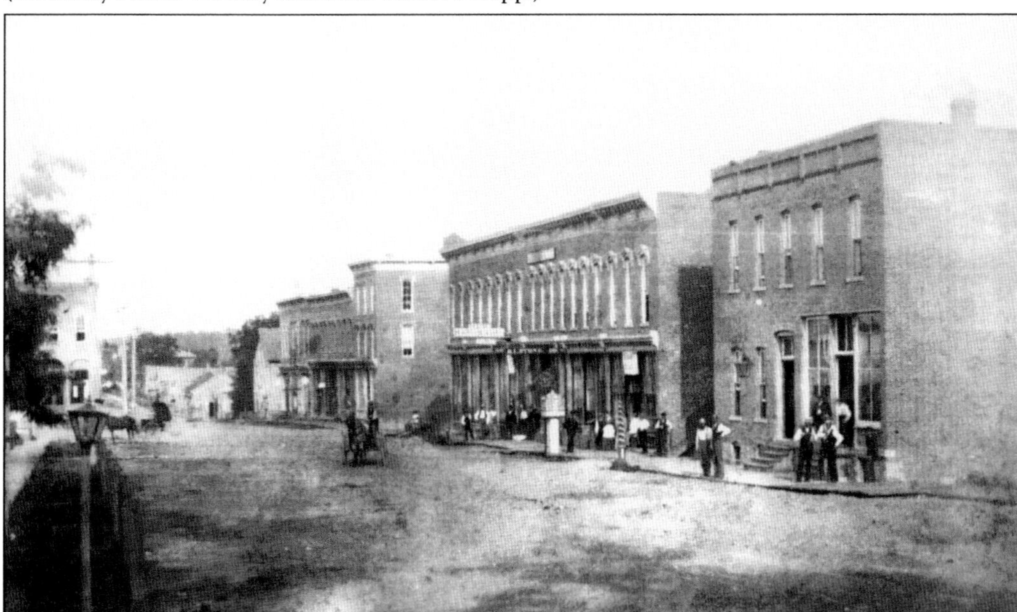

Brick buildings along Albion's Orange Street went up after a series of devastating fires leveled the original wood structures. In 1883, the *Albion New Era* editor pointed out, "We have been a resident of Albion for ten years, and during that period almost the entire business portion of the town has been burned over—and some of it twice." The Albion Fire Department was finally established in 1888. (NCHS.)

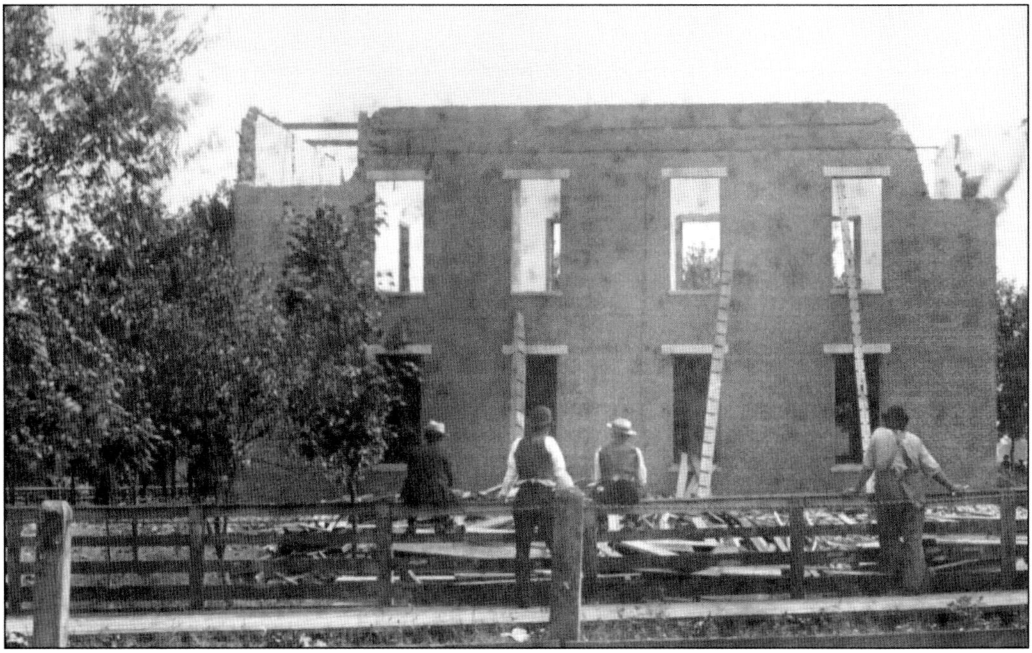

A crew tears down Albion's second Noble County Courthouse, which ran out of space after only 26 years. It had been constructed in 1861 to replace the first, which was destroyed by fire. Built by George Harvey at a cost of $11,000, it was demolished in 1887 and replaced with the current courthouse, which cost $114,062.41. (Courtesy Noble County historian Sarah Knopp.)

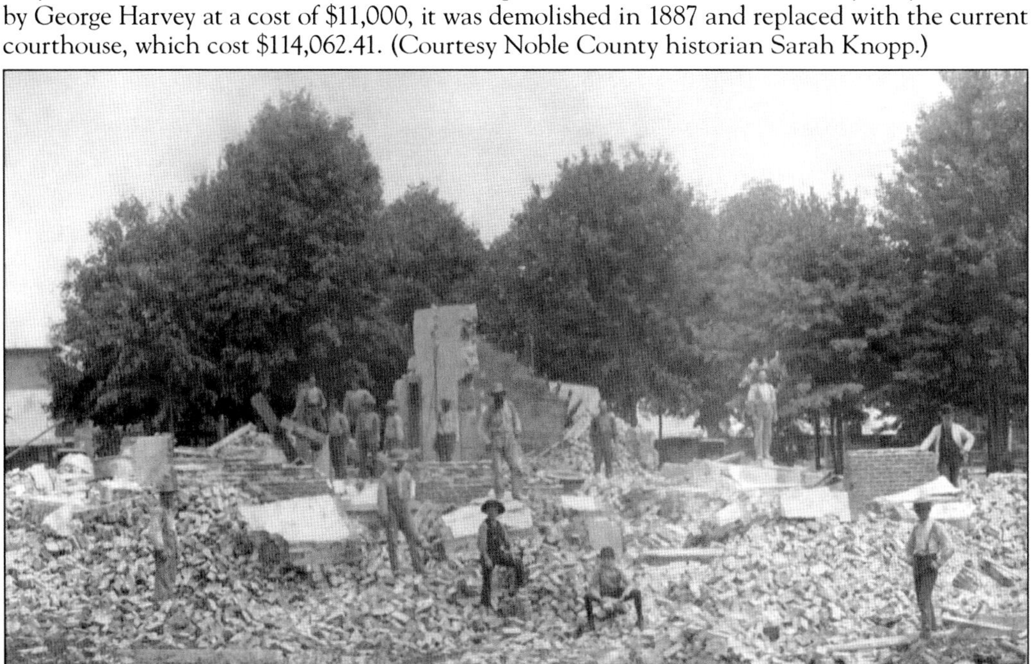

Only rubble remains of Albion's second Noble County Courthouse, demolished in 1887 after it ran out of room. The courthouse square was the geographic center of Noble County, until a two-by-six-mile section of the county's southwest corner was ceded to Whitley County. (Courtesy Noble County historian Sarah Knopp.)

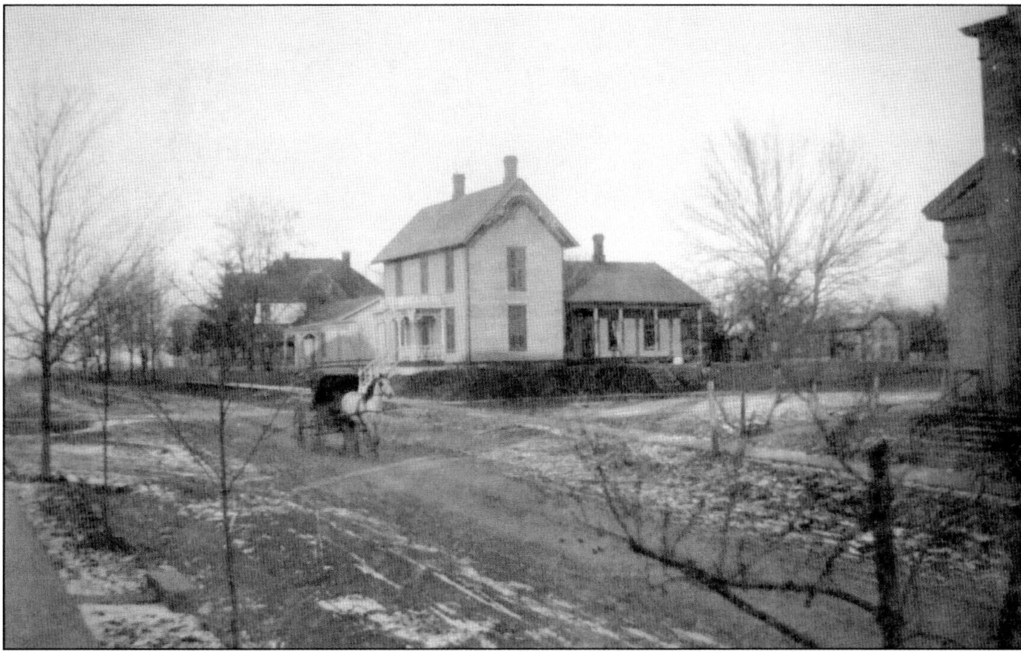

Albion's streets were a lot quieter when this c. 1880 photograph was taken. The buggy is headed south on Orange Street, passing Highland Street as it heads toward the courthouse square. St. Mark's Lutheran Church is on the right edge of the photograph; it and the house at the top of the hill still stand. Later, Orange Street would become part of Indiana State Route 9. (NCHS.)

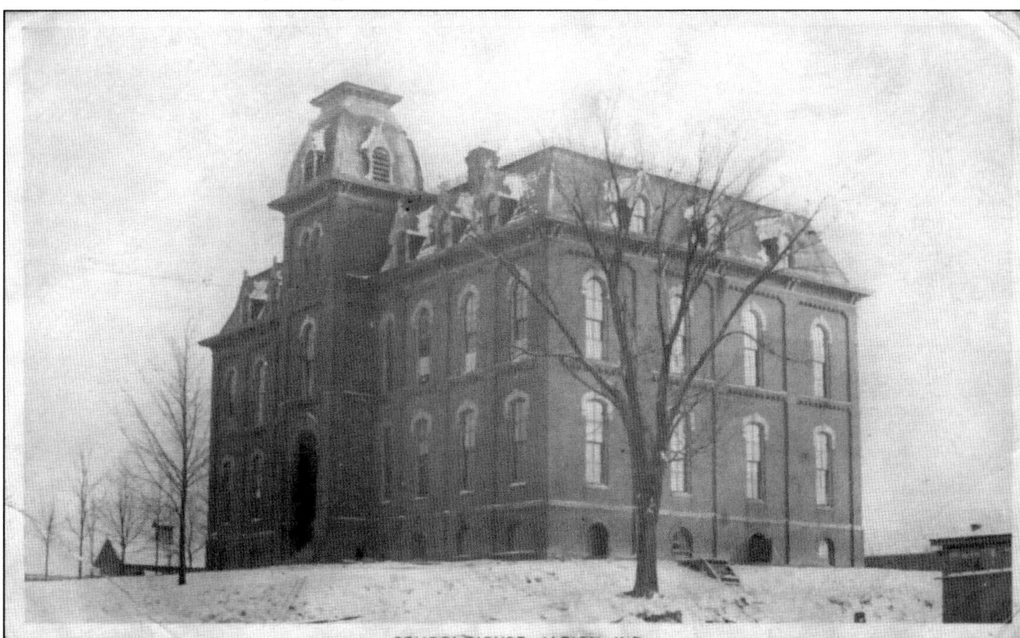

The three-story 1876 Albion schoolhouse stood on a hill on the southeast side of town, making it one of the most imposing structures in the community. When another new school was built on the east side of Albion in 1923, the old one was used for manufacturing for a time, then torn down in March 1969. An apartment complex is on the site now. (NCHS.)

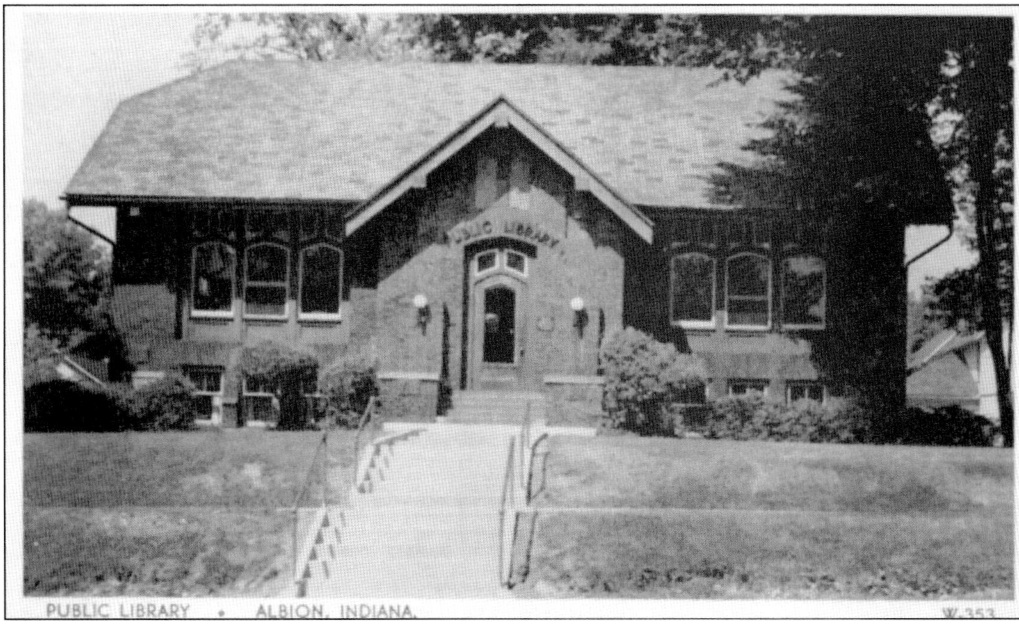

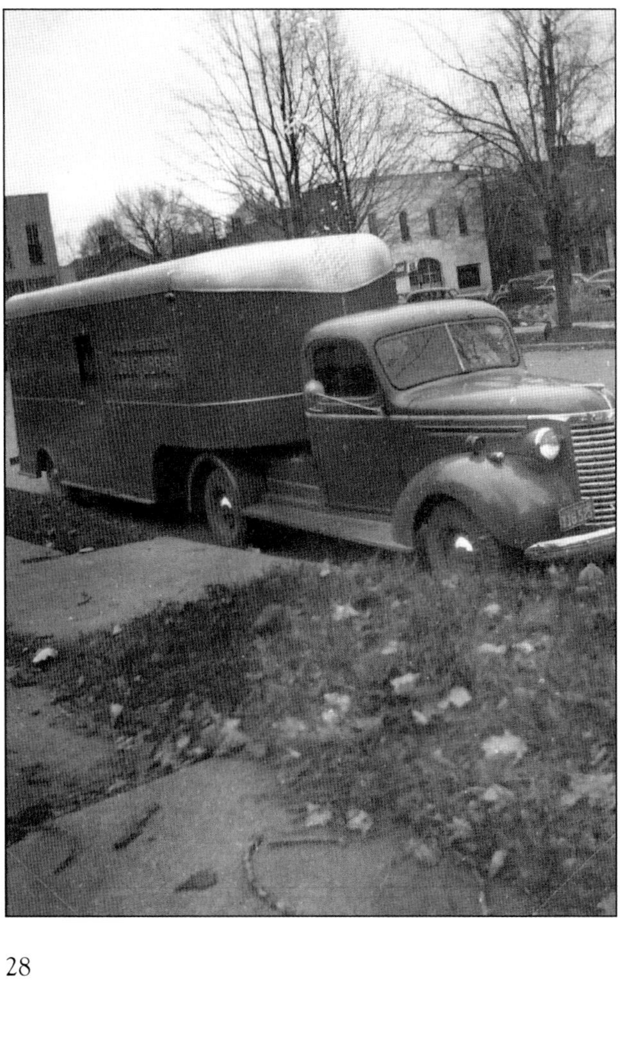

Between 1901 and 1918, Indiana received grants from Andrew Carnegie and the Carnegie Corporation that allowed for the building of 165 library buildings across the state. Albion's library opened on the courthouse square in 1916 thanks to a $10,000 grant, demonstrating Carnegie's emphasis on functionality and simplicity. Later, an addition was made to the front of the building that turned it into a three-level library. Now part of the Noble County Public Library system, the library was moved to a new building in 1995. The old Carnegie building and its addition still remain, housing the Noble County Prosecutor's Office. At left is the Albion–Noble County Public Library's first bookmobile, which was later replaced with a more maneuverable large van. (Above, NCHS; left, courtesy Ellen McBride.)

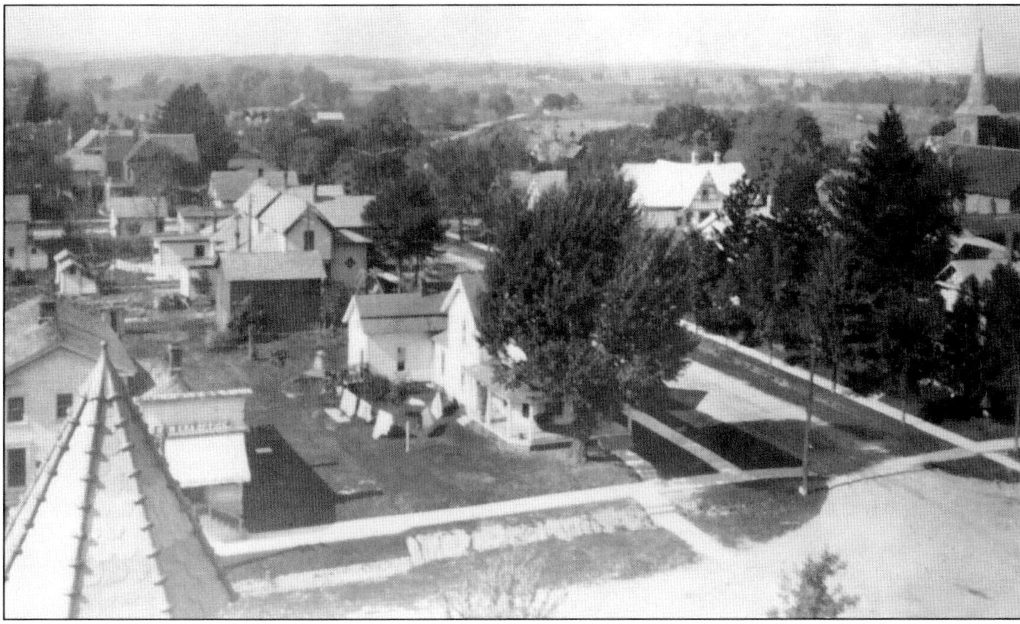

A photograph taken from the Noble County Courthouse, with a view toward the west, shows a glimpse of the *Albion New Era* office near the lower left corner, where the Albion Library would later be built. Established in 1872, the newspaper continues to be published as a weekly. The first newspaper in the county is believed to have been the *Noble County Star*, which published in Albion around 1850. (NCHS.)

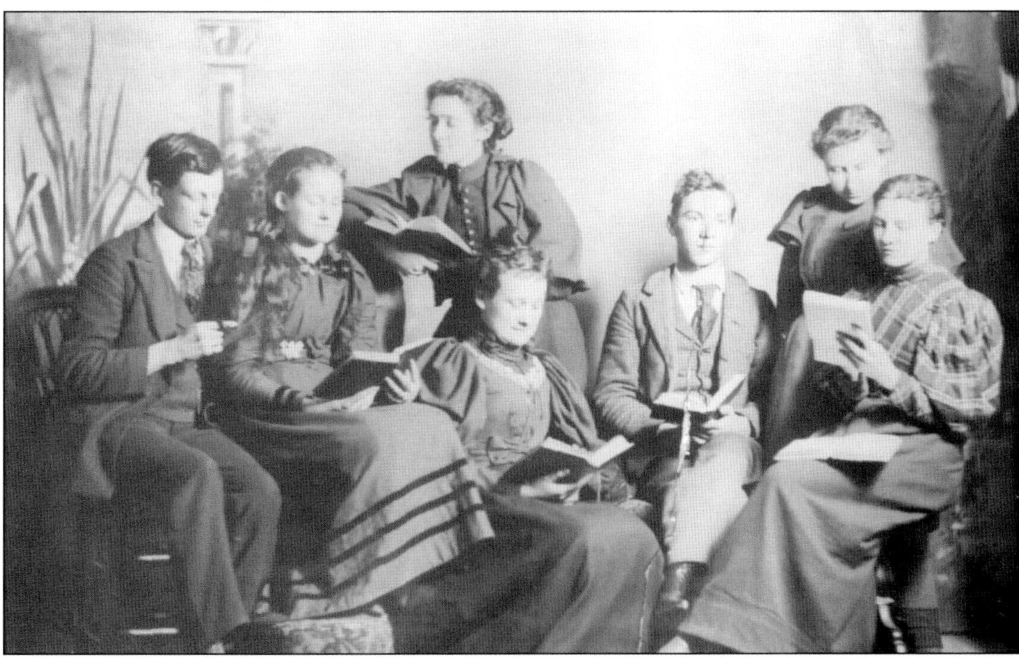

This gathering of Albionites includes Sam Kimmell, at far left. Kimmell was a teacher at the Burr Oak School, about five miles south of Albion, prior to 1909. The others in the photograph have not been identified but may be fellow teachers. The image was taken by John Alphius Harkless, a popular Albion photographer who died in 1917. (NCHS.)

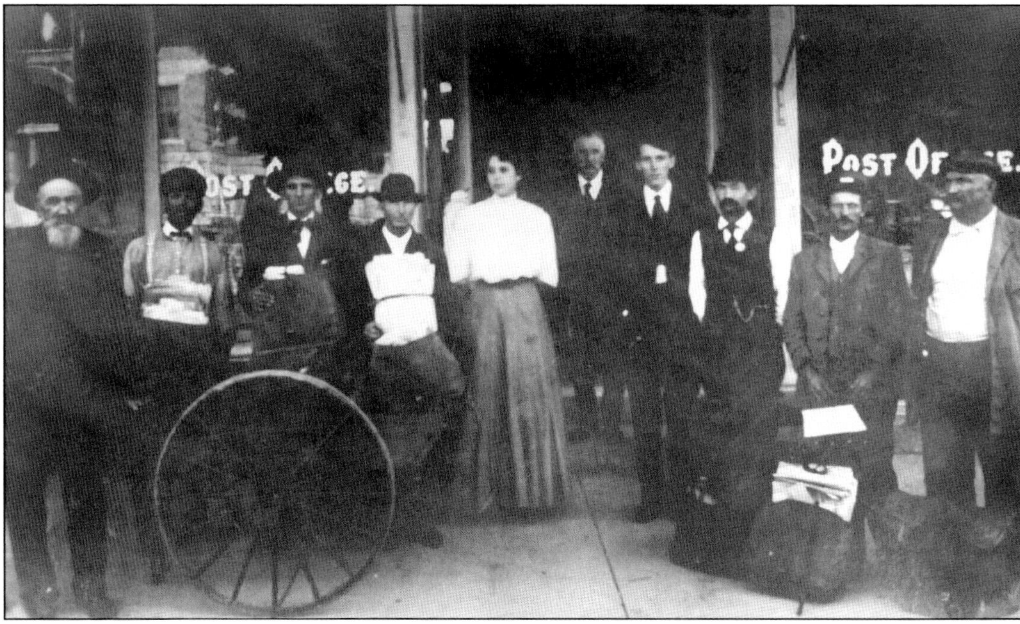

Albion's first post office was established on the south side of the courthouse square on August 19, 1847, with William Engle as the first postmaster. It is now around the corner: on January 31, 1965, the newest post office was officially dedicated at Orange and Hazel Streets. Engle stands at center rear, while others hold bags of mail. Later, a motorcycle was used for deliveries around Albion. (Courtesy Beth Shellman.)

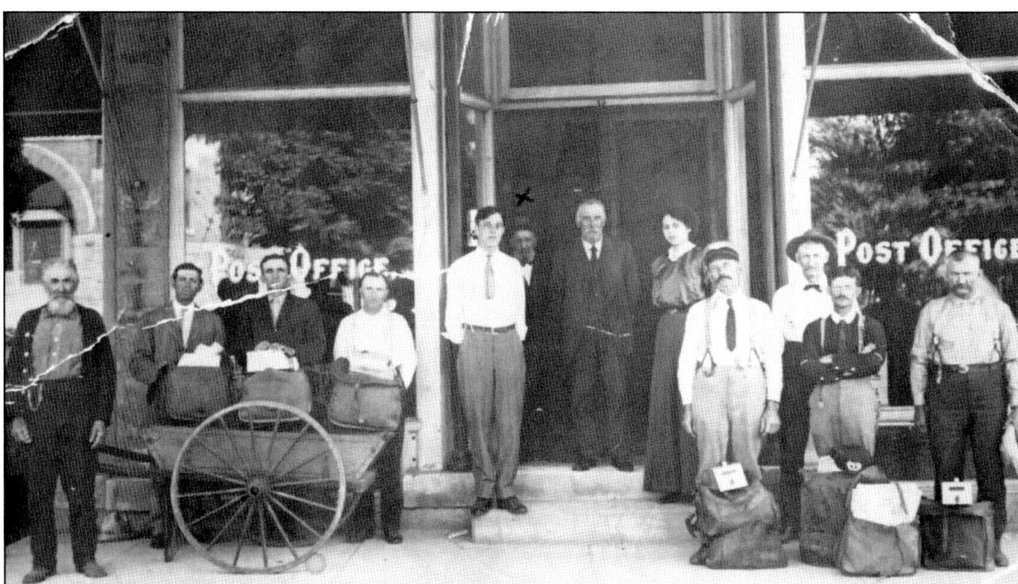

Albion Post Office workers stand ready at their North Orange Street location in the early 1900s. In the center is the 1906–1910 postmaster, John Cockley, and beside him is his daughter Mayme Cockley Sharpneck. The rural carriers, pictured with their bags, are, from left to right, Fred Ealbert, Myron Hursey, Herbert Cockley, Nathan Hathway, Bill Evans, and Albert McWilliams. Cockley worked at Black's General Store for 36 years. (Courtesy Noble County historian Sarah Knopp.)

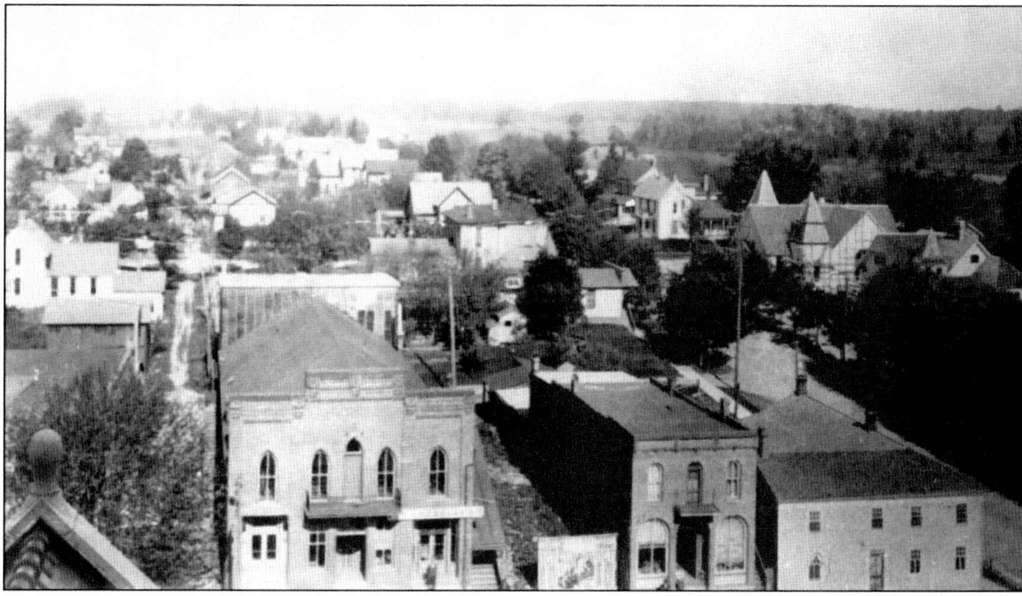

This northward view from the courthouse shows three Albion landmarks—Albion Opera House at lower left, with a billboard advertising plays to its right; the Worden House (Albion's first hotel), at lower right; and St. Mark's Lutheran Church, center right. (NCHS.)

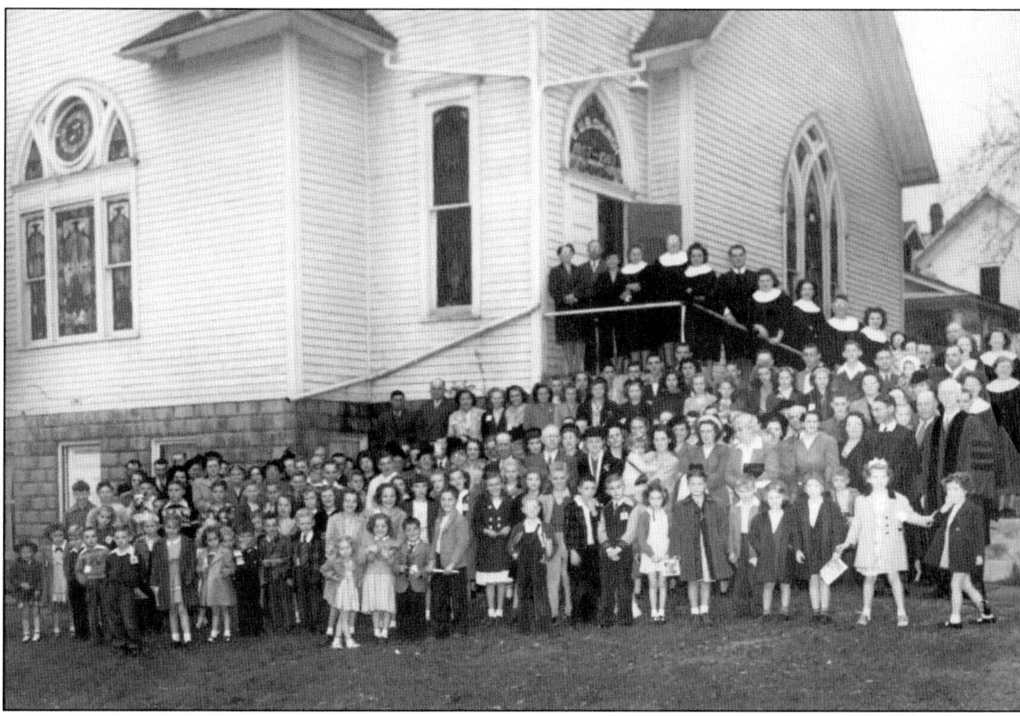

A congregation gathers before an 1867 Albion building that has seen many uses over the years. Originally the United Brethren Church at York and Main Streets, it later became Blessed Sacrament Catholic Church. When that congregation moved into a new building, the former church was turned into Albion Masonic Lodge No. 97, located across the street from the Noble County Old Jail Museum. (NCHS.)

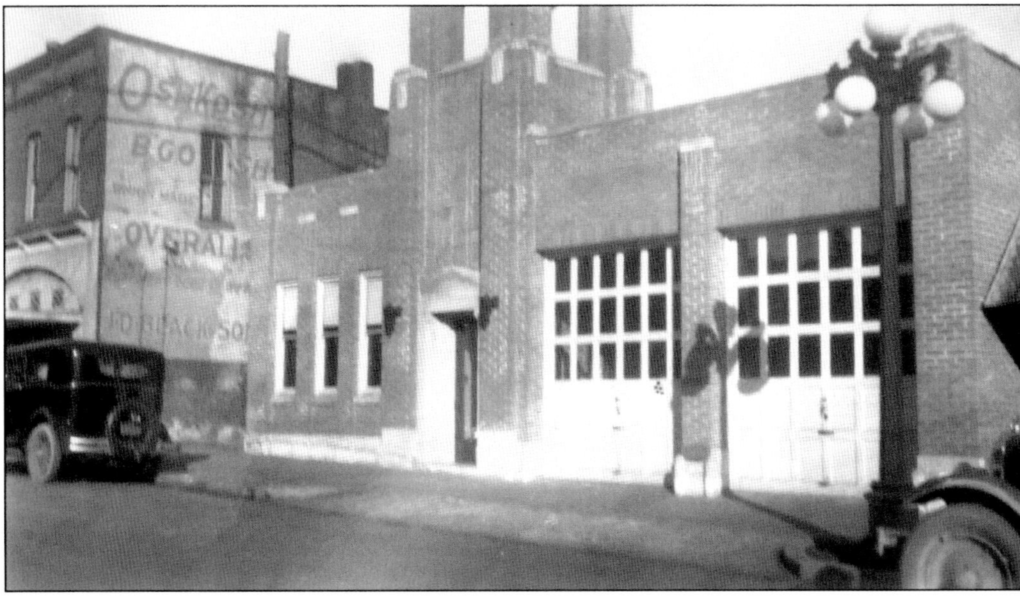

Albion Town Hall, a 1930s New Deal project, created jobs during the Great Depression. It was constructed by Hiatt Brothers, plumbed by P&H Co., and the heating system was installed by Albion Hardware Co.—all local companies. The building housed the Town of Albion administrative offices, the town board meeting room, and the fire department—until the early 1960s, when the fire department moved to a former auto dealership location next door. (NCHS.)

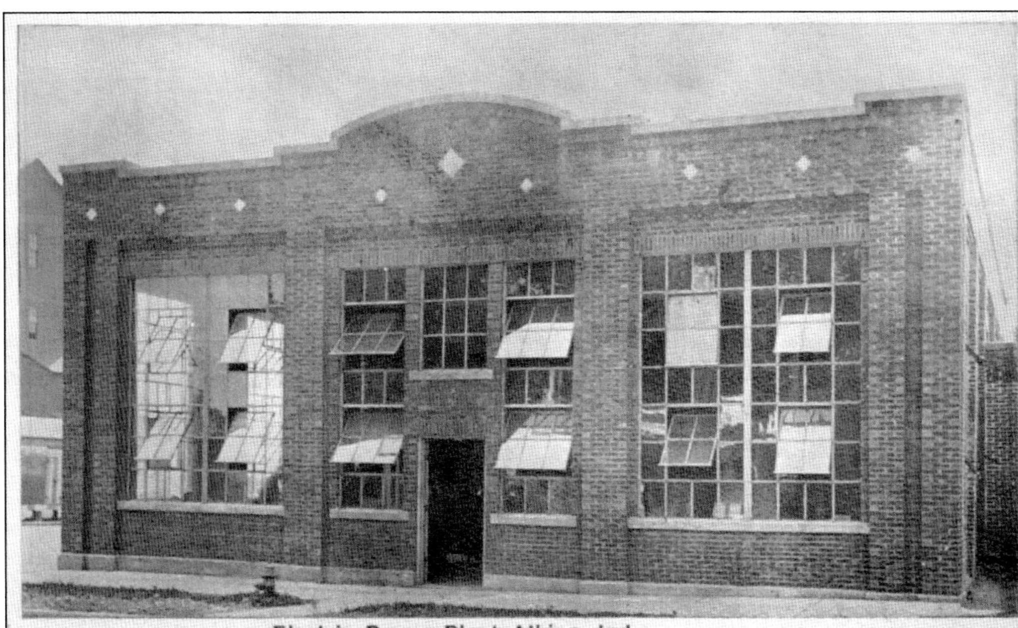

Albion's electricity was generated from a power plant along South Orange Street. One superintendent of the Albion Electric Light Plant was John W. Morr, a popular Albion doctor, who also served for a time as town treasurer and chairman of the Noble County Democratic Central Committee. The building was later the first location of the Lyall Electric Company, which became the largest employer in Noble County. (NCHS.)

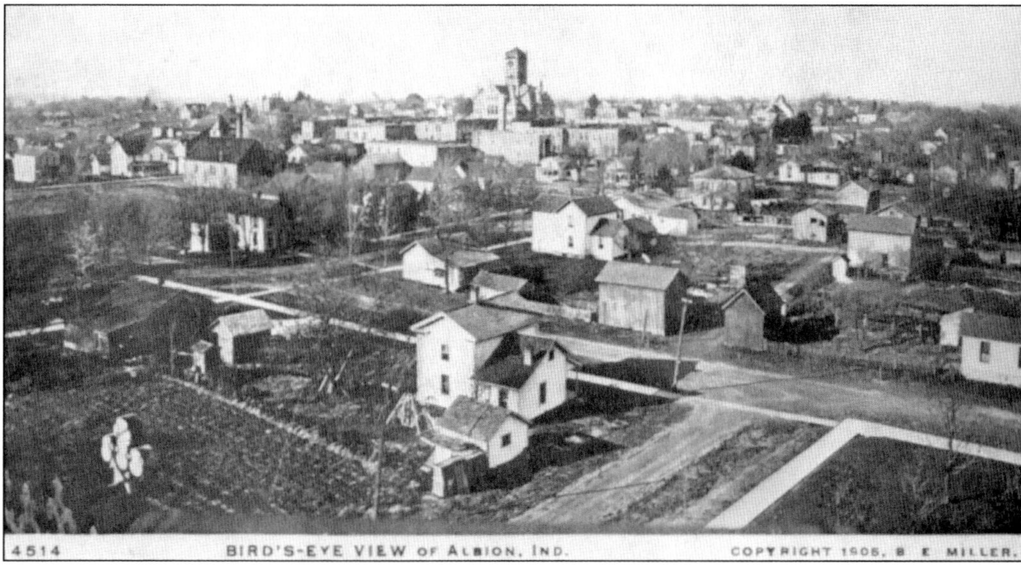

Many bird's-eye views of Albion were taken from the courthouse, but the view in this 1905 photograph looks out from the top of the Albion High School on the southeast side of town. Many of the buildings shown still exist, including the Noble County Courthouse itself in the background. (Courtesy Noble County historian Sarah Knopp.)

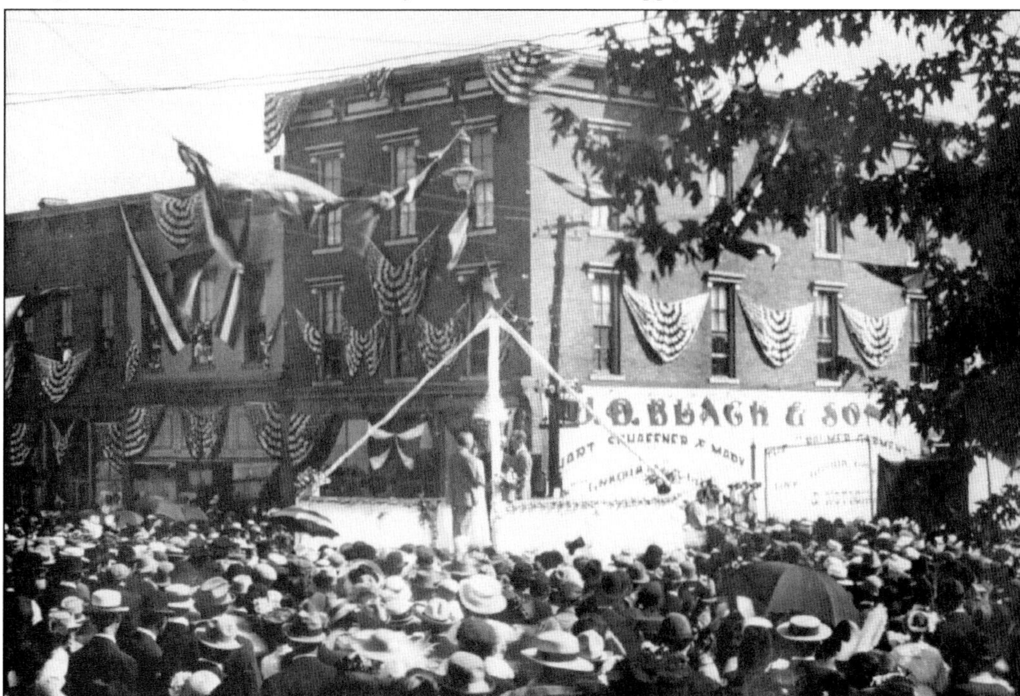

Before Internet or radio, any small-town events were big events. In this case, Albion's main intersection was closed off and a stage constructed so that everyone could witness the 1914 wedding of Zadel Fitch and Allan Brooks. Thanks to the building in the background, the intersection was sometimes referred to as "Black's Corner"; the Black family had by then been an ongoing Albion business interest for over 50 years. (NCHS.)

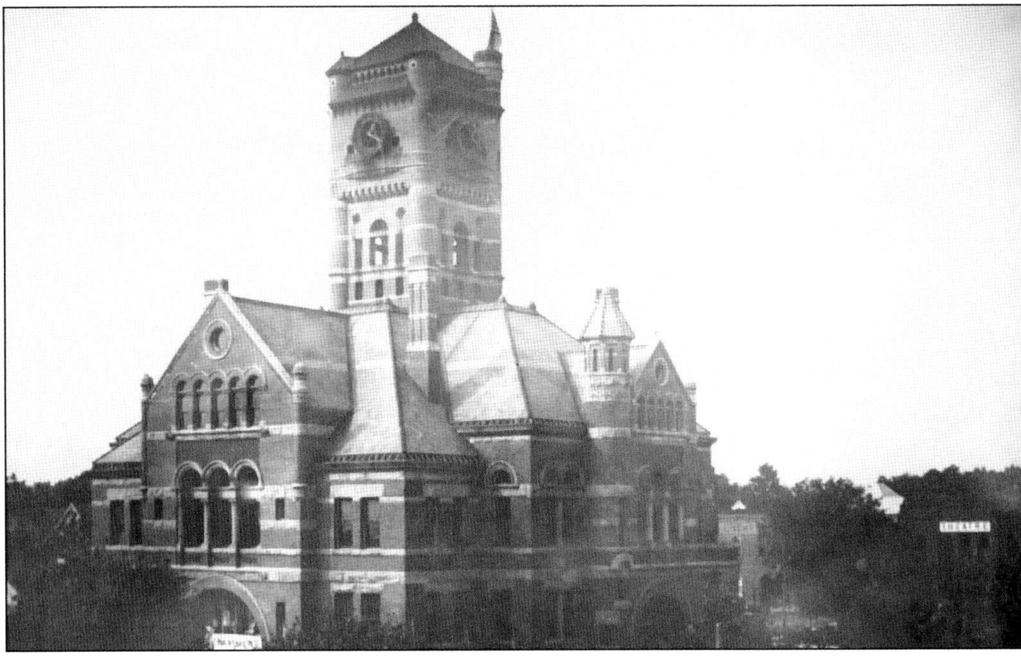

Ethel Skiver, of West Unity, Ohio, performed the "Slide for Life" as Madame La Fere. Hanging from her hair, La Fere would slide from the courthouse tower across Orange Street, landing in an alley beyond. But on September 25, 1908, the cable snapped, plunging her 75 feet into the street. Madame La Fere was taken to the Good Hope Hospital, a building that still stands nearby, and later died. (NCHS.)

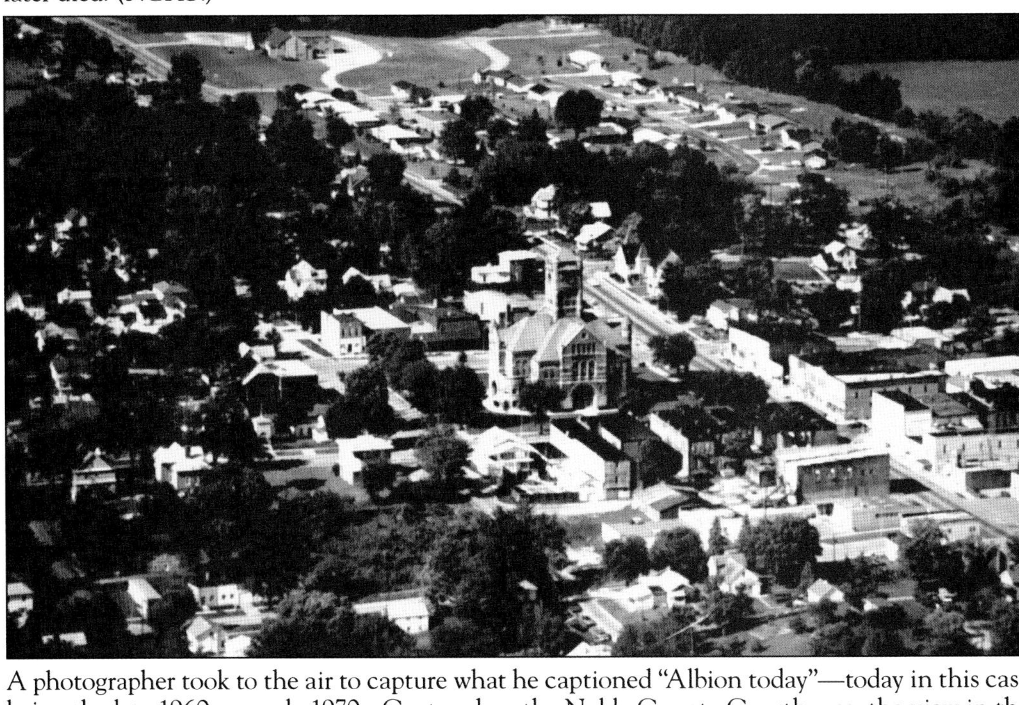

A photographer took to the air to capture what he captioned "Albion today"—today in this case being the late 1960s or early 1970s. Centered on the Noble County Courthouse, the view in the photograph looks toward the northeast. (NCHS.)

Three

Business—From Wood to Brick

Early Midwest settlers were self-sufficient trailblazers. But when enough people gathered together to form a community, businessmen arrived to serve the needs of others.

So it is not surprising that Joel Bristol, heading the first family of settlers in Noble County, ended up a businessman. First, Bristol erected a large cabin on the south side of the Fort Wayne–Goshen Road, northwest of what would become Merriam. With so many settlers passing by, he turned the home into a tavern, where immigrants could stop for a rest or spend the night. Noble County's first business lasted from around 1827 until 1831.

Bristol later tried to start his own town, founding Noblesville in 1849. Although a small combination grocery store/saloon was established there, he found few takers. Bristol died the next year, but the community struggled on. Since there was already a Noblesville Post Office in Indiana, the town is now known as Merriam.

Providing a place for travelers to stay was a common first business on the frontier. Two such establishments along the Fort Wayne–Goshen Road were Stone's Tavern (now a historic site) and Kimmell House (now a bed-and-breakfast). Mills also quickly went up, especially sawmills to supply lumber for new homes and businesses. When a small gathering of settlers came together, they would petition for a post office.

In 1902, A.T. McDaniel built a store in Merriam that came to be known as the Uncle Sam Store. Hoosiers claim that the original Uncle Sam, symbol of the country, is buried in the nearby Merriam Chapel cemetery. In that dispute, the US Congress sided with Troy, New York.

The other necessary businesses for isolated rural towns are predictable: blacksmith shops, shoemakers, grocery, hardware, and drugstores. Needed professions included carpenters, masons, butchers, barbers, doctors, and dentists. Both are partial lists, but there was always a new entrepreneur ready to fill a business gap.

Industry also came, of course, especially when it involved agriculture. Over the years, many of those wooden businesses burned down, often in fires that razed whole blocks, but the intrepid businessmen switched to brick and kept coming back.

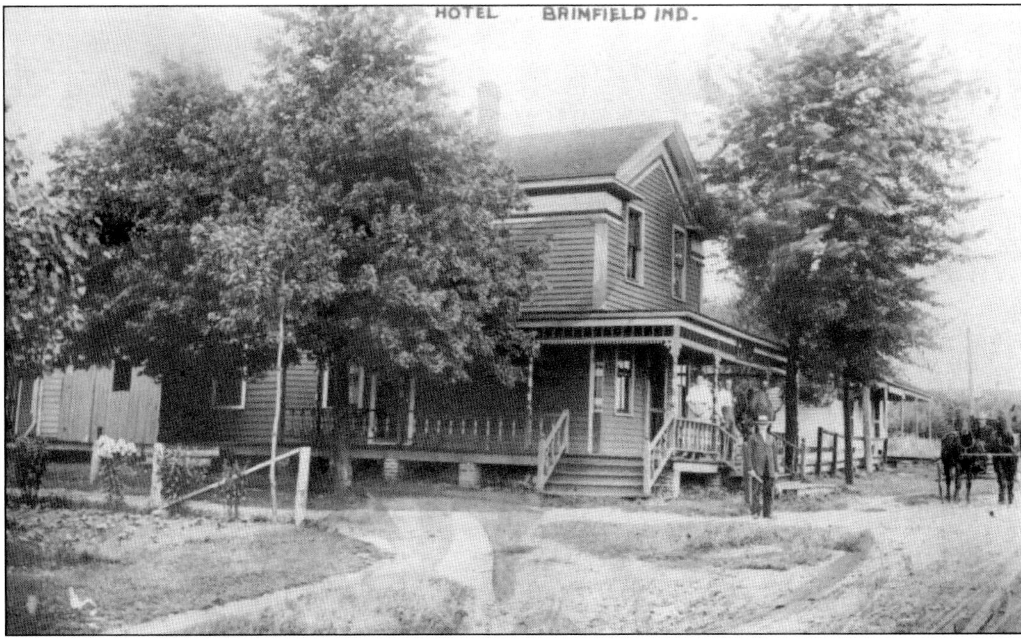

The hotel of A.C. Emahiser stands in Brimfield, in the early 1900s. It replaced a larger hotel that burned down around 1894. Emahiser was a founding member of the Brimfield Odd Fellows in 1881 and was one of several businessmen in Brimfield who profited from first the railroad, then a US highway passing through the town. Many businesses followed, although most of them have since closed down. (Courtesy Marcia Garrett.)

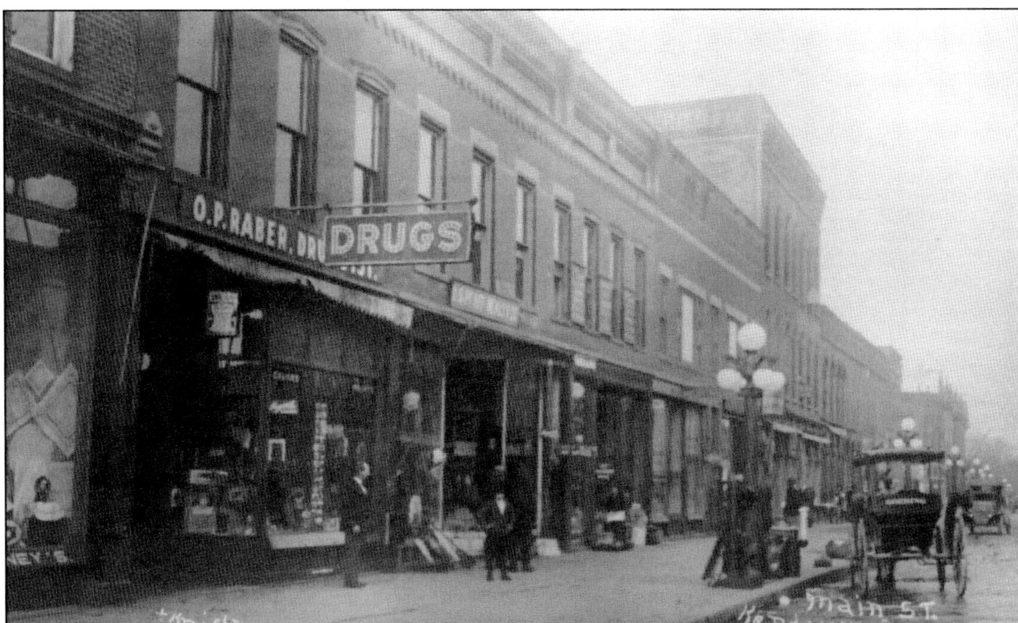

Oliver P. Raber moved his drugstore from Corunna, east of Noble County, to Kendallville in 1902 and took over the business of druggists W. and J.R. Bunyan. When Raber retired, he handed it over to the pair of Weldy and Reiley. (Courtesy Mike Mapes.)

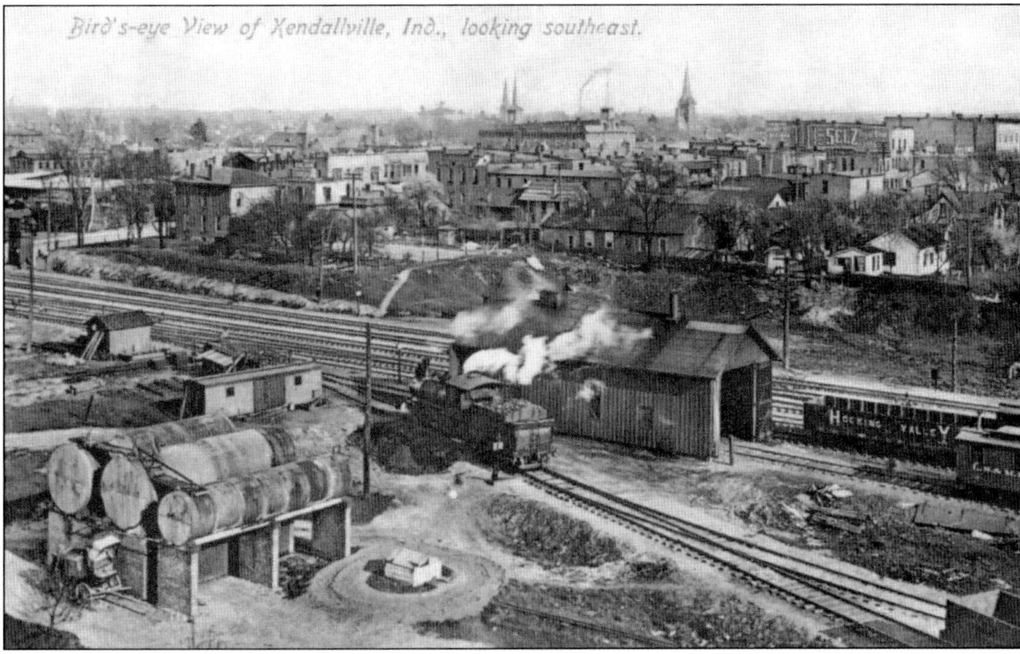

Kendallville's busy downtown and the railroad area north of it are seen in this 1908 photograph. (Courtesy Mike Mapes.)

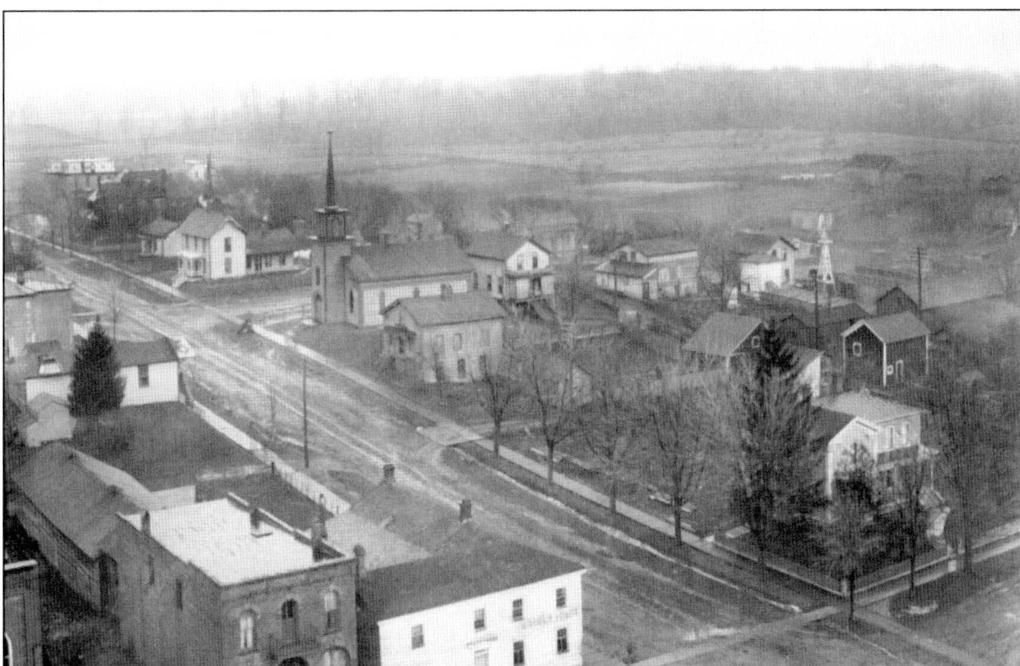

The Worden House, bottom center in this 1890 view looking northeast, was Albion's first hotel. After the county seat was relocated, the building is believed to have been moved to Albion in pieces from Port Mitchell, three miles south. By 1861, there were three hotels in Albion—the Mansion House, run by J.R. Sloan; the Worden House, owned by G.E. Worden; and the Tenant House. (Courtesy Noble County historian Sarah Knopp.)

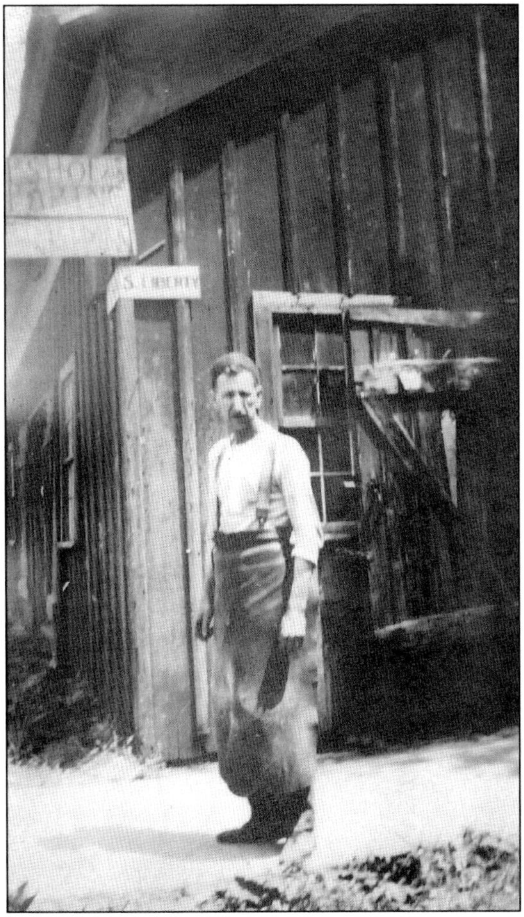

Simon Merriman shows off his blacksmith's shop at Liberty and Main Streets in Albion. He took over the operation of Nicodemus and Haney in the former Beck Blacksmith Shop in 1918 and later moved north on Liberty. The original location became a Chevy garage, then Noble REMC, and today is the Central Noble School District superintendent's office. Merriman had a son, Carl, who was a painter, and a daughter, Ruby Pierce, who worked at Black Mercantile. Ruby and her husband later owned a pool house and ran a family restaurant for many years. Simon passed away at age 98, but the family business presence in Albion remains, thanks to descendant Don "Duber" Merriman, who owns Doc's Hardware. (Both, courtesy Helen Swanson.)

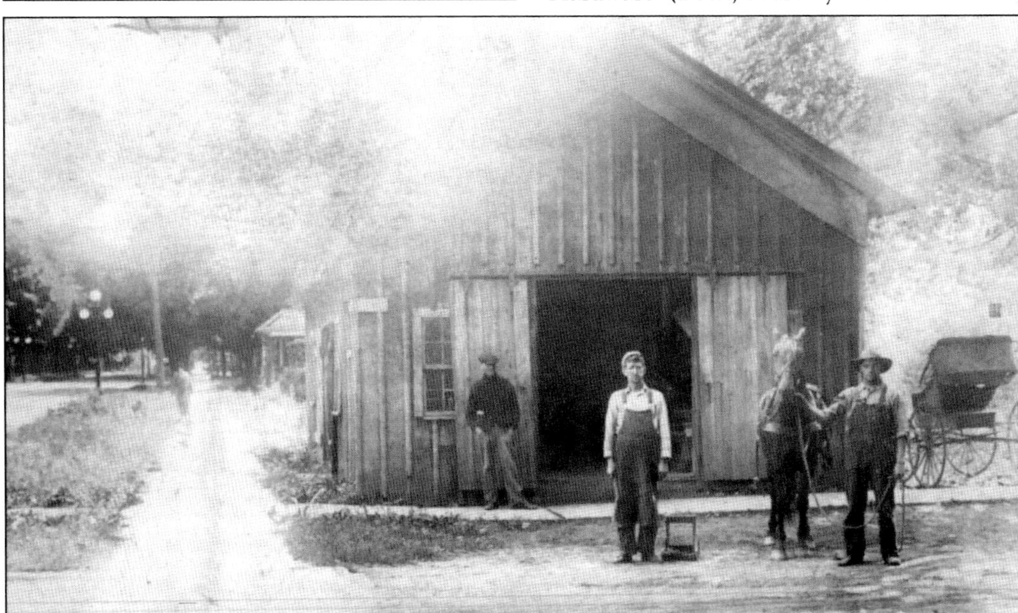

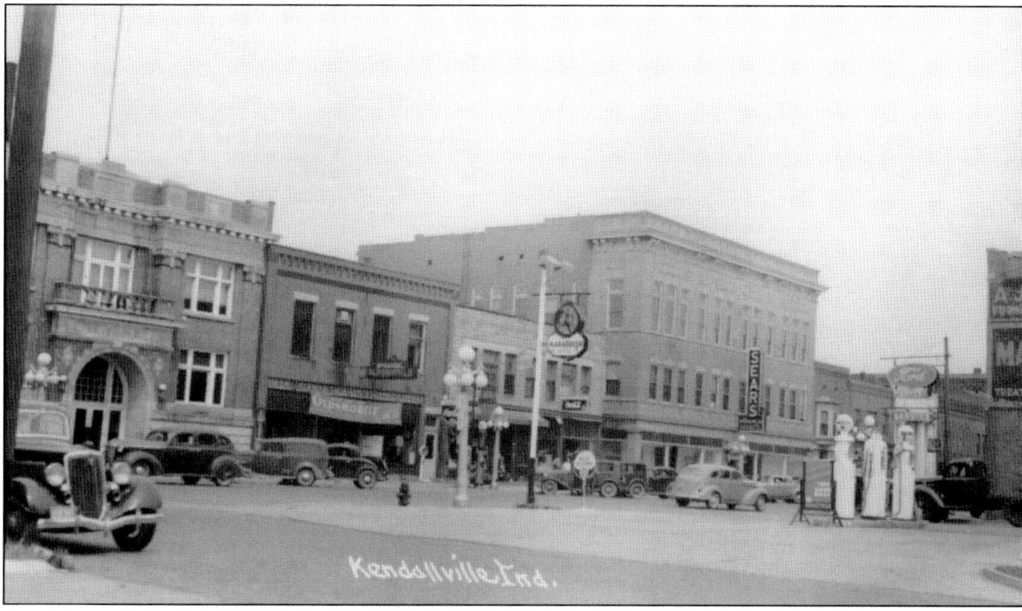

The above 1943 photograph of downtown Kendallville shows the city hall on the left, followed by an Oldsmobile dealer and Shell station, while Sears occupies a three-story building farther right. Gas pumps across the street reveal a station that is still in business, as a convenience store. Sears later moved to a store farther north by the railroad tracks, then to an appliance store on the north end of the city. The photograph below shows the same area, about 20 years earlier. Although businesses have changed, little else except the style of cars is different. The post in the middle of the street reminds drivers to keep to the right. (Both, courtesy Mike Mapes.)

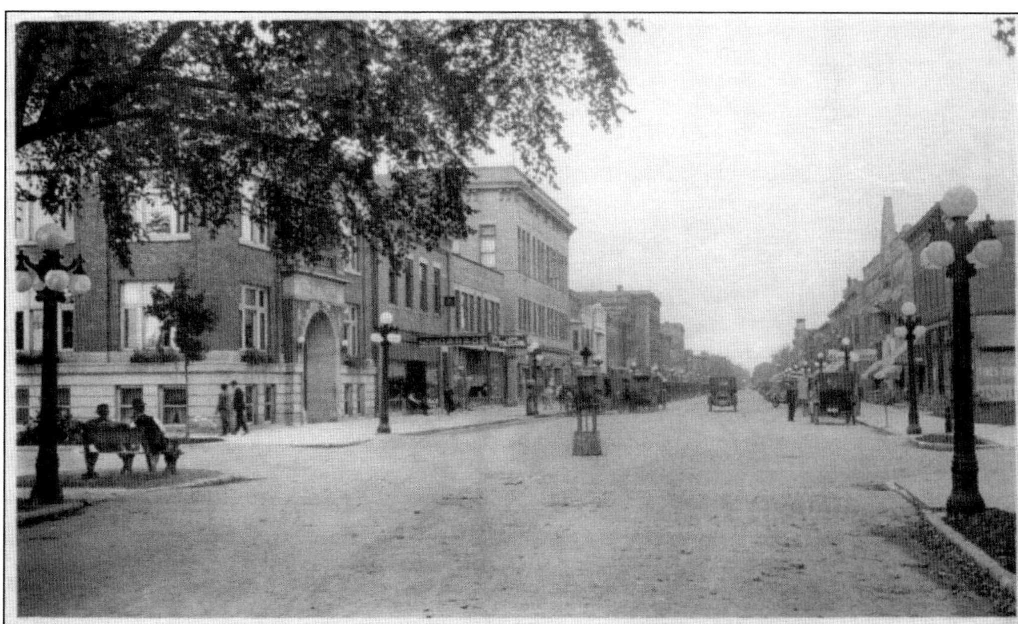

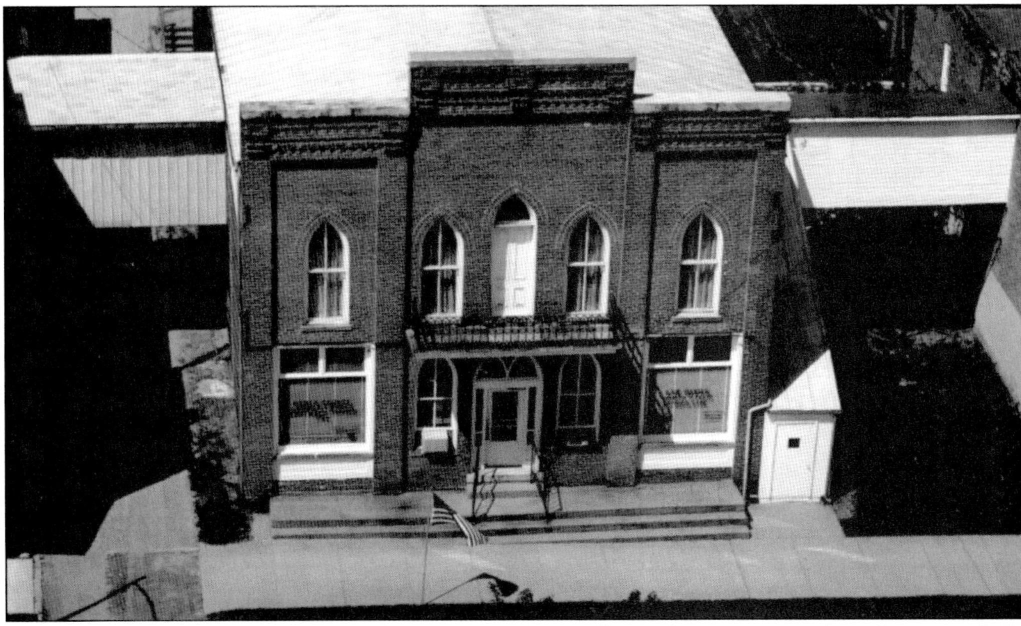

The Albion Opera House was built in 1879 and was almost lost in 1931 when fire gutted the upstairs. The building held a wide variety of events and businesses, including newspapers, roller-skating, theater, dances, basketball games, and political gatherings. When the present courthouse was built in 1887, county offices moved across the street to the Opera House, and high schools held graduation ceremonies there. Excel Furnishings constructed second-story bridges to buildings on either side to display their furniture. In 2014, the building was sold to the Noble County Courthouse Square Preservation Society, which intends to pass it on to a new generation of users. The photograph below shows an iconic view of Albion, looking north from the courthouse tower around 1890 with the Albion Opera House at center right. (Above, NCHS; below, courtesy Noble County historian Sarah Knopp.)

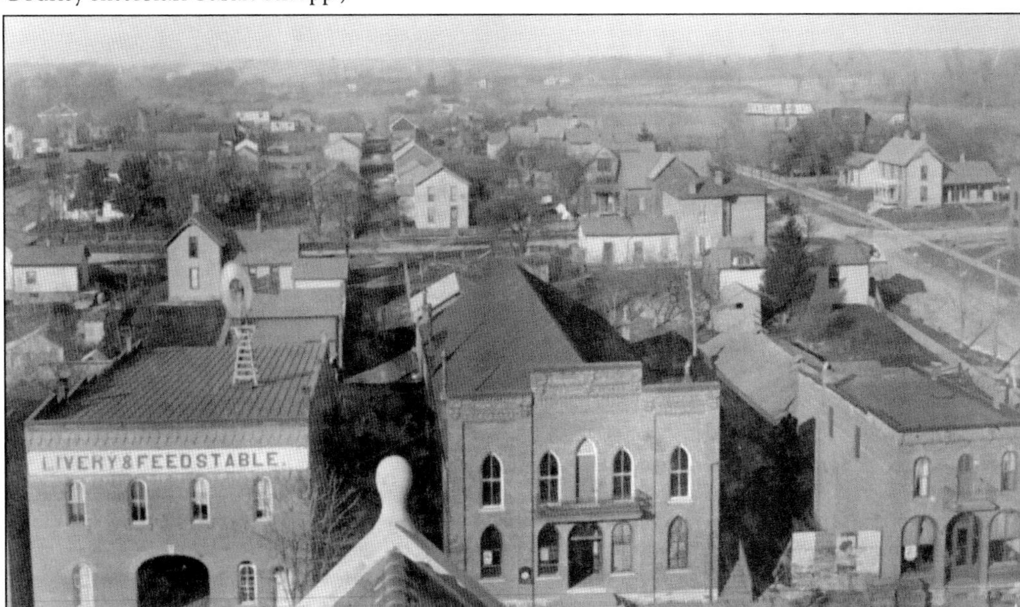

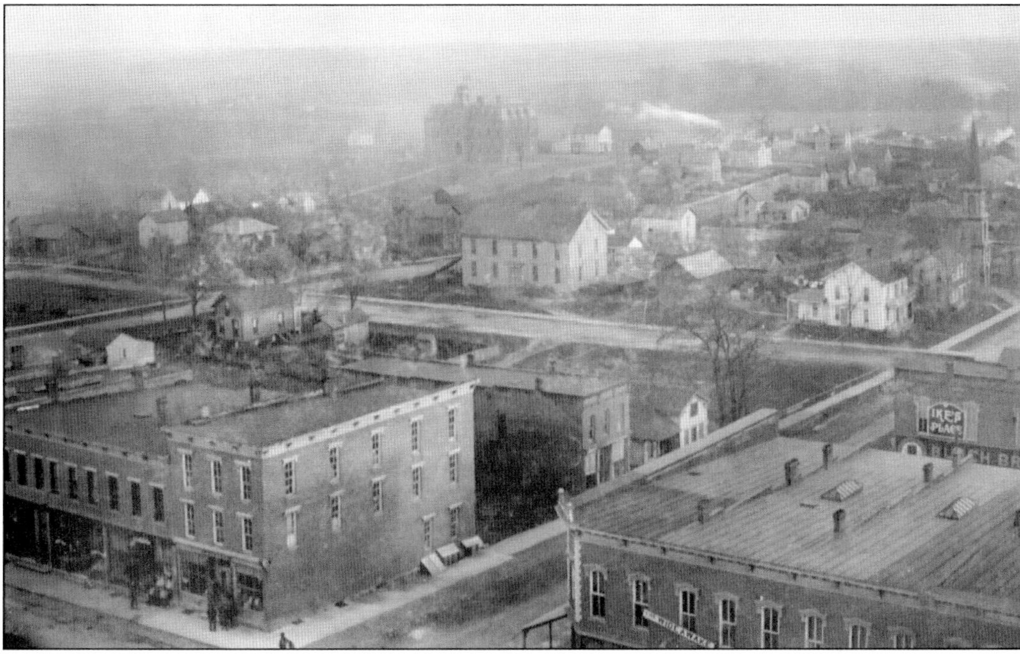

A view from the courthouse southeast shows the Albion School in the background, a seminary near the center, the Black Building lower left, and, lower right, the Wide Awake Grocery. The Wide Awake was run by Cornelius B. Phillips in what was once known as the Clapp Block. Phillips spent two terms as Noble County auditor. (Courtesy Noble County historian Sarah Knopp.)

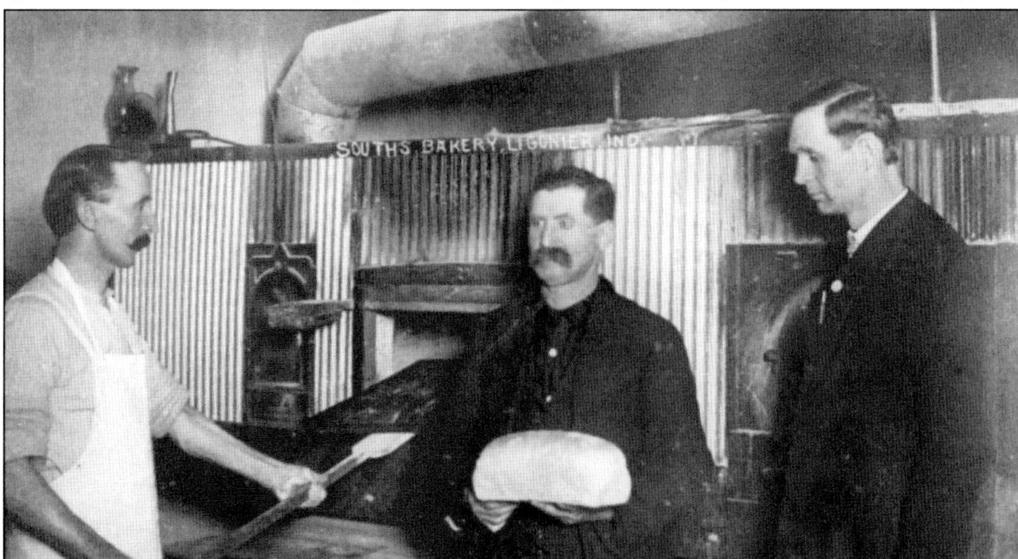

Workers show their wares at South's Bakery, in Ligonier. Food has always been associated with the city: settlers arrived to find beds of wild strawberries. In 1952, Ligonier began celebrating Strawberry Valley Days. The name of the event later changed to the Ligonier Marshmallow Festival, because a major employer in the area was Kidd's Marshmallow. Between Kidd's Marshmallow and Kendallville's Kraft plant, at one time two-thirds of the country's marshmallows were made in Noble County. (STHS.)

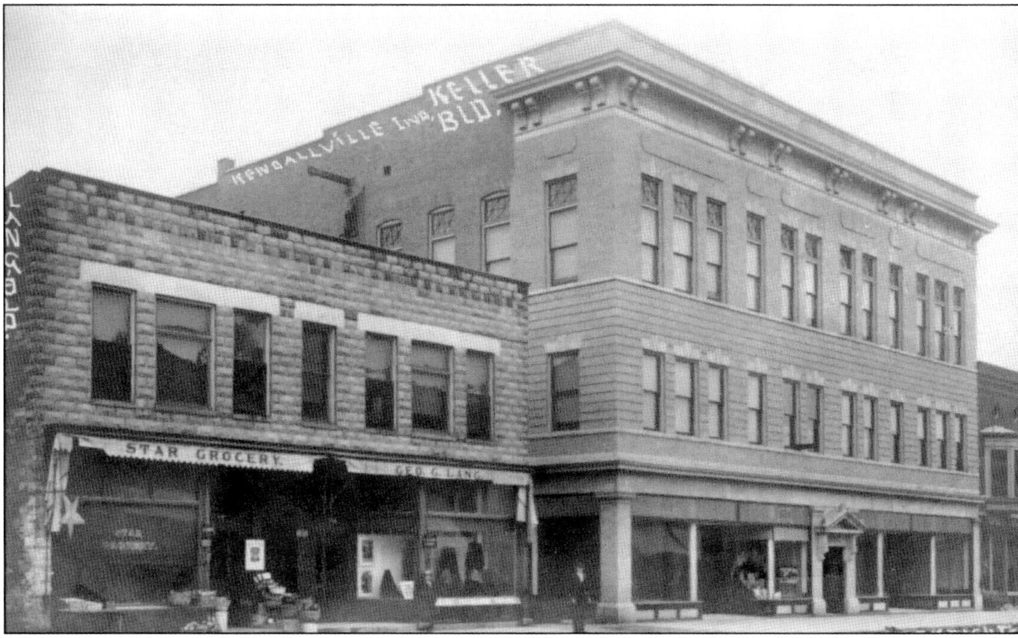

The three-story Keller Building in Kendallville was erected in 1870 by Jacob Keller, a German Jewish businessman. It started as a dry goods store and, in 1889, became a bank that two years later incorporated as Noble County Bank and Trust. On the left is the Star Grocery, run by George Lang. (Courtesy Mike Mapes.)

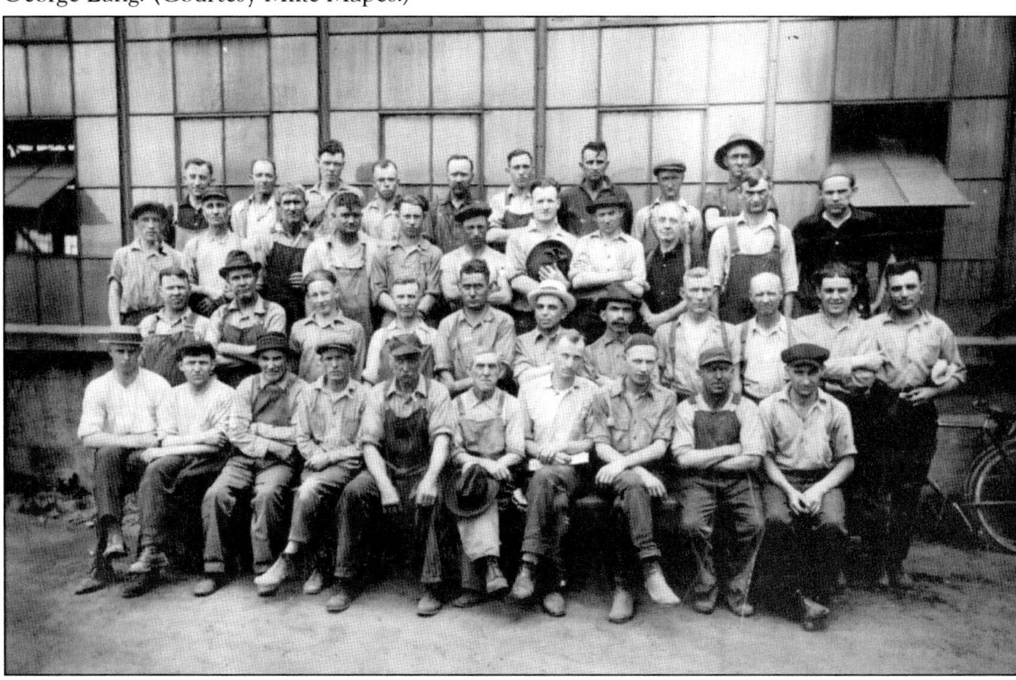

A crew from Newnan Foundry in Kendallville poses for a photograph in the late 1910s. After changing ownership, the industry that is now called Dalton Foundry was shut down almost 90 years later. As of 2015, the foundry complex was being torn down and prepared for new business opportunities. (NCHS.)

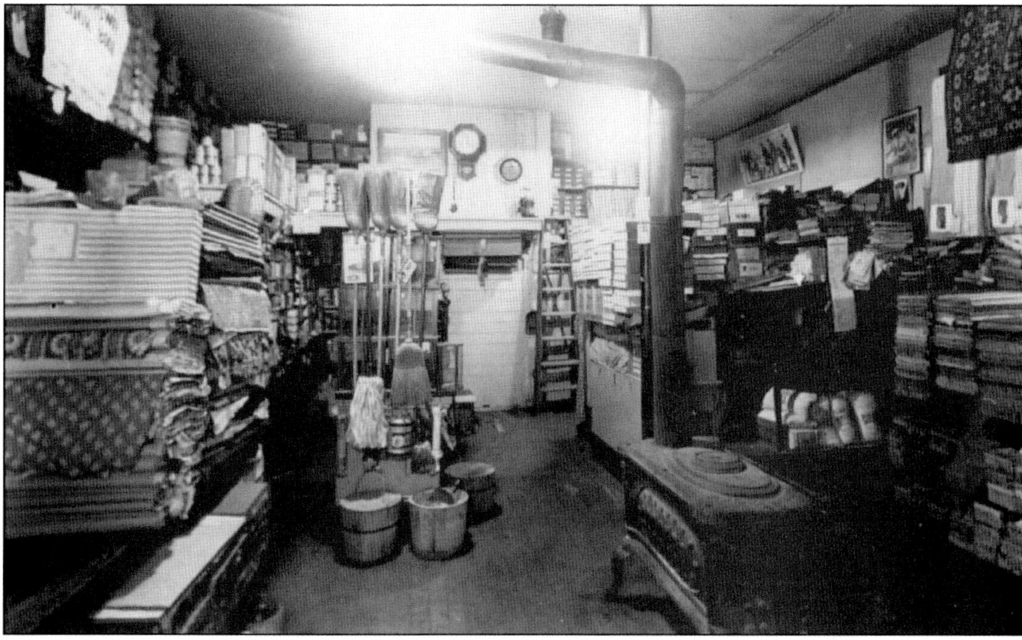

Berger and Sons naturally considered itself to have the finest hardware in Northern Indiana, and it certainly had a wide selection in a deep, if not wide, store. The hardware store was on the east side of the Noble County Courthouse square in Albion, south of the alley between a bank and the Albion Post Office, and not far from a second hardware store. In 1881, Jesse Davis Berger came to Albion from his hardware store in Cromwell and purchased the hardware stock of Markey and Walters on Main Street. In 1891, he moved to the east side of the square, to a building that eventually became the Albion Hardware Co. When the hardware store was turned over to P.J. Stanley in 1911, it was one of the oldest establishments in town. (Both, NCHS.)

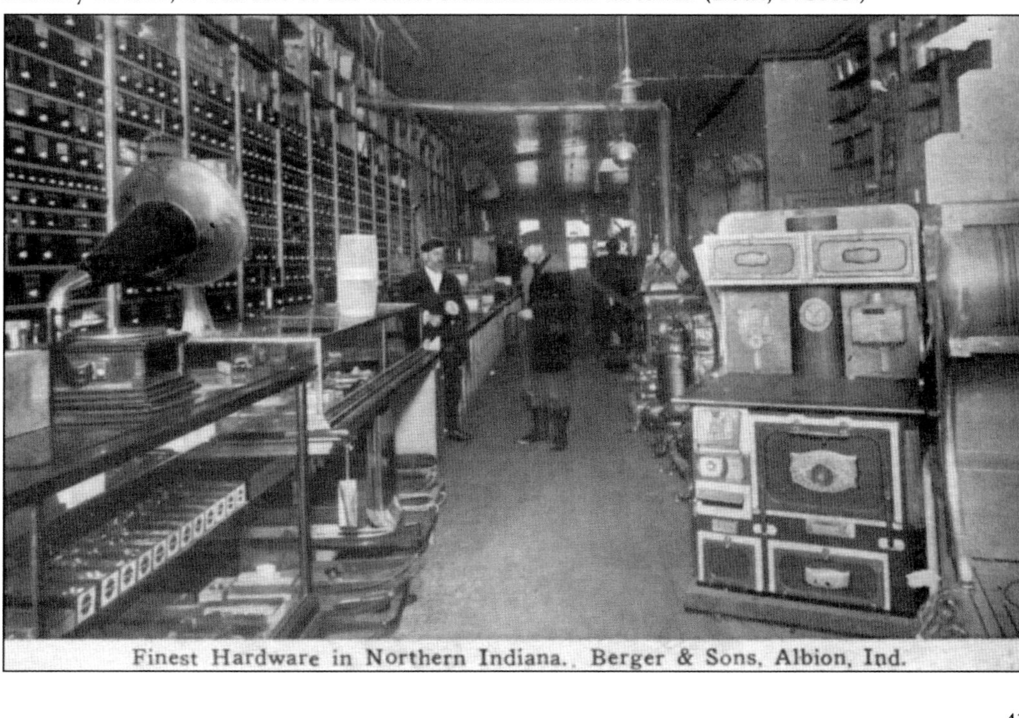

Finest Hardware in Northern Indiana. Berger & Sons, Albion, Ind.

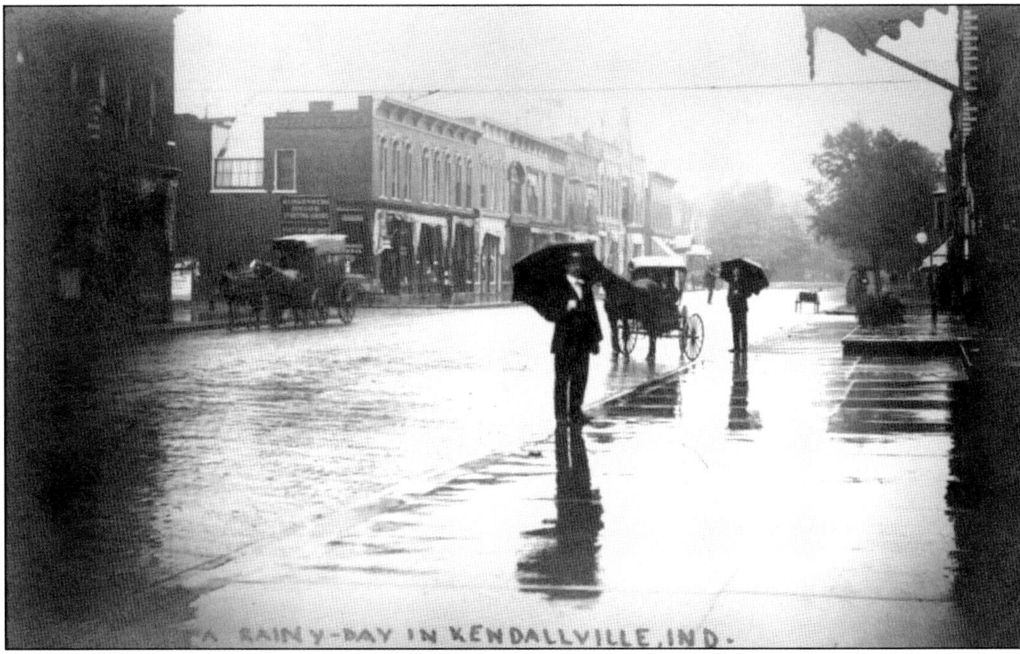

The limits of photography at the time made rainy-day photographs rare, but this one was shot in downtown Kendallville in the late 1800s. Near center left is Klinkenberg Drugs, which was established in 1889 and stayed open for the next 111 years. (Courtesy Mike Mapes.)

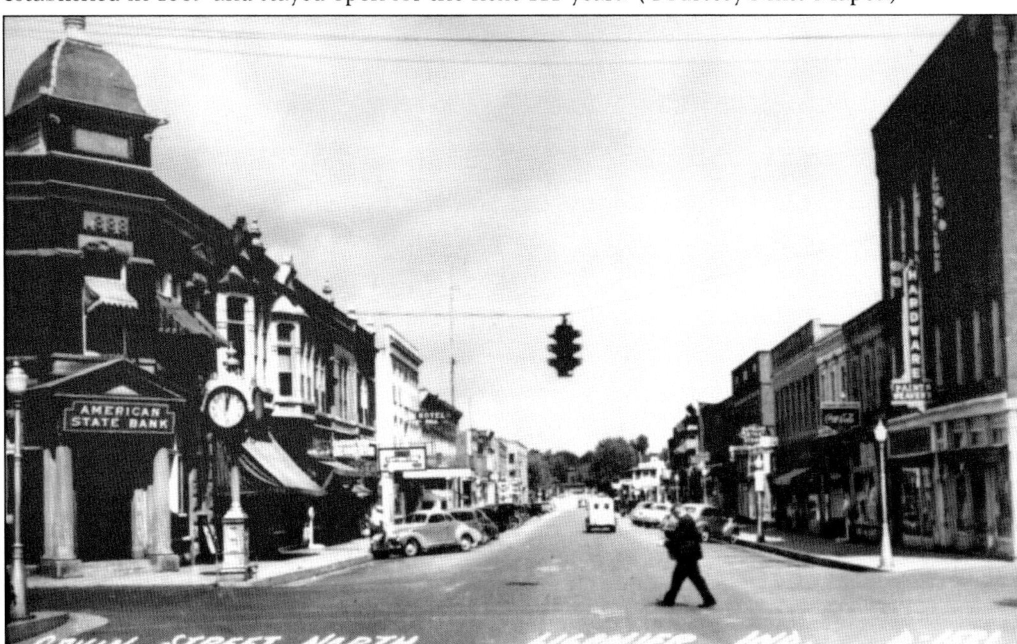

The American State Bank building on Cavin Street no longer exists, but Ligonier has grown into Noble County's second-largest community. Jewish immigrants began settling there in the 1850s, and 40 years later over a quarter of the population was Jewish. Main Street was called Little Jerusalem and was lined with Victorian homes. On Main Street, Congregation Ahavath Shalom built a synagogue. That building later became the Ligonier Public Library. (STHS.)

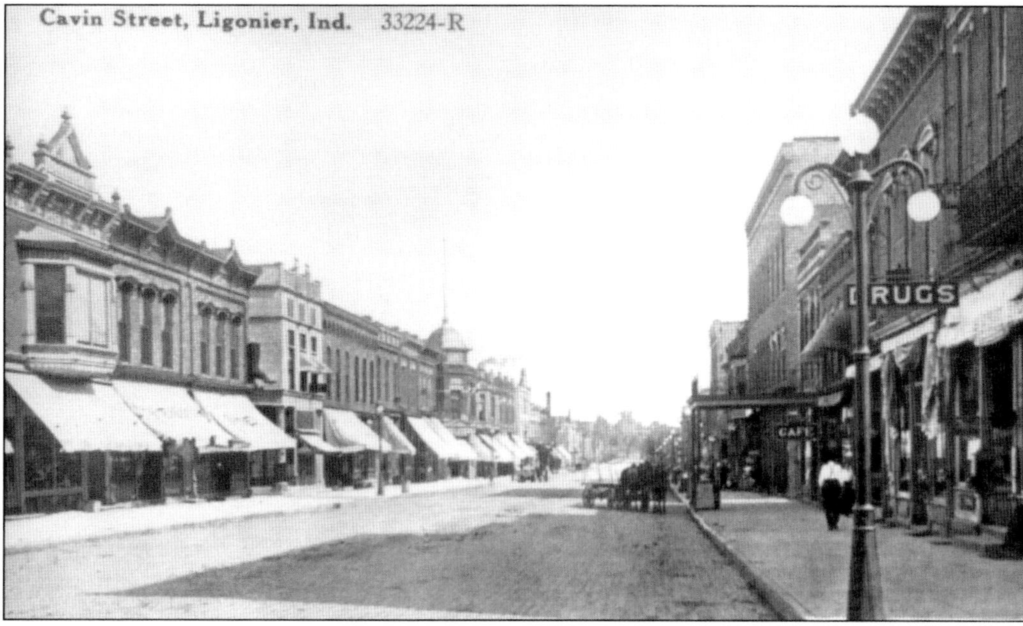

Downtown Ligonier is booming in these photographs from around the turn of the 20th century. The city was laid out in 1835—a year before Noble County was organized—by Isaac Cavin, who was later immortalized by having the main street named after him. Some of the earliest settlers made their homes on the rich soil of Perry's Prairie, and found strawberries growing in abundance along the banks of the Elkhart River, where Ligonier now stands. Legend has it that Native Americans dumped animal bones there, making the soil rich for the berries. Another village, Rochester, was a short distance southeast but faded away when the railroad went through Ligonier. (Both, STHS.)

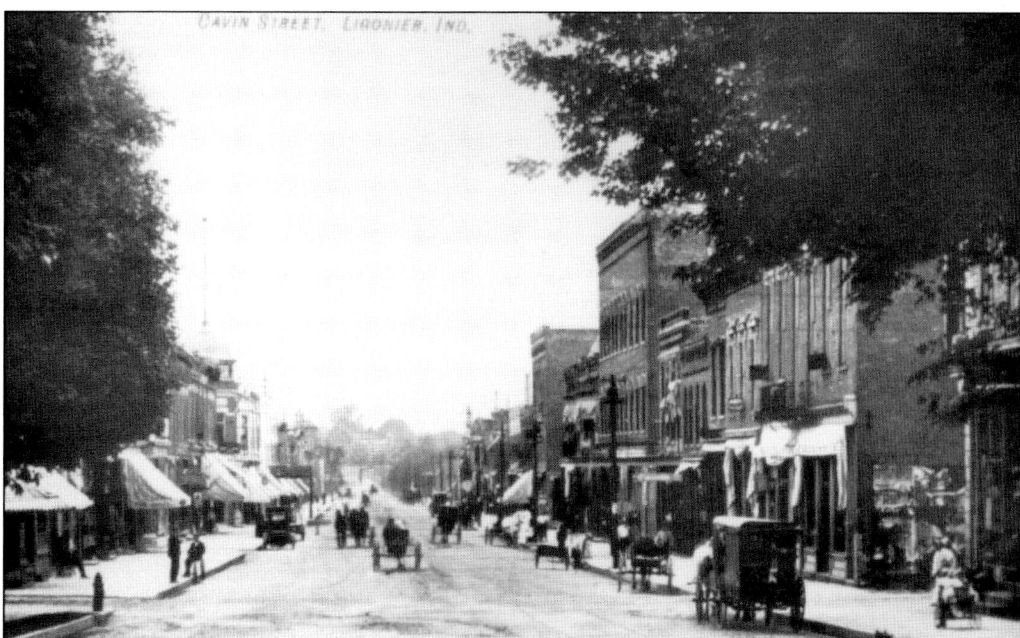

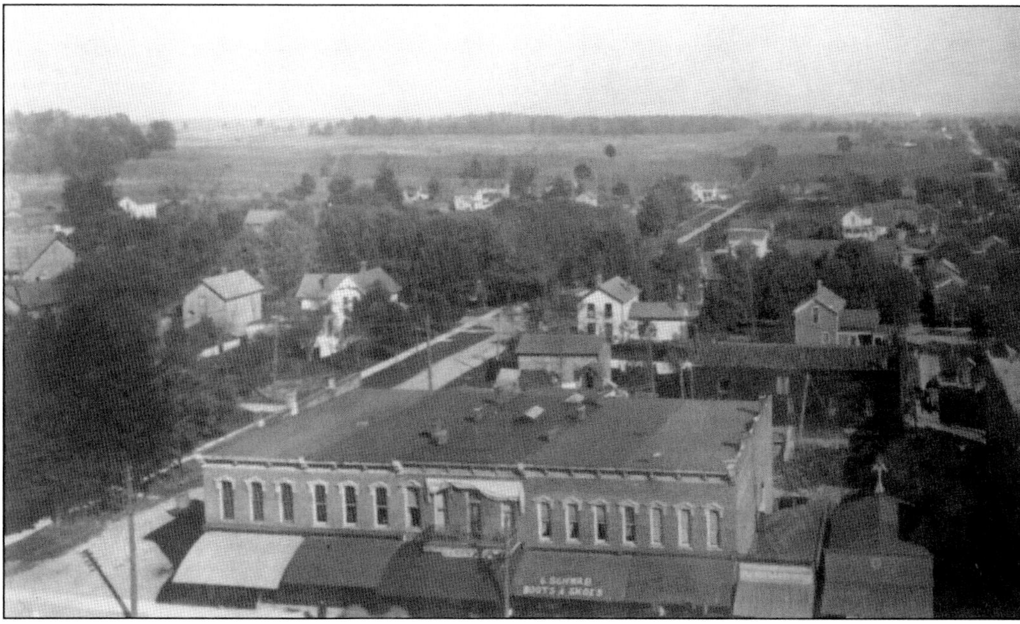

Businesses on the east side of the Noble County Courthouse square include the boot and shoe shop of Gottlieb Schwab. Schwab came to America in 1866 and moved to Albion in the mid-1880s after his Wawaka shop was destroyed by fire. When he died in 1926 at age 82, he was the oldest businessman in town. A hardware store is left of the Schwab shop, near the location Doc's Hardware occupies today. (NCHS.)

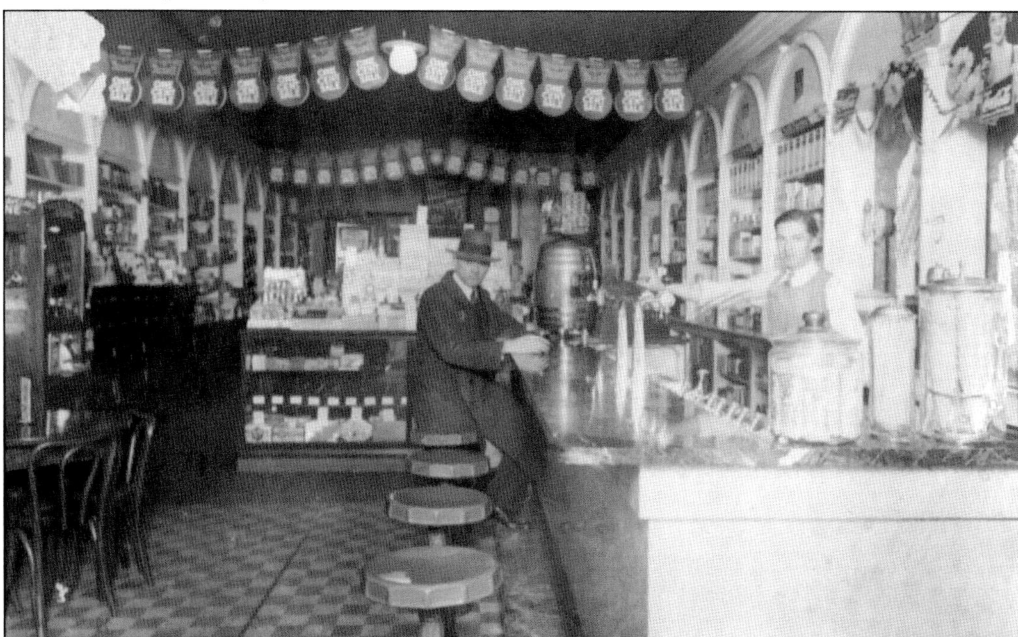

Soda jerk Glen Black serves a customer at Halferty Drug Store, on the south side of the courthouse square. Halferty was open for many years and is still a legend to older Albionites, who fondly remember waiting in long lines for ice cream at a nickel a cone. Black, a 50-year Albion businessman, later helped establish Chain O' Lakes State Park. (Courtesy Noble County historian Sarah Knopp.)

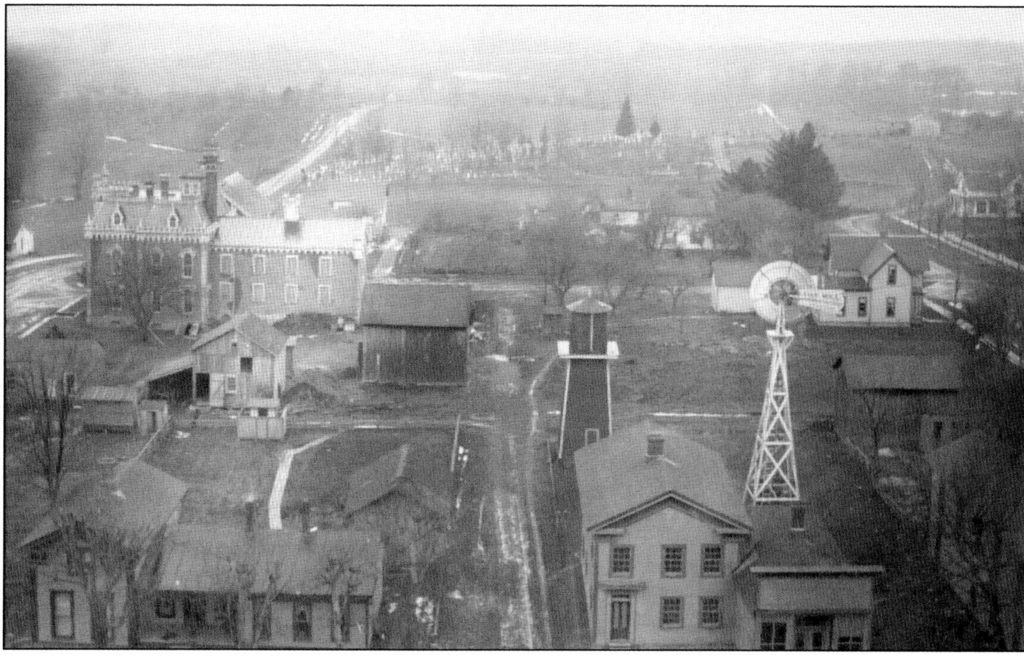

A late 1800s view from the courthouse shows the Noble County Jail center left and the Albion Cemetery—now Rose Hill Cemetery—in the distance. The windmill is from Flint and Walling, a company formed in Kendallville in 1866. Flint and Walling began manufacturing water pumps and windmills in 1874. In 1878, it patented the Star Windmill, one of which is seen here. (Courtesy Noble County historian Sarah Knopp.)

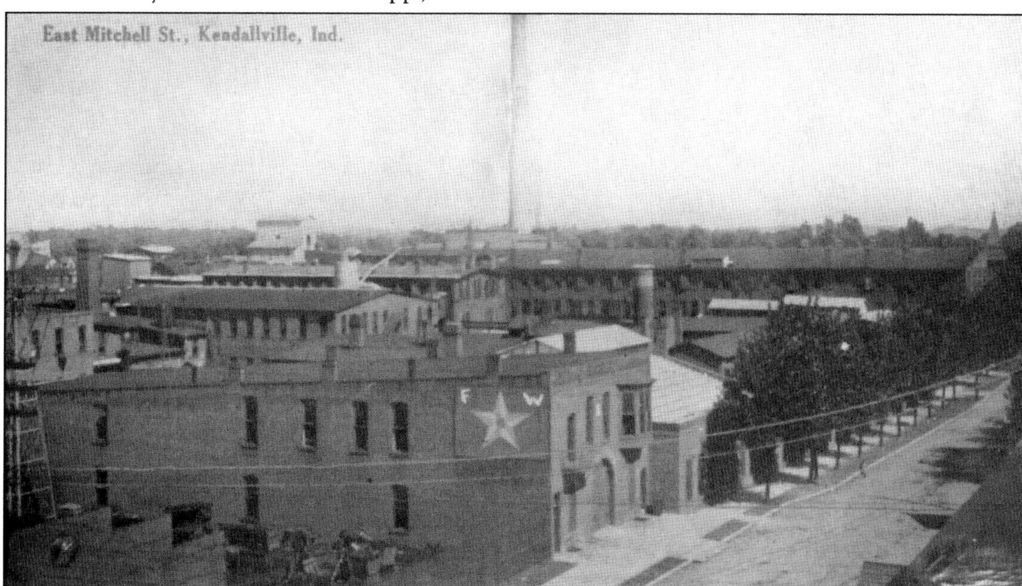

A star on the side of Kendallville's Flint and Walling plant advertises its most popular windmill model, which was made from 1878 until 1954. At one point, more than 30 windmill manufacturers were located within 50 miles of Kendallville, sending their products around the world. The Kendallville Windmill Museum, later named the Mid-America Windmill Museum, was established in 1992 to preserve that heritage and now displays 52 windmills. (Courtesy Mike Mapes.)

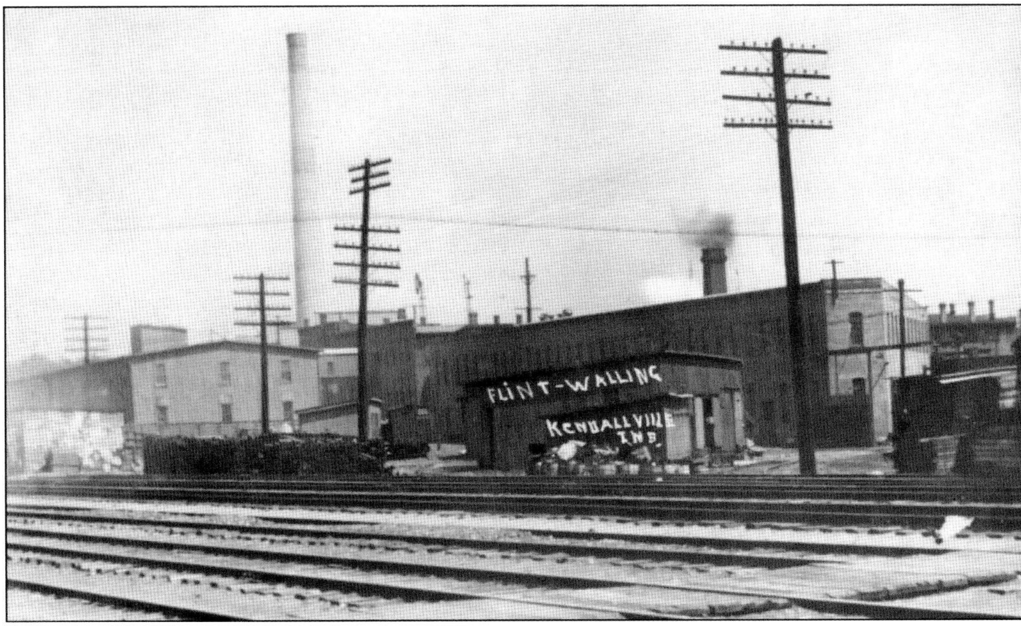

Simeon Flint and David C. Walling met in Norwalk, Ohio. Both were machinists, and in 1866 they moved to Kendallville and bought into the metalworking shop of William Hildreth. Hildreth had started a foundry in 1854, and with the new partners began producing agricultural implements. By 1874, Flint, Walling & Company was manufacturing water pumps and windmills that were shipped worldwide for decades. (Courtesy Mike Mapes.)

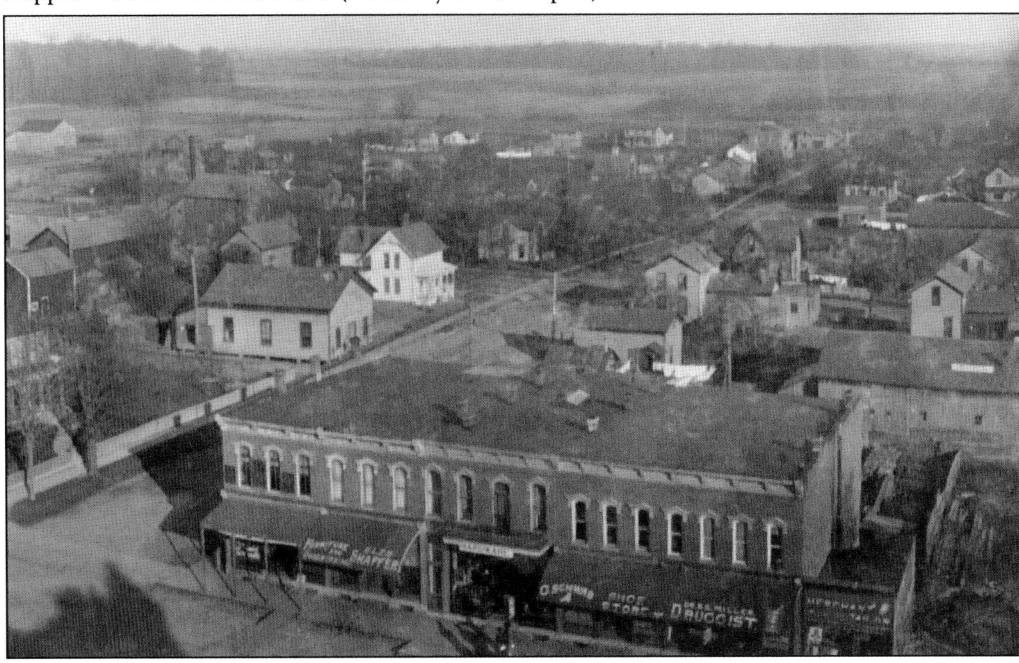

The south side of the courthouse square shows a variety of 1890-era businesses, including a furniture store run by the undertaker, Elza Shaffer; a hardware store; G. Schwab's shoe store; and Dr. B.E. Miller, druggist. At the far right is a small tailor shop. (Courtesy Noble County historian Sarah Knopp.)

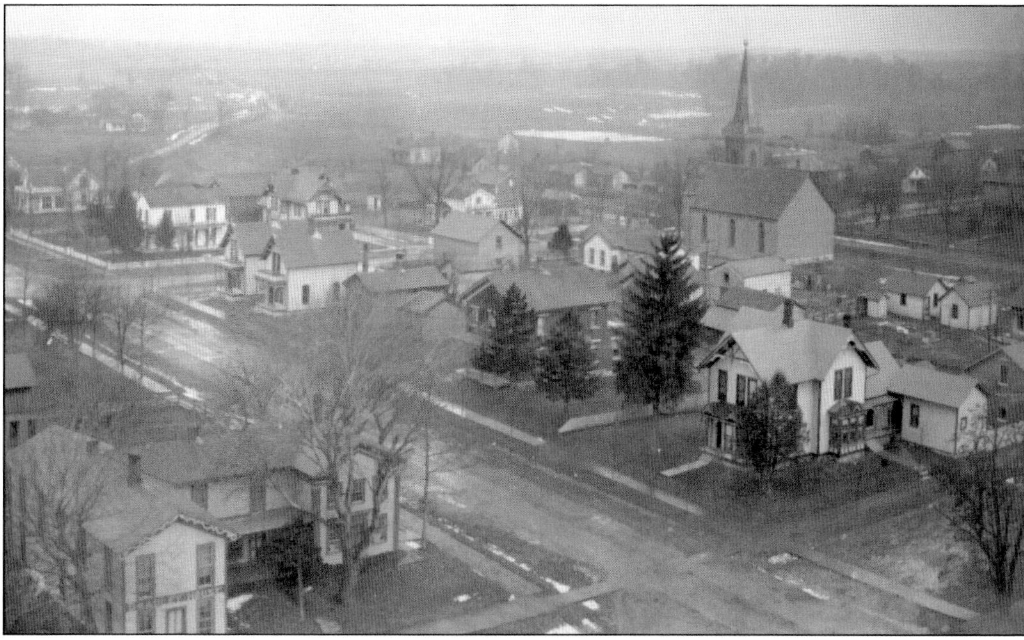

The Bradley House, one of Albion's early hotels in the late 1800s, is seen on the bottom left of a photograph taken from the courthouse tower. The First Presbyterian Church at Oak and Highland Streets is at center right. (Courtesy Noble County historian Sarah Knopp.)

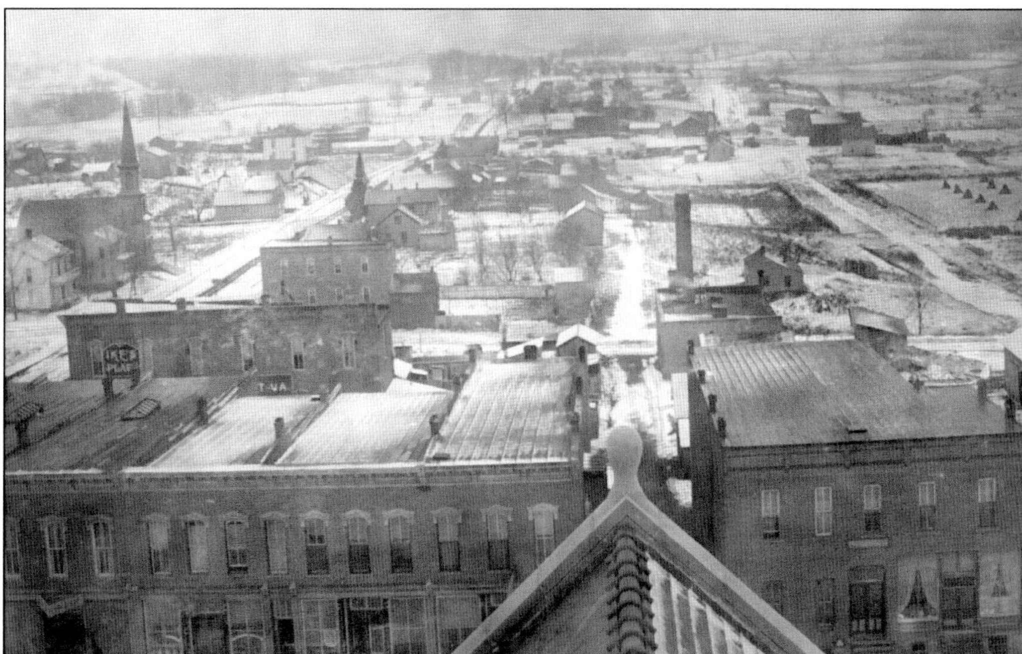

Winter settles over southern Albion in this 1894 photograph. At bottom right is the Williams House, built in the early 1880s. It was later run by the Rumbaugh family, then housed several businesses, including the Albion License Branch and Ron's TV and Appliance. Pictured directly behind it is the heating plant for Noble County Courthouse, which is now the Albion Eagles building. (Courtesy Noble County historian Sarah Knopp.)

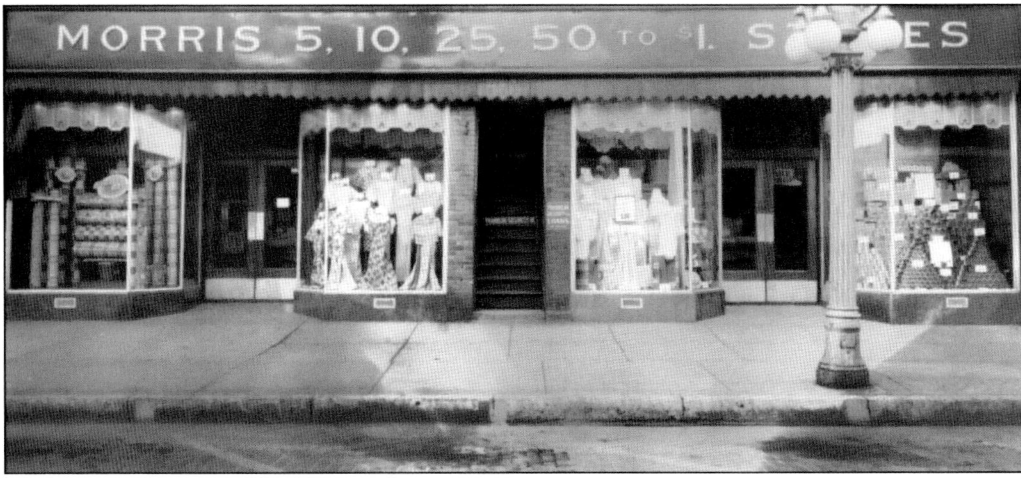

In 1951, Murphy Co. purchased the Morris 5&10 Cent stores in Indiana, Illinois, and Ohio. Kendallville's Main Street shop was one of the 71 Bluffton-based variety stores purchased, and it was replaced by a G.C. Murphy Store. In 1985, Murphy merged with Ames Department Stores; Ames had a store on the north side of Kendallville until the company went bankrupt. (Courtesy Mike Mapes.)

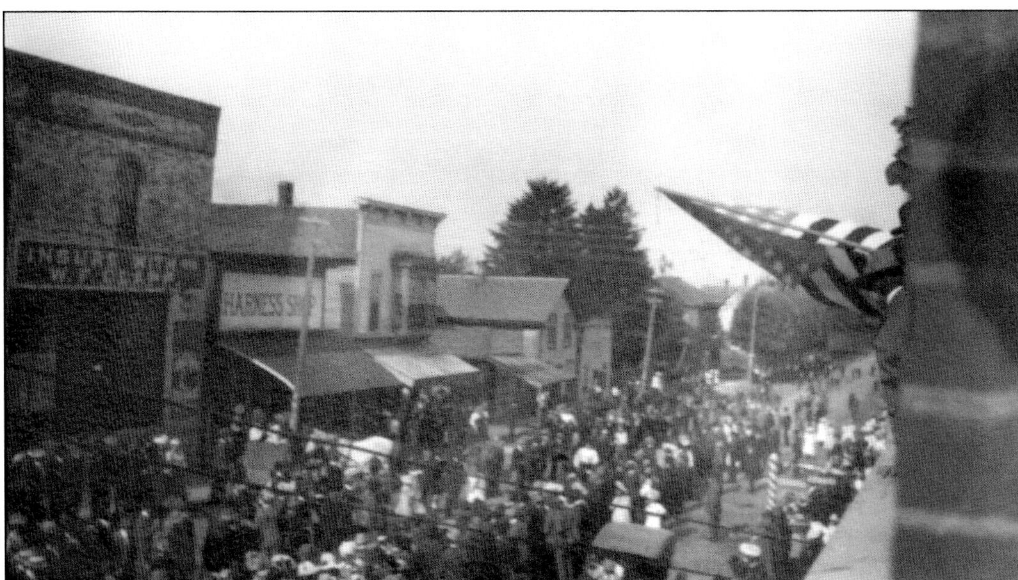

Crowds throng Albion's East Main Street in the summer of 1901, seen from an upper story of the Black Building at Main and Orange Streets. In small towns, any celebration tended to bring out the whole population. The building to the left was the insurance office of W.F. Clapp. The building next door was a harness shop owned by P.A. Sunday, who was Albion's first town marshal. (Courtesy Linda Shultz.)

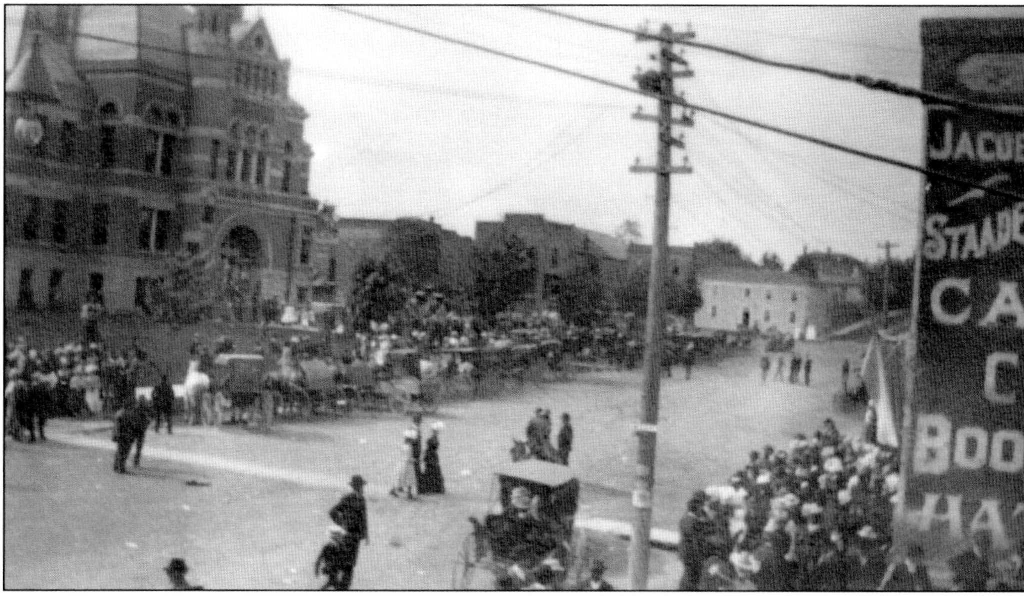

Albion buzzes in the summer of 1901, in a photograph taken from the Black Building with a view looking northwest. The Noble County Courthouse is to the left, the Albion Opera House at center, and the Worden House to the right on Jefferson Street. Directly behind the Worden House is a home that now houses the Brick Ark Inn, a bed-and-breakfast. (Courtesy Linda Shultz.)

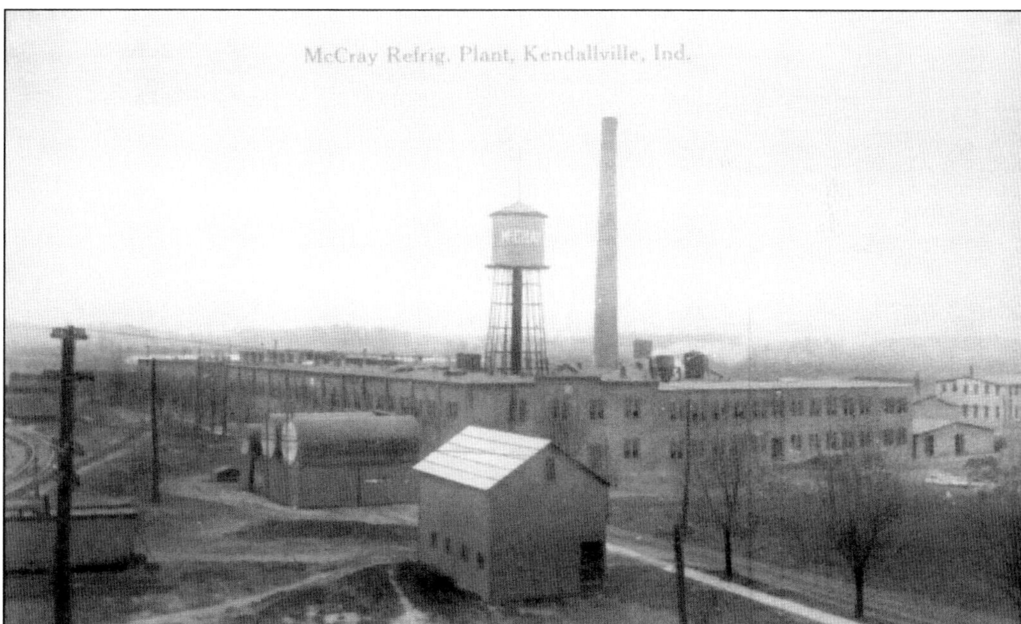

The McCray Refrigeration Plant is booming in this 1921 photograph. The McCrays started out in 1868 dealing in eggs, meat, and poultry. They soon began looking for ways to preserve their products. McCray Refrigerators were shipped around the world from a plant that grew from 2,500 square feet to 310,000 on seven acres. (Courtesy Mike Mapes.)

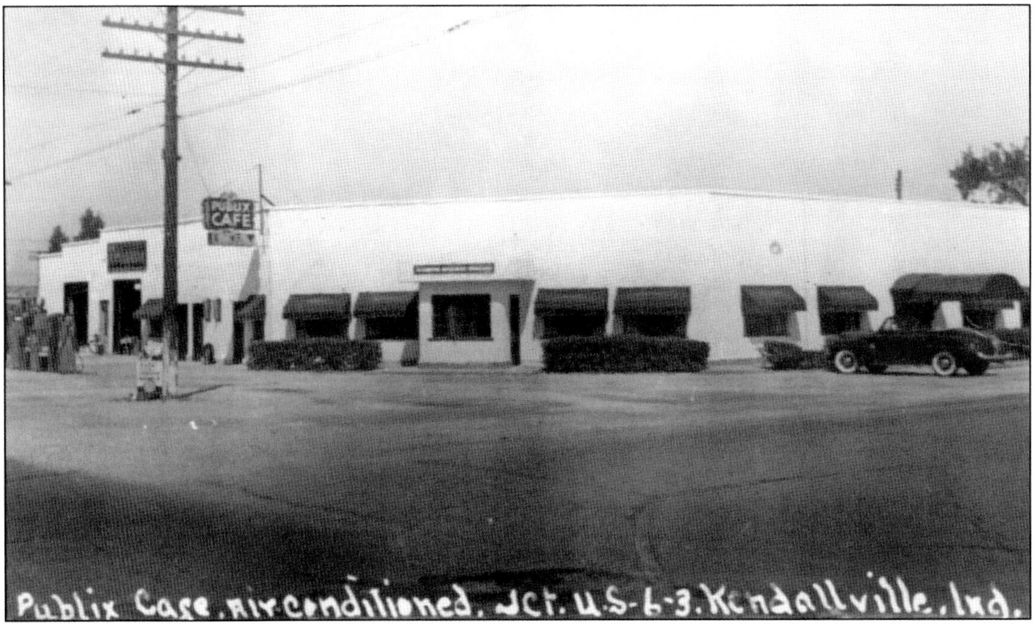

The intersection of US 6 and SR 3 in Kendallville was a great business location, occupied for many years by Gardner's Publix Corners. At one time, the area boasted a café, motel, gift shop, Phillips 66 station, and Buick sales and service, all under the Publix name. In this photograph, gas pumps are on the far left, near a Firestone sign. (Courtesy Mike Mapes.)

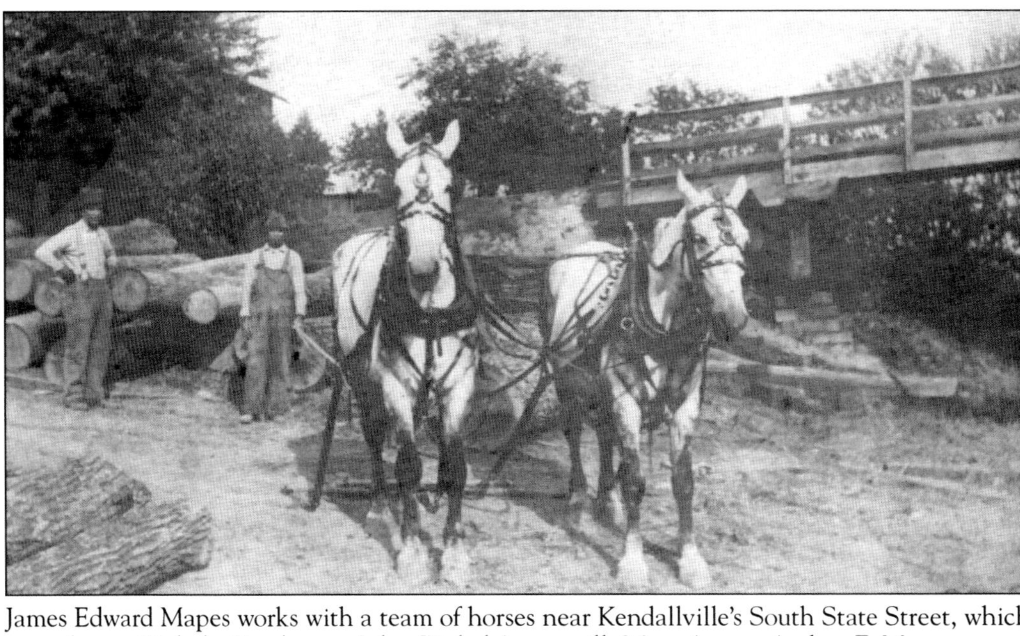

James Edward Mapes works with a team of horses near Kendallville's South State Street, which passed over Diebele Creek near John Diebele's sawmill. Mapes's son, Arthur F. Mapes, wrote Indiana's official state poem and was named state poet laureate. (Courtesy Mike Mapes.)

Four

Agriculture and a Rural World

Most people who immigrated to the west went for land, and often they wanted it for farming. Agriculture was and (to an extent) still is king in Indiana, and Noble County settlers were soon engaged in draining swamps and cutting down trees to make fields. Even occupants of the Poor House, established first east of and then northwest of Albion to house the destitute and infirm, tended fields and cows while staying there.

That is one reason why western Noble County was settled first, along the Fort Wayne–Goshen Road. Many of the earliest settlers came to Perry's Prairie near Ligonier, which was already clear of thick forest and had rich soil. Strawberries already grew in abundance around what became Ligonier. Rumor had it that was because Native Americans discarded animal bones there, fertilizing the soil. Farther south, the soil in the Wolf Lake area was perfect for tubers such as onions, which became the primary crop in the area.

Shipping those onions caused Kimmell, north of Wolf Lake, to boom. In fact, businesses supporting agriculture went up all across the county, and towns grew to support the surrounding farms. Those towns often were established near bodies of water, where hydraulic force could power mills, or near railroads, which could transport farm products.

Most residents out of town at the time were farmers. If a wagon was seen going down a rural road, it was likely to be carrying either crops or supplies for the farm. At one time, a main road entering Albion from the west was paved—but only the eastbound side. The pavement allowed heavy farm wagons to come into town without sinking into dirt or mud; on the way back from town, they were lighter and did not need such a hard surface. It is now called Albion Road, but some people still refer to it as the Halfway Pavement.

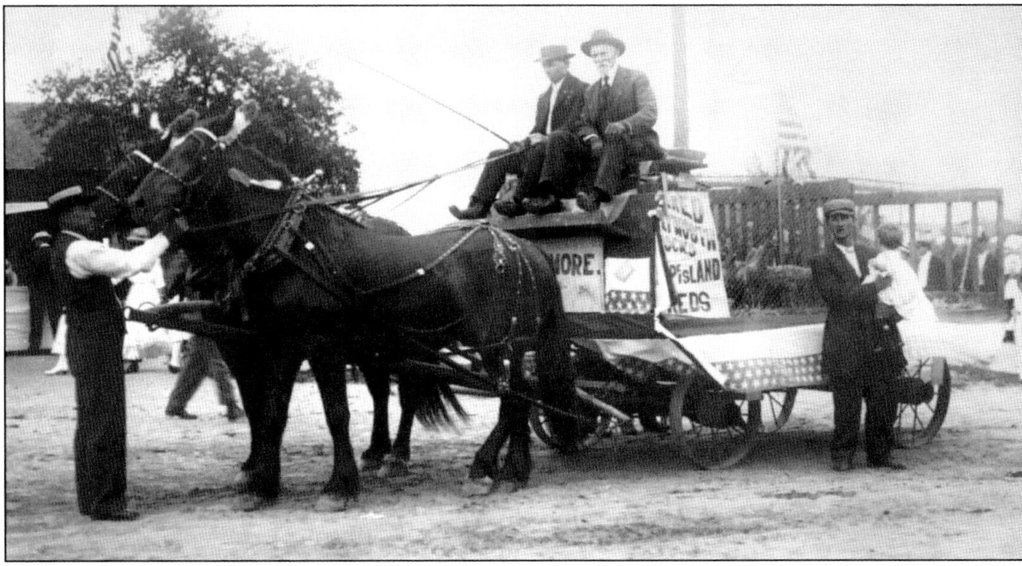

"Granddad" Moore and his son Otto show off their farm goods in the 1908 Wolf Lake Onion Day Parade. Their prizewinning Rhode Island Red chickens demonstrated that there was more to southwest Noble County farming than onions, though that is what most fields around Wolf Lake were growing at the time. Onions were harvested in June and July, then hauled by horse-drawn wagon to the Kimmel train depot for shipping. (Courtesy Mike Mapes.)

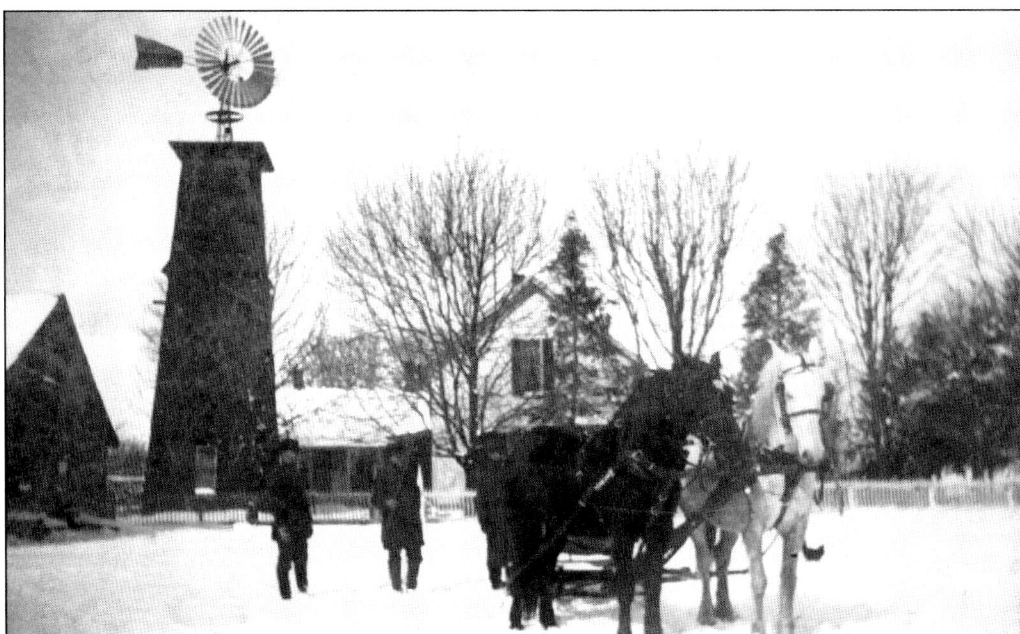

A team of horses goes to work at the Theodore P. Kesler Farm near Brimfield, in north central Noble County, near the turn of the 20th century. Kesler was a Civil War veteran, and his grandfather was reportedly a hero of the Revolutionary War. (NCHS.)

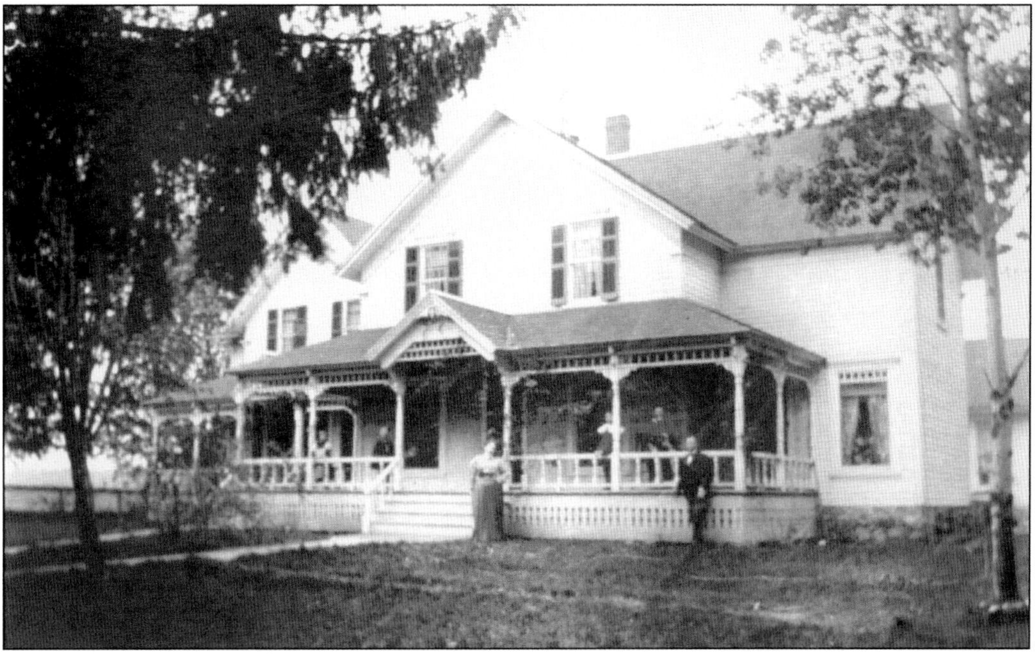

A relaxing moment was captured at the Theodore P. Kesler home along US 6, near Brimfield, in the late 1800s. After growing up as an early settler in Michigan, Kesler served in the Civil War, then came to Noble County to help construct the Lake Shore Railroad. He built this home in north central Noble County in the 1870s and lived there until his death in 1904. (NCHS.)

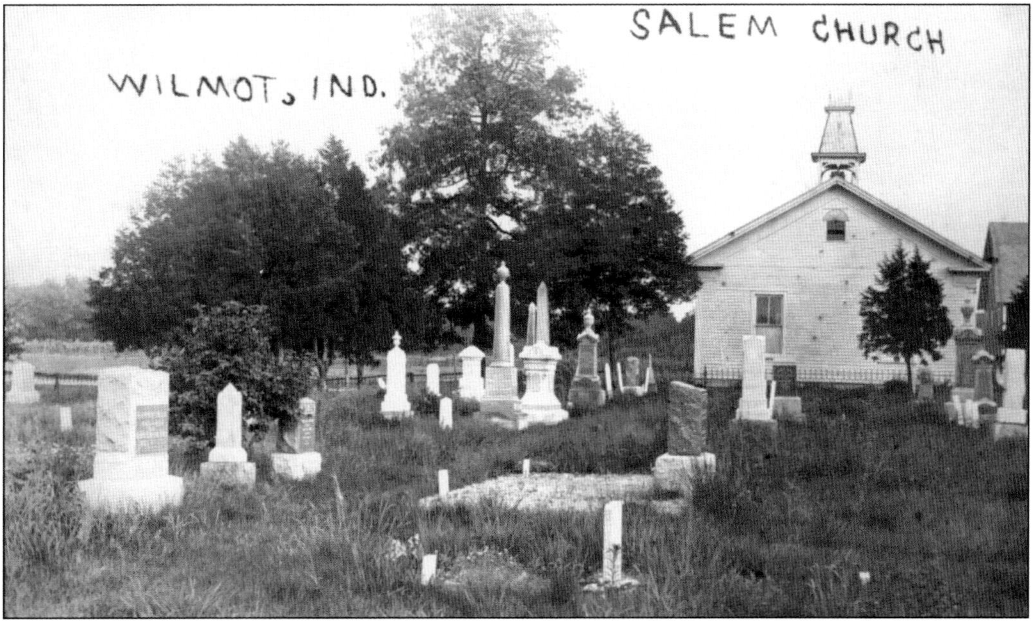

Salem Church and its accompanying cemetery are near the village of Wilmot, in the extreme southwest corner of Noble County. Near the headwaters of the Tippecanoe River, Wilmot was named to establish a post office in the rural area. Although that office was discontinued in 1911, Wilmot at times had a water mill, telephone exchange, general store, and a few other businesses along with the homes. (Courtesy Mike Mapes.)

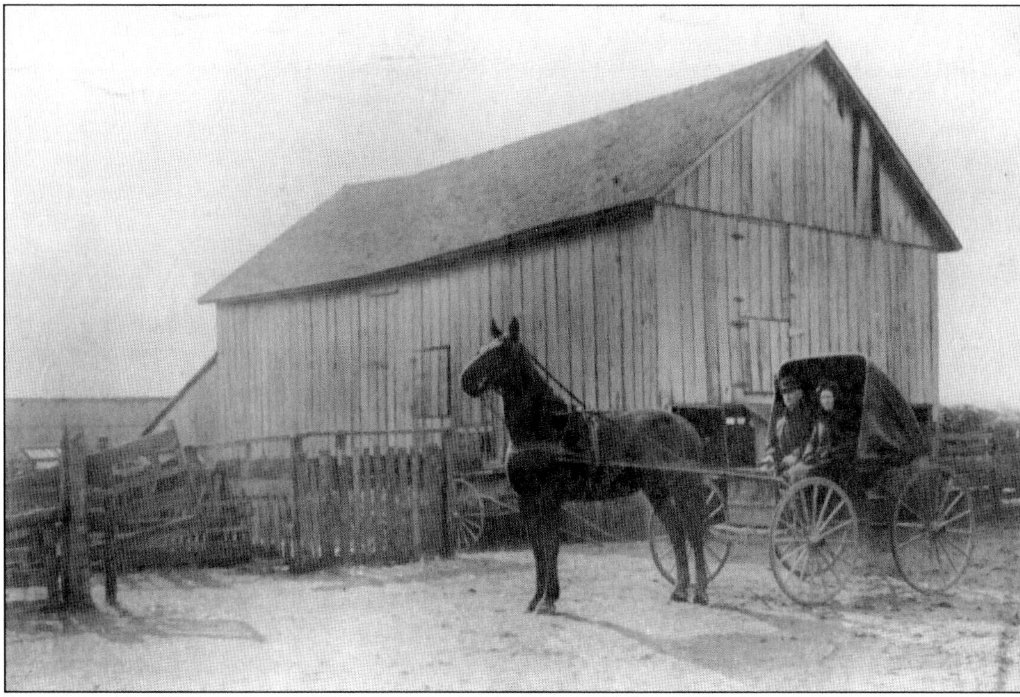

Rollin Blackman of rural Albion and his wife prepare for a ride at their York Township farm in the early 1900s. The Blackmans moved to Noble County from Pennsylvania, sometime before 1838. (NCHS.)

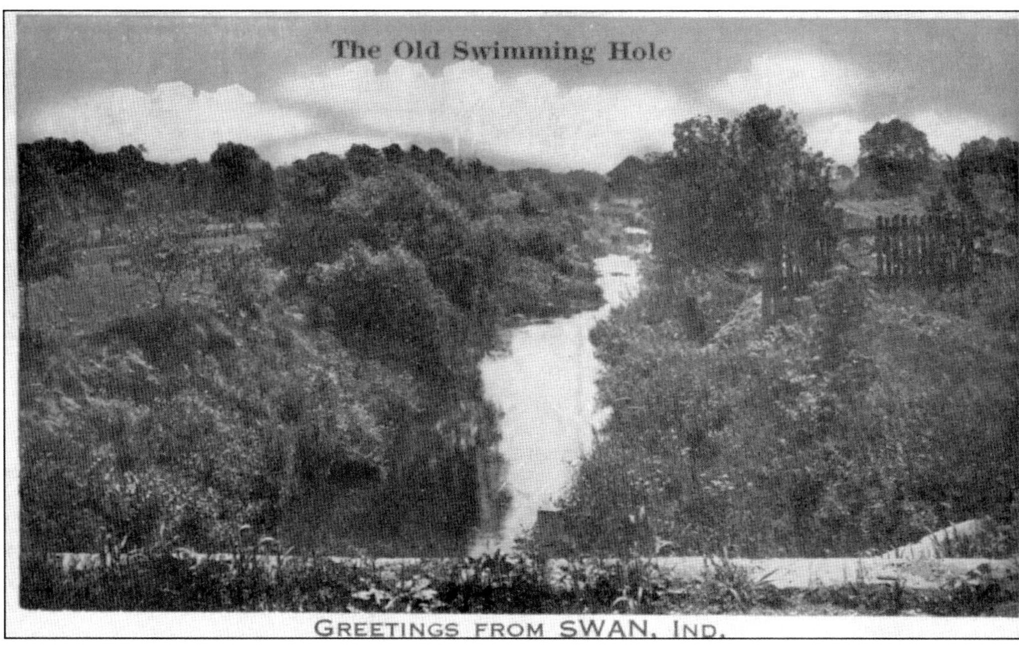

The terrain of southeast Noble County was largely the result of deposits from an ancient glacier, which produced rich soil and fairly level land, as in this Swan Township landscape. In other areas of the county, glacial movement caused ridges and pothole-like lakes. (Courtesy Vern Christlieb.)

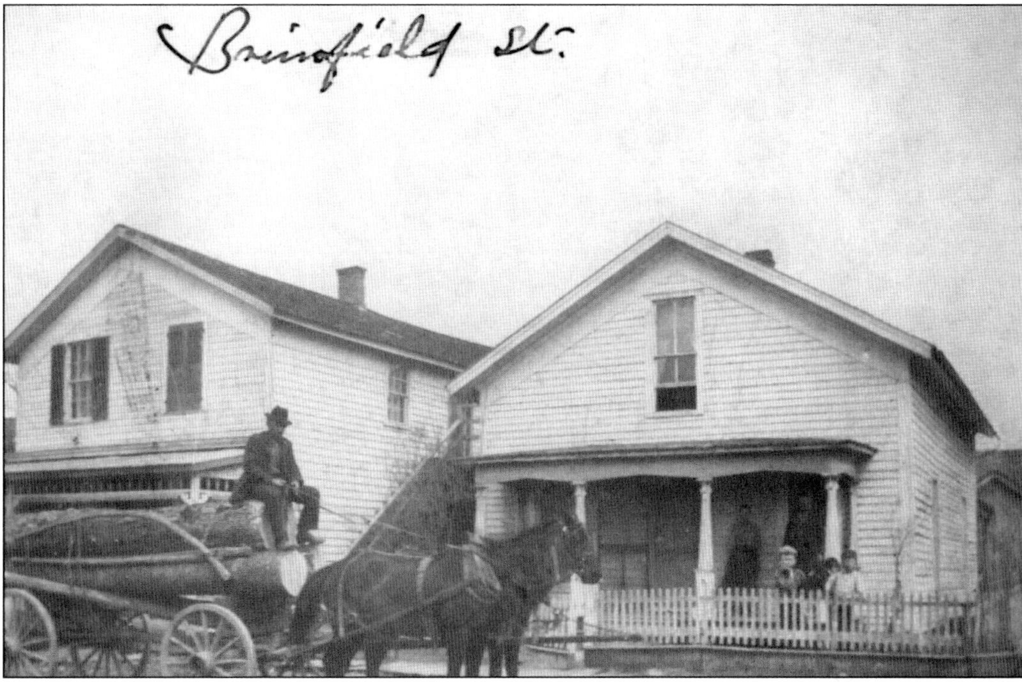

A logging wagon pauses in front of a home occupied by the parents of Wilbur Loy, who in 1890 was a student at Brimfield School. The lumber industry looms large in Brimfield history; Frick Lumber Company, the town's largest employer, has been there since 1924. (Courtesy Marcia Garrett.)

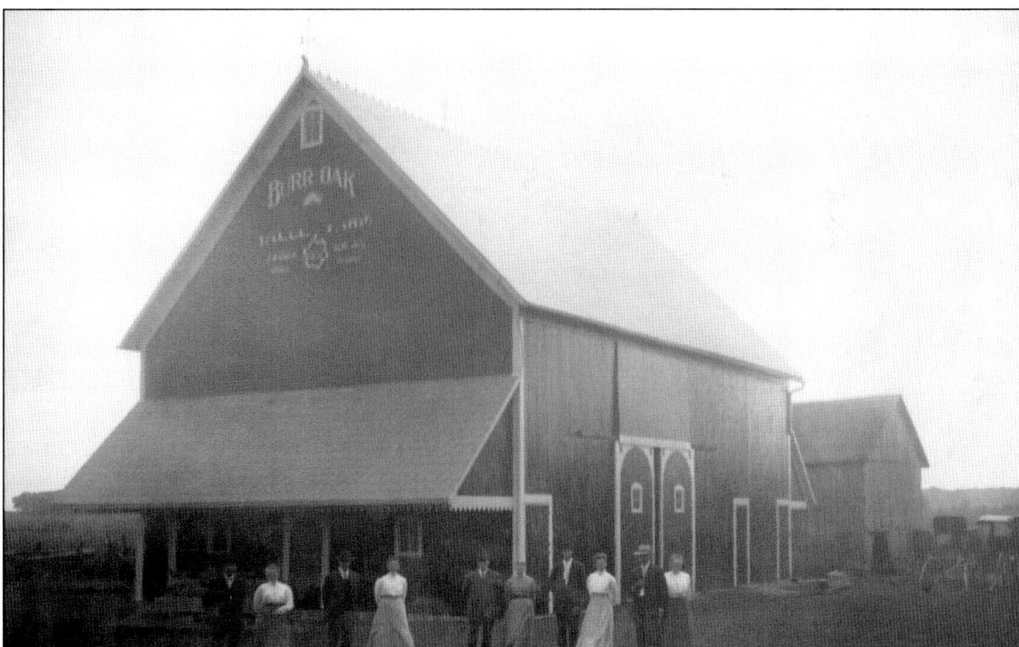

Burr Oak residents stand in front of a 1910 barn, not far from town. Burr Oak, in southwest Noble County near where the first settlers located, is believed to be the location of the first "real" schoolhouse in the county, built in 1840. (NCHS.)

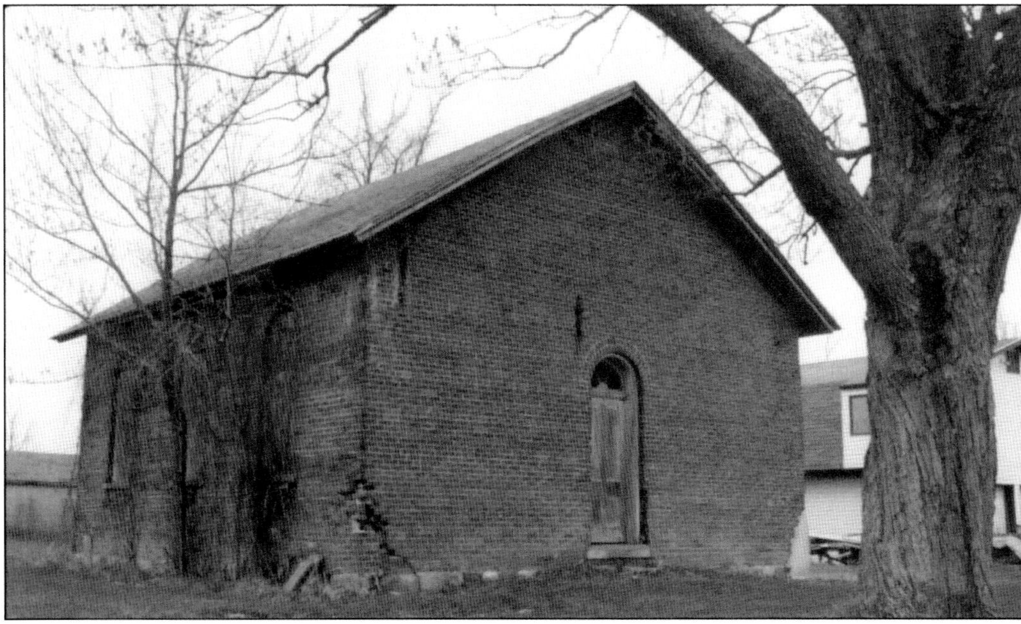

The Swan Center School, in southeast Noble County, was typical of one-room schools built in the early 1900s for rural students. During the 1908–1909 school year, it had 21 students who were taught by Melvin Yarian. Swan was a whistle-stop station for the county's second railroad, the Grand Rapids & Indiana. The line was extended south from Michigan, reaching Fort Wayne by 1872. (NCHS.)

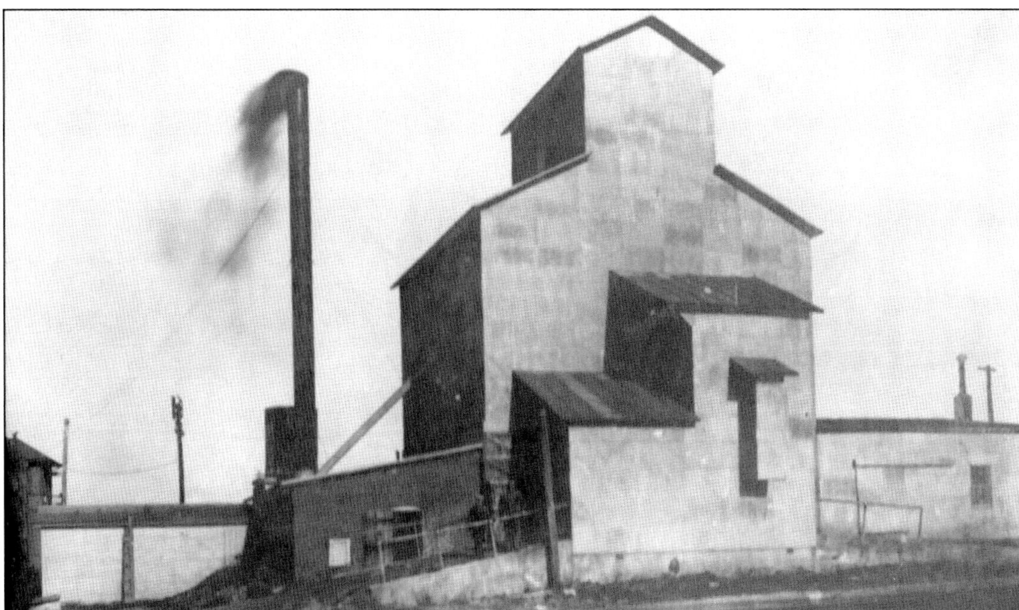

It would not be an agricultural community without a grain elevator, like this one in Kimmell. After losing its county seat position (as Sparta), Kimmell gained importance as an agricultural shipping center when the railroad passed through. Today, one of the town's main attractions is the Kimmell House Inn, a brick Italianate Victorian home built by state representative Orlando Kimmell. Gaerte Grain maintains the community's agricultural tradition. (NCHS.)

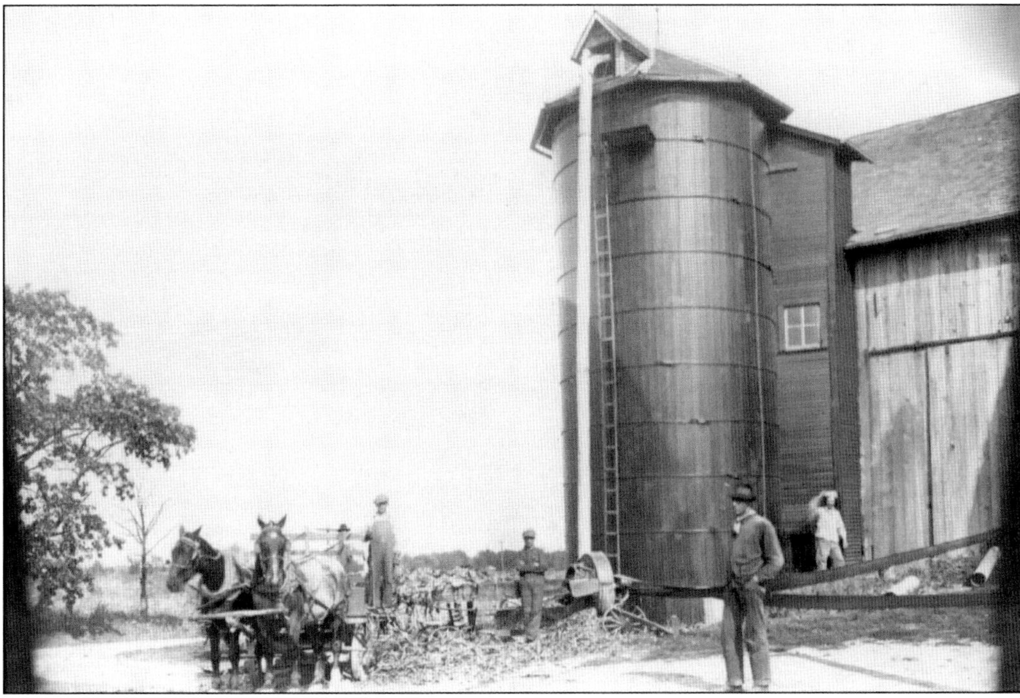

Around 1910, farmers pause for a photograph before going back to work in rural Noble County. Horses and strong backs still provided the power for agriculture, although steam-powered farm equipment was becoming more popular. (NCHS.)

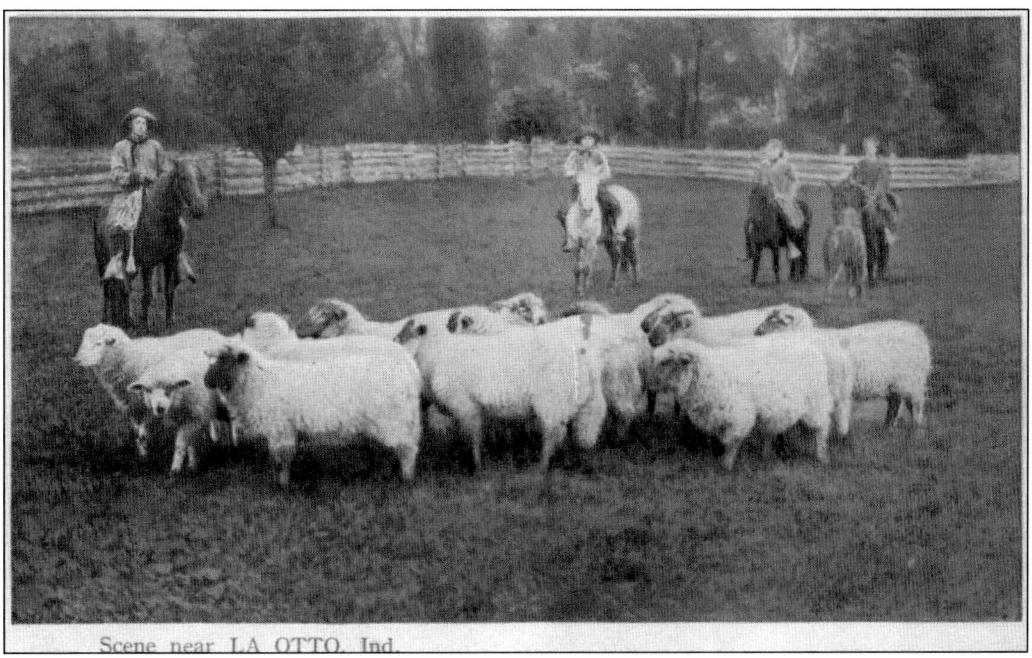

Sheepherders show off their flock in southeast Noble County. Today, cattle and hogs are much more common in the county. Whiteshire Hamroc, a hog farm near Albion, produces thousands of hogs every year and does business with a firm in China. (Courtesy Vern Christlieb.)

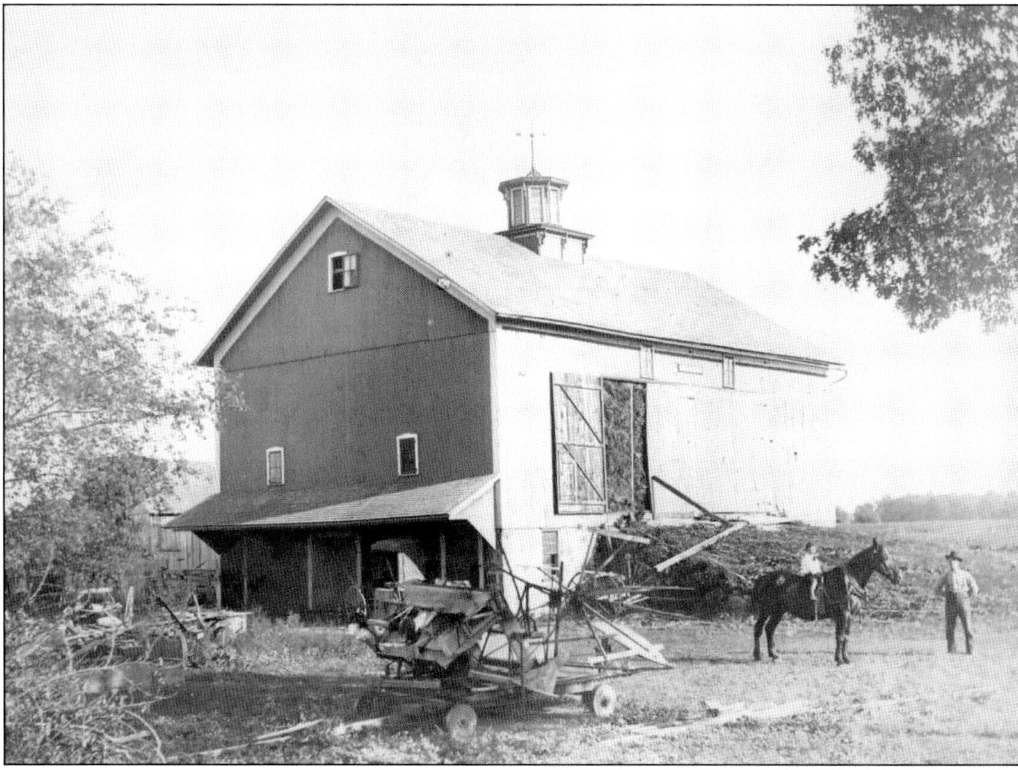

A farmer's child gets a ride on a horse that was probably more used to pulling plows for a living, in this typical Noble County farm scene from around 1910. (NCHS.)

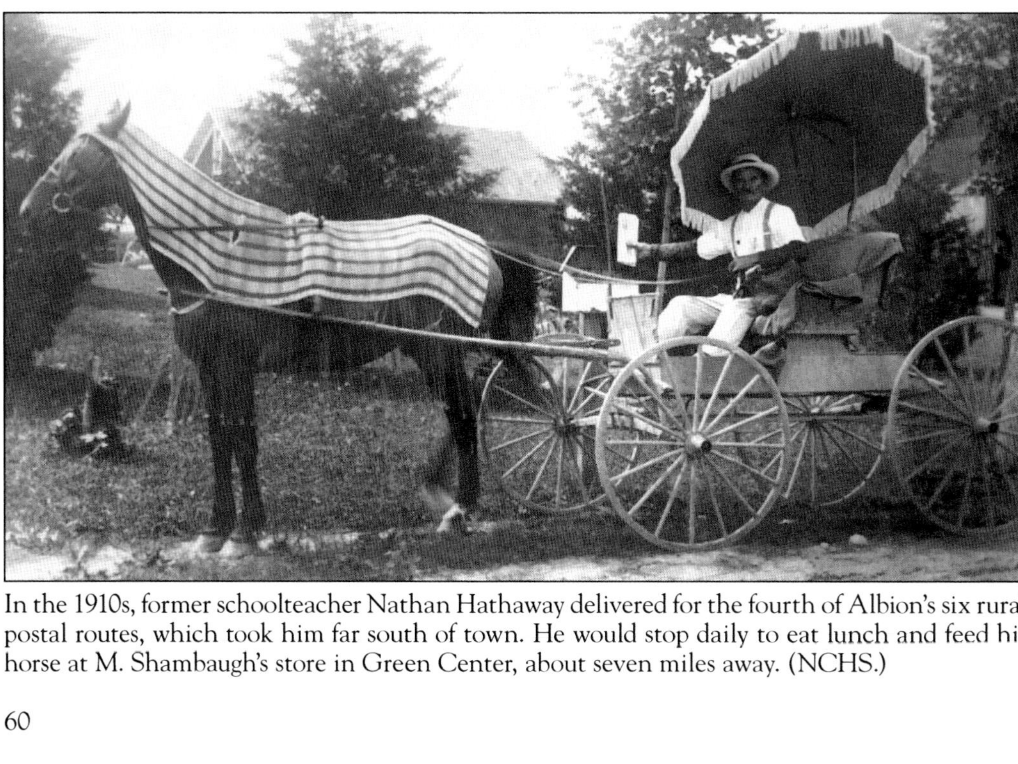

In the 1910s, former schoolteacher Nathan Hathaway delivered for the fourth of Albion's six rural postal routes, which took him far south of town. He would stop daily to eat lunch and feed his horse at M. Shambaugh's store in Green Center, about seven miles away. (NCHS.)

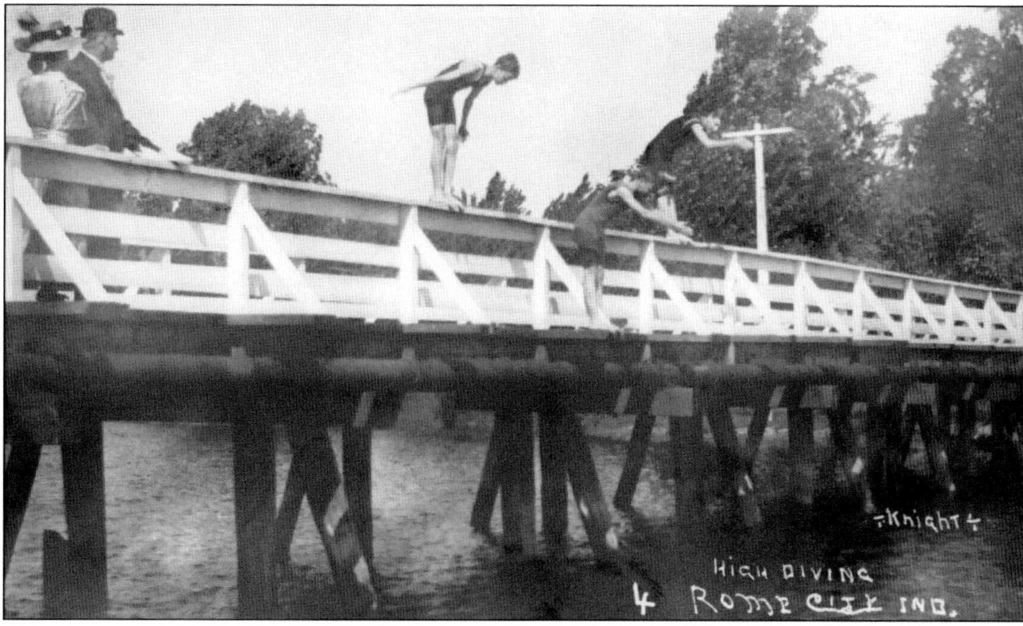

Kids dive off a bridge over Sylvan Lake in 1918, under the watchful eyes of an adult couple. Swimming remains a popular pastime in Noble County, which features numerous lakes, rivers, and streams. (Courtesy Mike Mapes.)

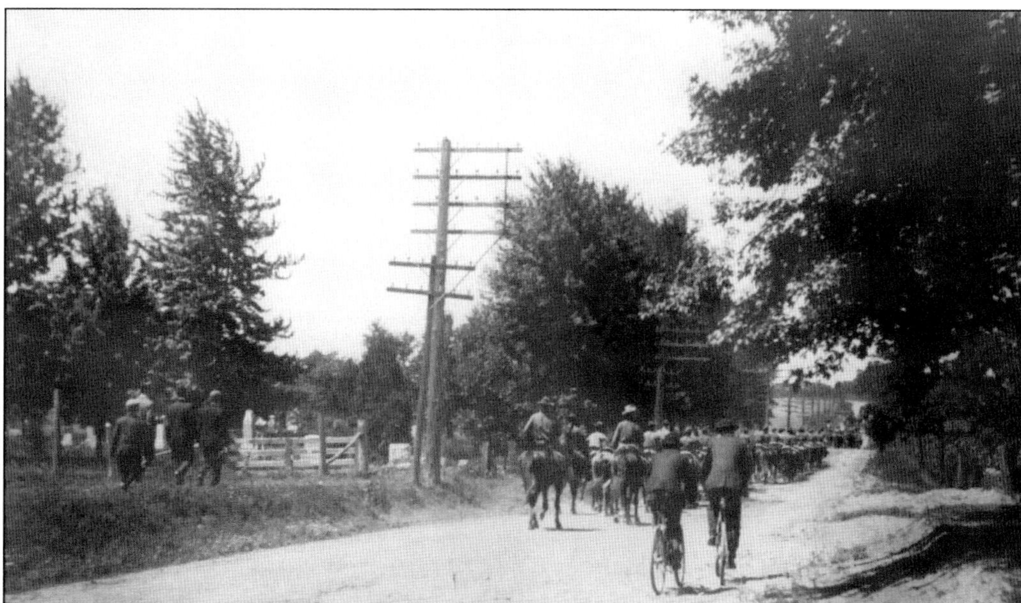

A group of 300 soldiers on horseback caused a stir when they passed through Avilla sometime around the time of World War I. (Courtesy Mike Mapes.)

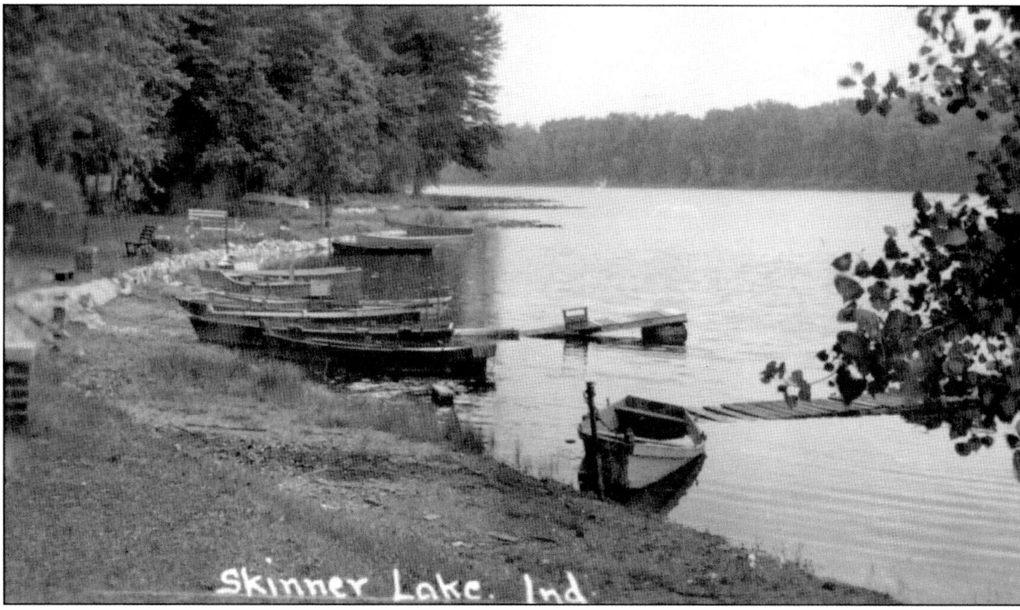

World War II must have seemed far away when this photograph of Skinner Lake was taken in 1942. Three miles east of Albion, the 125-acre lake drains 10,000 acres of surrounding land, most of it agricultural. A small community sprang up on the south side of the lake early in Noble County's history, but eventually most of the businesses left, leaving homes around the lakeshore. (NCHS.)

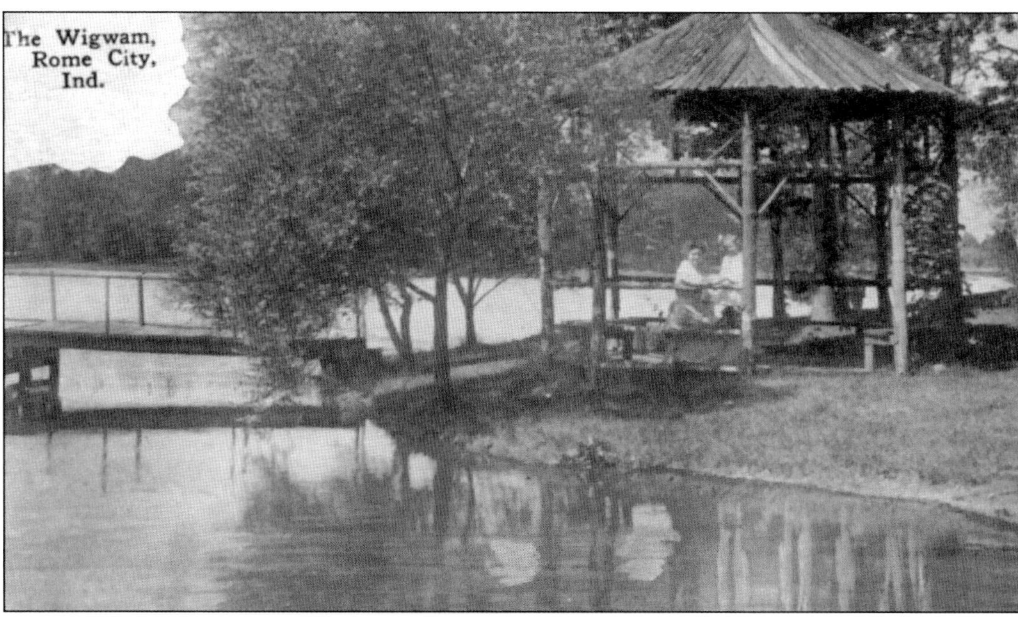

A family enjoys some relaxation time on the edge of Sylvan Lake in 1912. (Courtesy Mike Mapes.)

Five

Schools and Churches

After starting a new town in Noble County, the founders set out to provide for churches and schools. Sometimes, churches and schools became practically interchangeable. It was not uncommon for public schools to meet in churches and for congregations to hold their services in schools until they could put up a house of worship.

An early settler reported that the first sermon preached in Noble County was in the summer of 1832, when a Presbyterian minister from South Bend held a service on Perry's Prairie, near Ligonier. An organized church was started in 1836 at Haw Patch, on the border between Noble and LaGrange Counties. One year later, sessions of both school and church were held in a log cabin that was later called Salem Chapel. That was purported to be the first building put up in the county that was not originally a residence.

In 1888, by some counts, there were 54 churches in Noble County. But in 1874, there were 73 one-room schools, spread out by state law so that no student had to walk too far to get to class. At that time, 4,555 students were counted in the county, with 628 of those in high school. An example of one-room schools, the 1915 Stanley Schoolhouse, stands inside Chain O' Lakes State Park and has been preserved as a historical classroom.

The old schoolhouse in Kendallville was turned into a hospital for sick soldiers during the Civil War. While being treated there, several soldiers died of smallpox. The building later burned, and rumor had it that the citizens torched the building out of concern that later students would catch the disease.

Schools have now consolidated, and there are only four public school systems serving Noble County—West Noble, Central Noble, East Noble, and Smith-Green. There are also eight private schools, the largest being Oak Farm Montessori School in Avilla. As for churches, just about every denomination is represented. A synagogue was built in Ligonier in 1871, but as the Jewish population of that city shrank it was also turned into a church and eventually became the Ligonier Public Library.

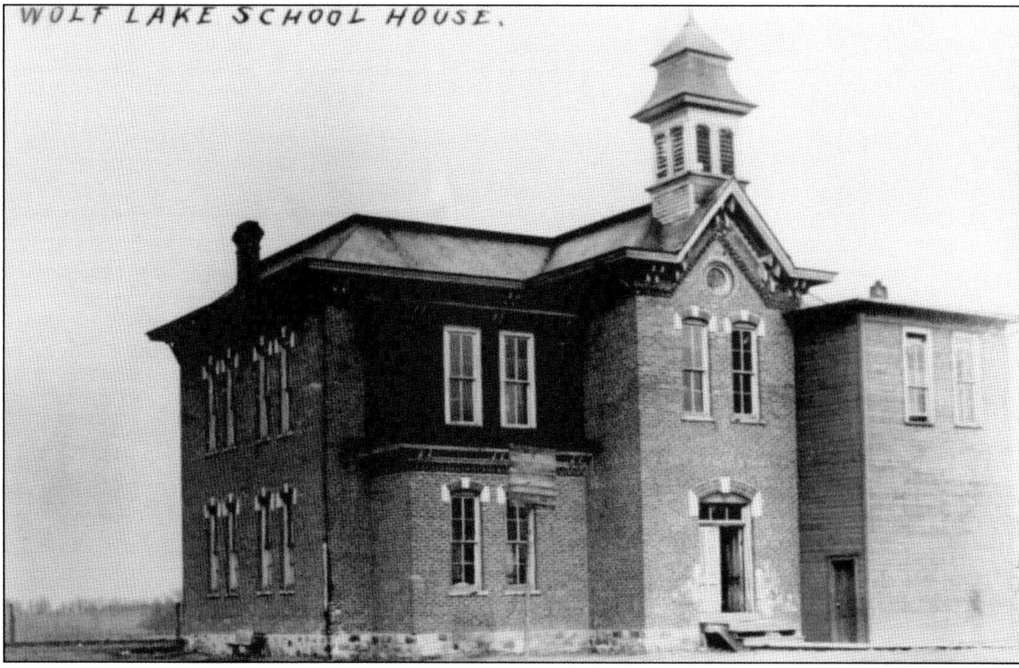

The 1882 Wolf Lake Schoolhouse was far from the first one in Wolf Lake, which (as might be supposed) was named after the nearby body of water in 1836. In addition to being the first town in Noble County, Wolf Lake is thought to be the location of the first meeting in the county to recruit soldiers at the beginning of the Civil War. (NCHS.)

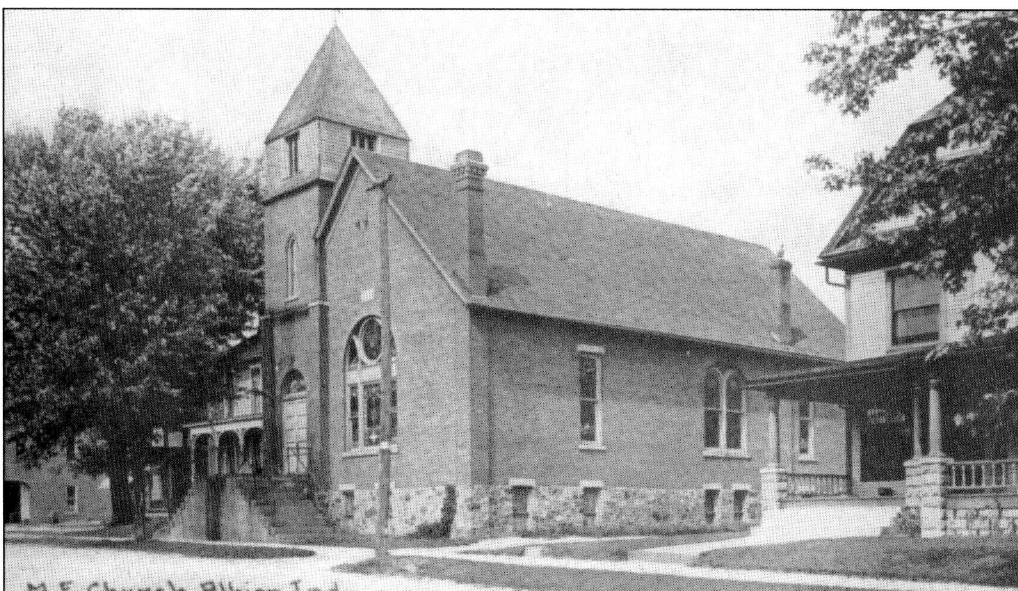

Albion's Methodist Episcopal church was founded in 1847, but it was not until 1875 that the congregation built its own church, three blocks south of the courthouse square. In 1898, it was replaced with this impressive brick building at a cost of $4,300. Although there are now two Methodist churches in town, nothing remains of the South Orange Street building but a historical marker. (NCHS.)

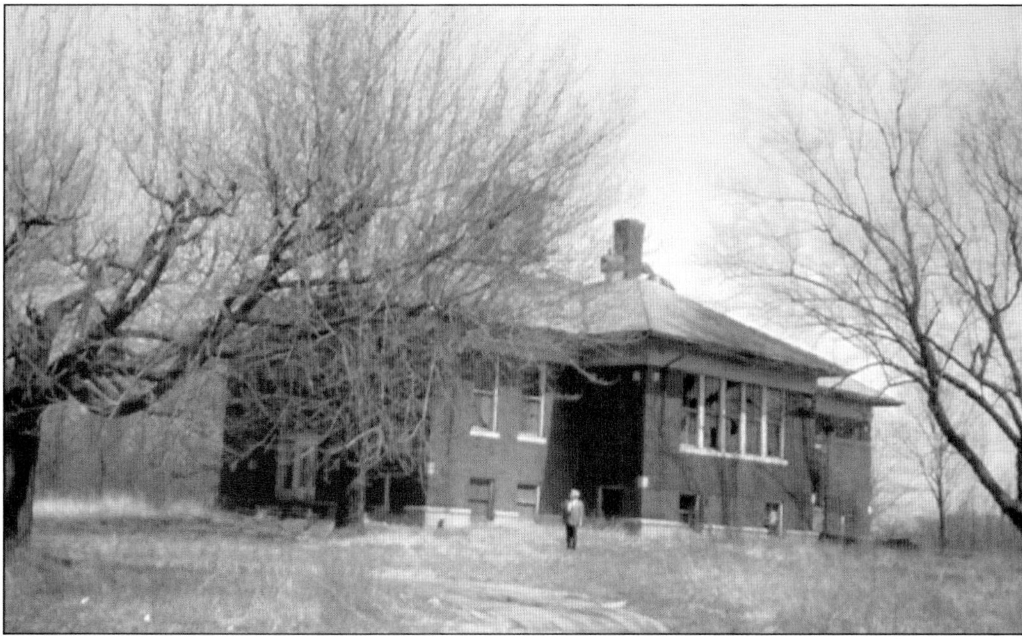

Although still standing as of 2015, the 1921 Brimfield School building has been abandoned for many years. An attempt was made to turn the building on the north side of the town into apartments for farmworkers, but that effort was abandoned. As of this writing, the building is unused and usually unnoticed in a grove of trees. (NCHS.)

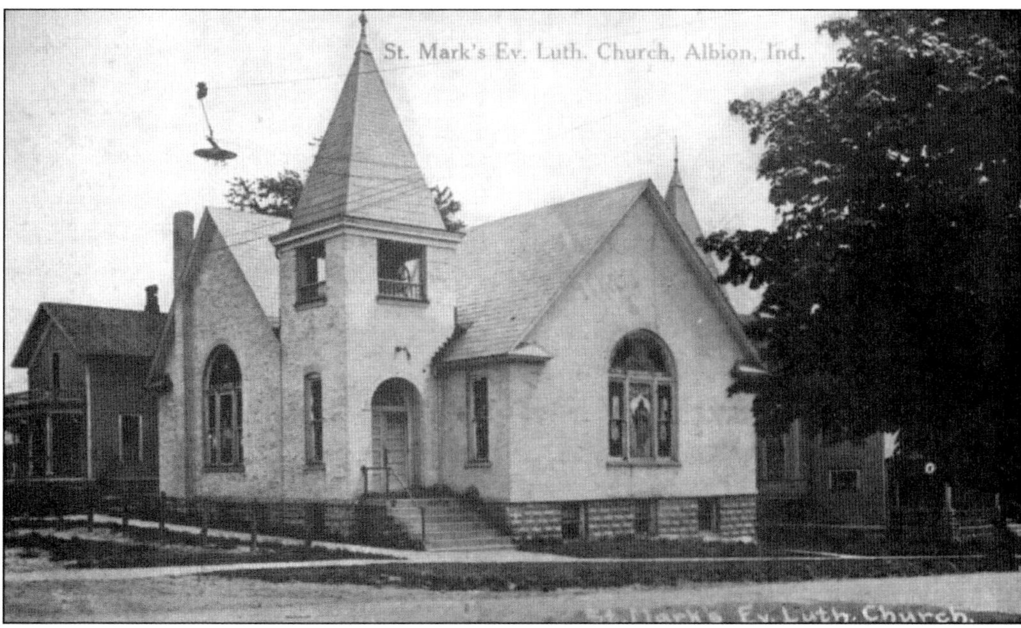

Albion's first Lutheran church was built in 1855, although the Evangelical Lutherans organized in 1848. St. Mark's Evangelical Lutheran Church has been lowered to grade, remodeled, and added to many times since but still stands on North Orange Street, near one of the highest points in town overlooking the courthouse square. The church served as a courtroom for a time after the Noble County Courthouse burned in 1857. (NCHS.)

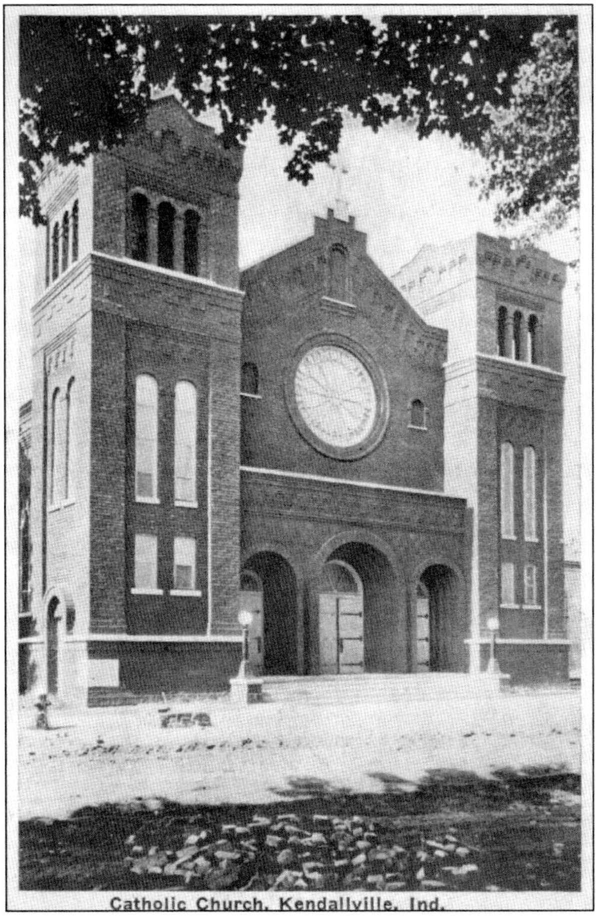

The Immaculate Conception Catholic Church still stands on Diamond Street in Kendallville. Catholics in Kendallville traveled to Avilla to worship until Immaculate Conception was organized in 1897. (Courtesy Mike Mapes.)

The Albion High School marching band performs in the gym to a large crowd. The band's members were from the classes of 1949–1953. In 1957, the school became Albion-Jefferson High, and in 1969 it combined with Wolf Lake High School to form the Central Noble School District. (Courtesy Ellen McBride.)

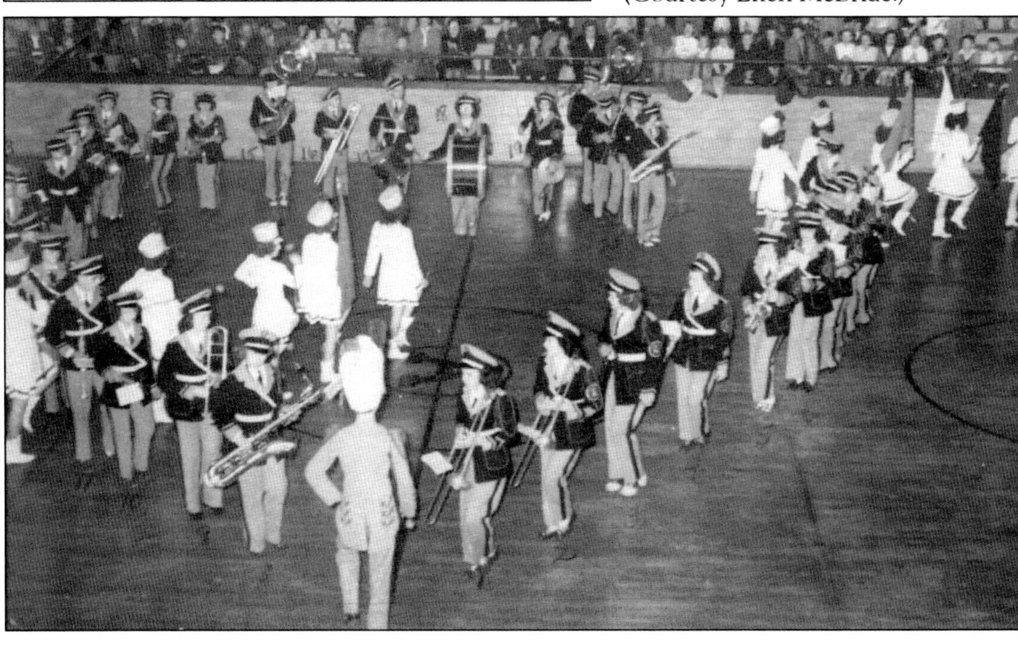

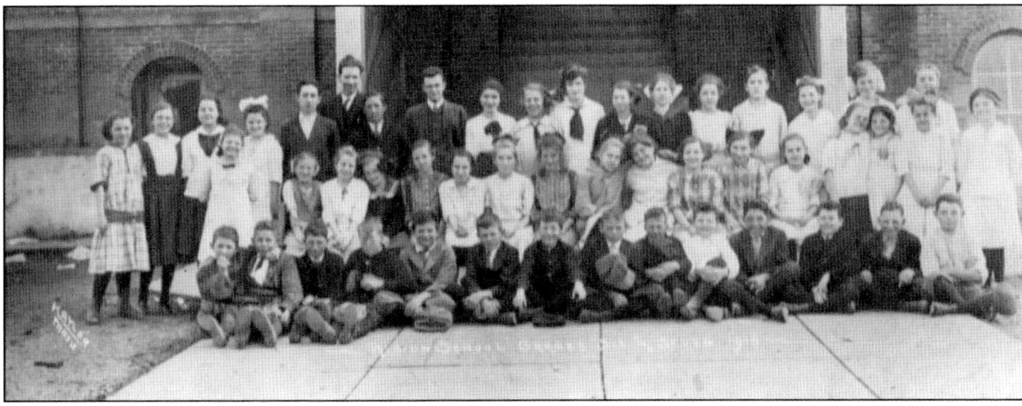

Sixth graders and seventh graders from the Albion School pose in front of the building in the mid-1910s. (NCHS.)

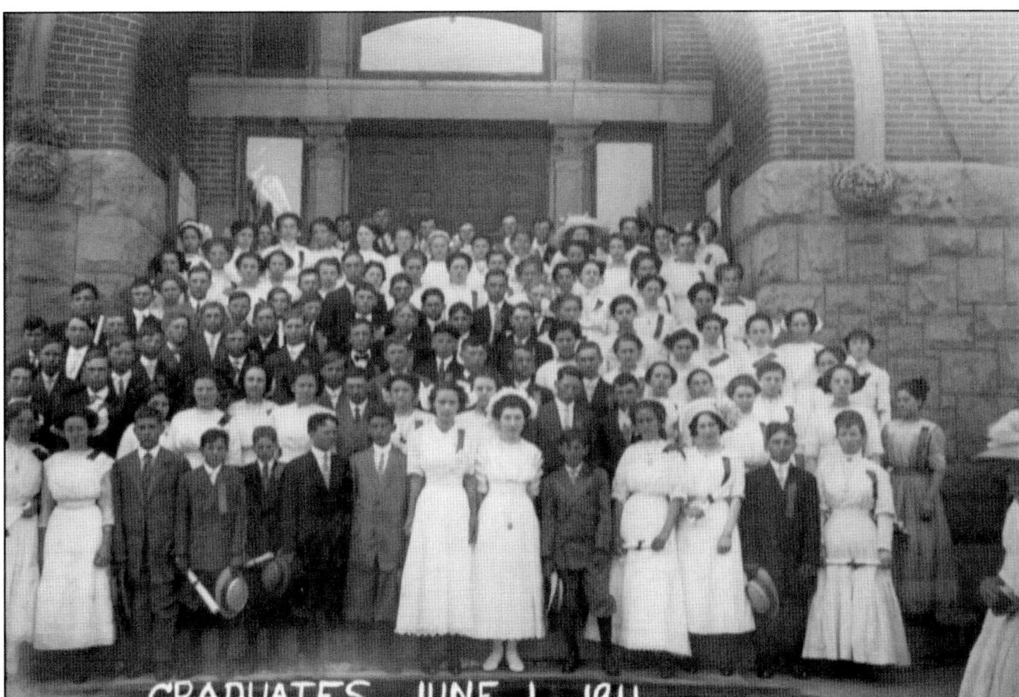

High school graduates gather in front of Noble County Courthouse after their commencement in 1911. In the early 1900s, classes from all over the county held their graduations in Albion, often at the Albion Opera House on the north side of the courthouse square. A photograph with the imposing courthouse in the background was the logical next step. (NCHS.)

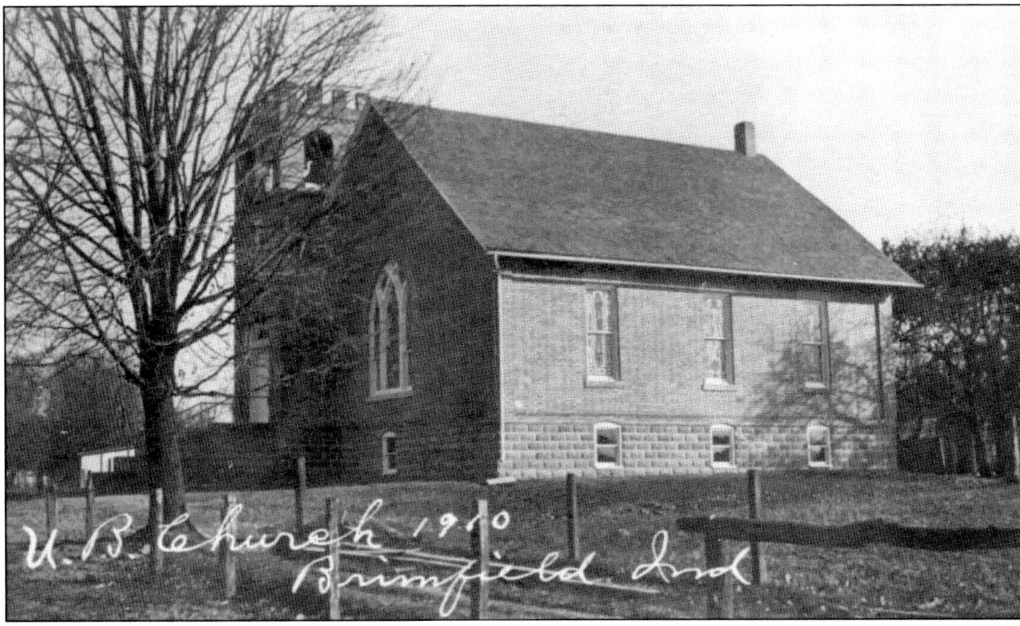

Seen above in 1910 and below after one of its many renovations, the Brimfield United Methodist Church celebrated the 125th anniversary of its building in 2002. The congregation started meeting in the Brimfield Schoolhouse around 1867 and decided to build its own church in 1875, at a cost of $2,700. Rev. David Hartman was the first pastor. There were additions in 1952 and 1965, as well as several remodelings that included the removal of a bell tower. When new pews were purchased, the wood of the old pews was preserved in a foyer partition. (Both, courtesy Marcia Garrett.)

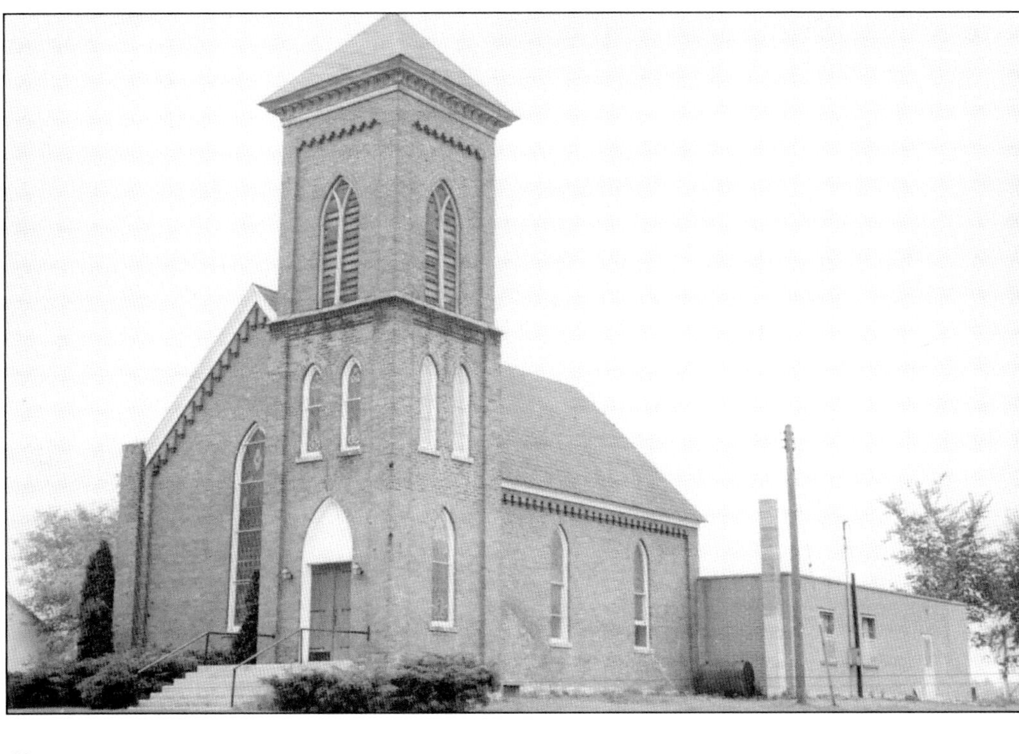

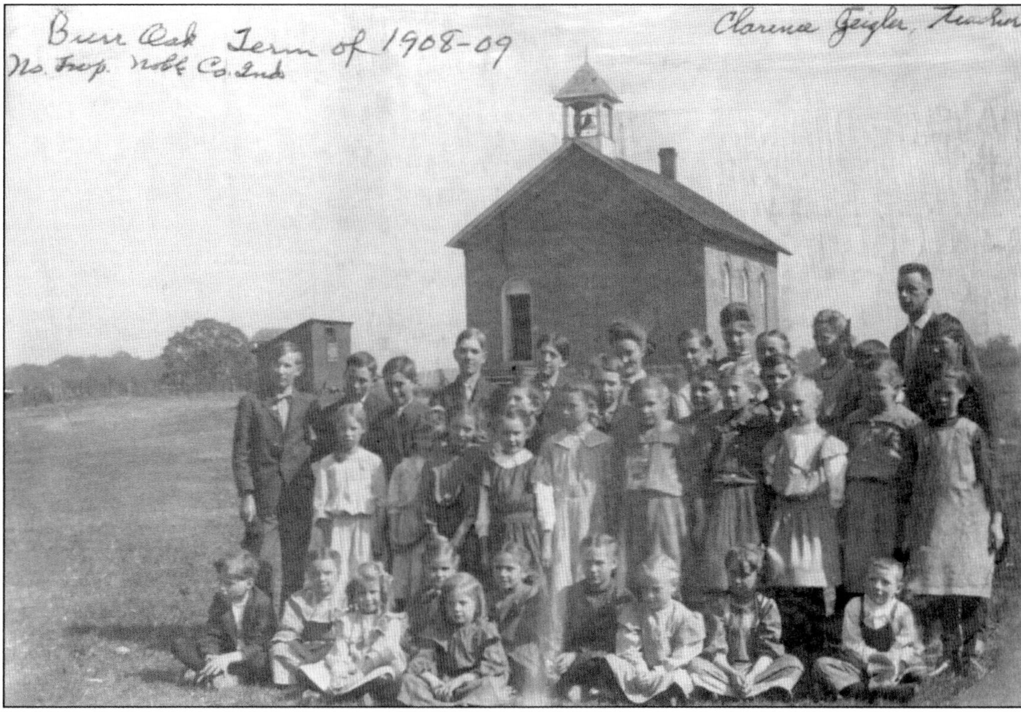

Burr Oak School students gather for their class photo for the 1908–1909 term. Clarence Geigler was the teacher for the one-room school, in southern Noble County. The school building was erected in 1881, and the last classes were held there in 1923. (NCHS.)

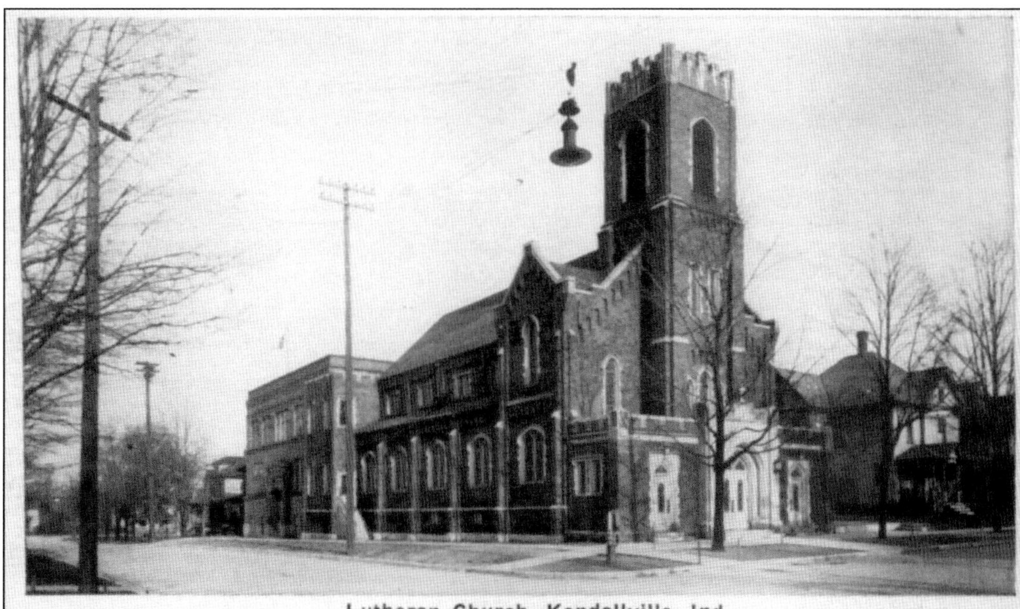

St. John Lutheran Church built its first Kendallville church in 1862 and replaced that frame building with a brick structure in 1873. After fire destroyed that church, the first portion of the current building was dedicated in 1925. It has been added to several times since and now houses a school in addition to the original church. (Courtesy Mike Mapes.)

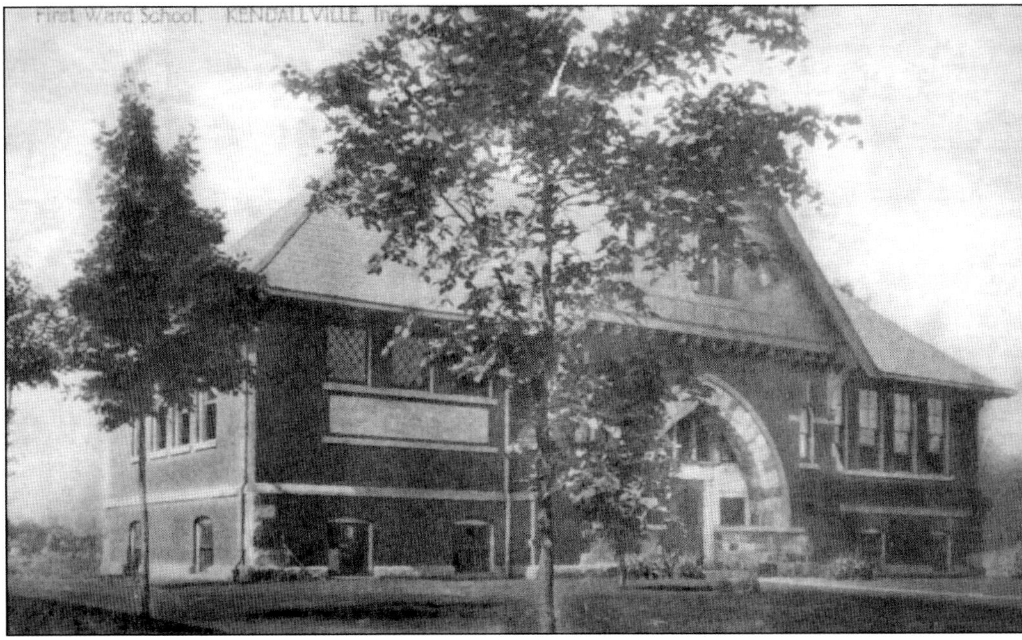

The First Ward School in Kendallville is seen in this 1910 image. It was also known as the North Ward School. (Courtesy Mike Mapes.)

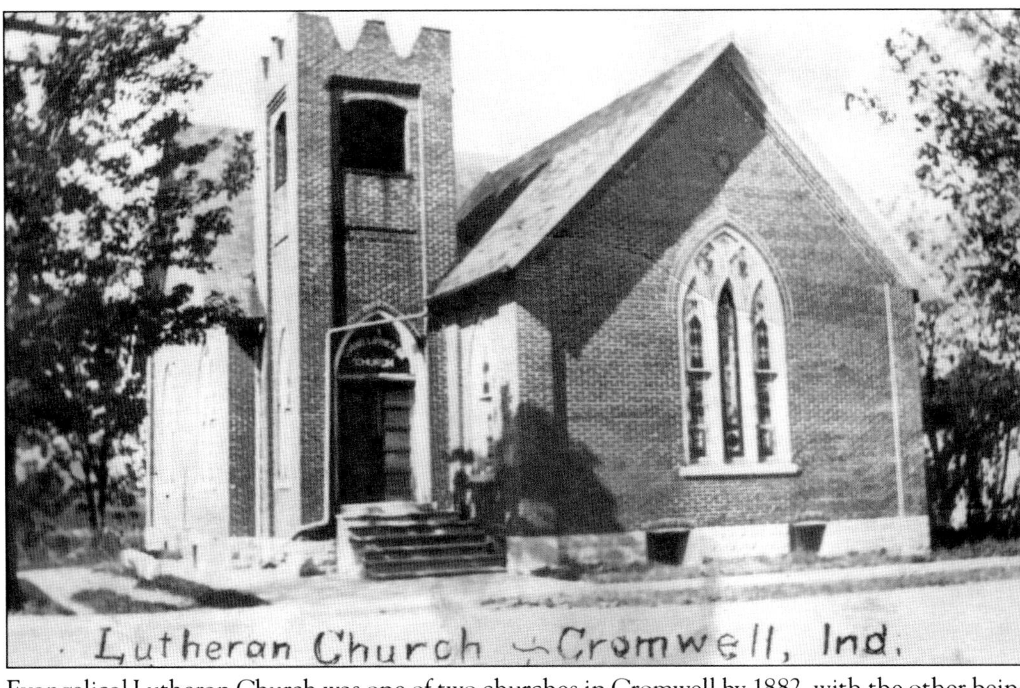

Evangelical Lutheran Church was one of two churches in Cromwell by 1882, with the other being a Methodist church. Both were built around 1870, after an attempt to establish a single union church failed. (STHS.)

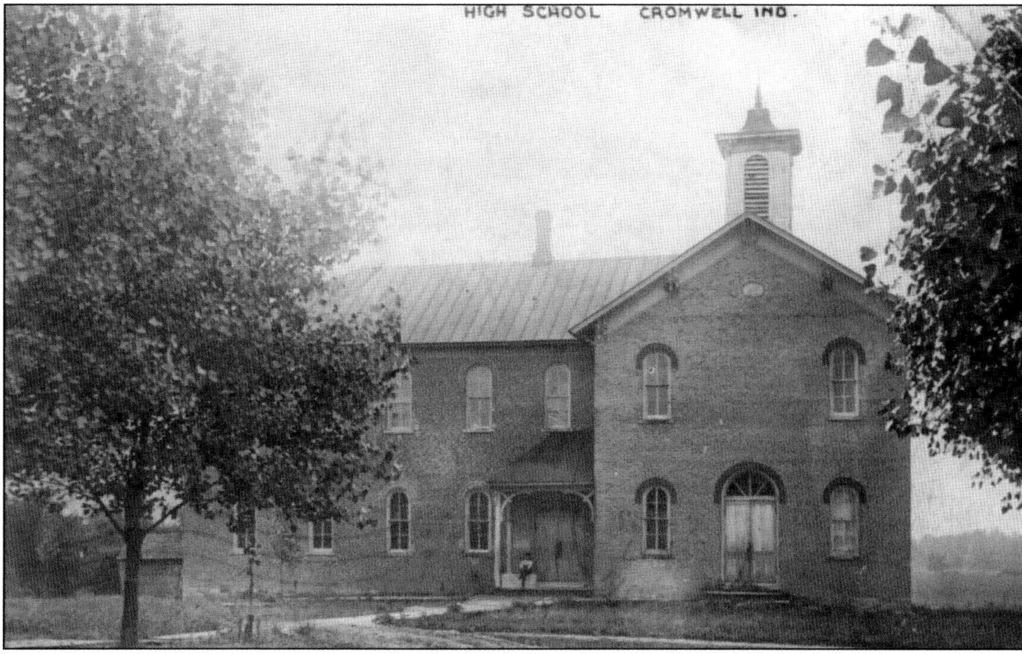

The Cromwell High School pictured above was built around 1880 and later replaced by a new school, shown below under construction in 1911. Although it did not have a stint as county seat or a location on the Fort Wayne–Goshen Road like Sparta (later Kimmell) did, Cromwell benefited from the B&O Railroad line. Platted in 1853, it is now the smallest incorporated town in Noble County. Harrison Wood, who had served Noble County as sheriff and probate judge, platted out 28 lots and named the town after Oliver Cromwell. The first school in town was a 20-foot-square log house, built where the Cromwell Railroad depot would later be constructed. (Both, STHS.)

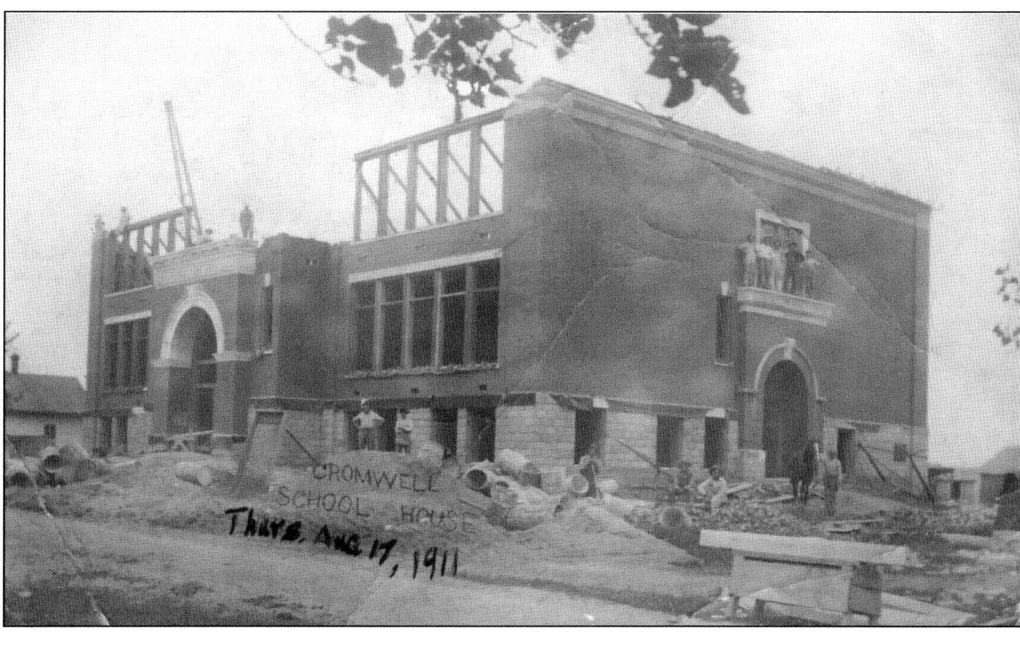

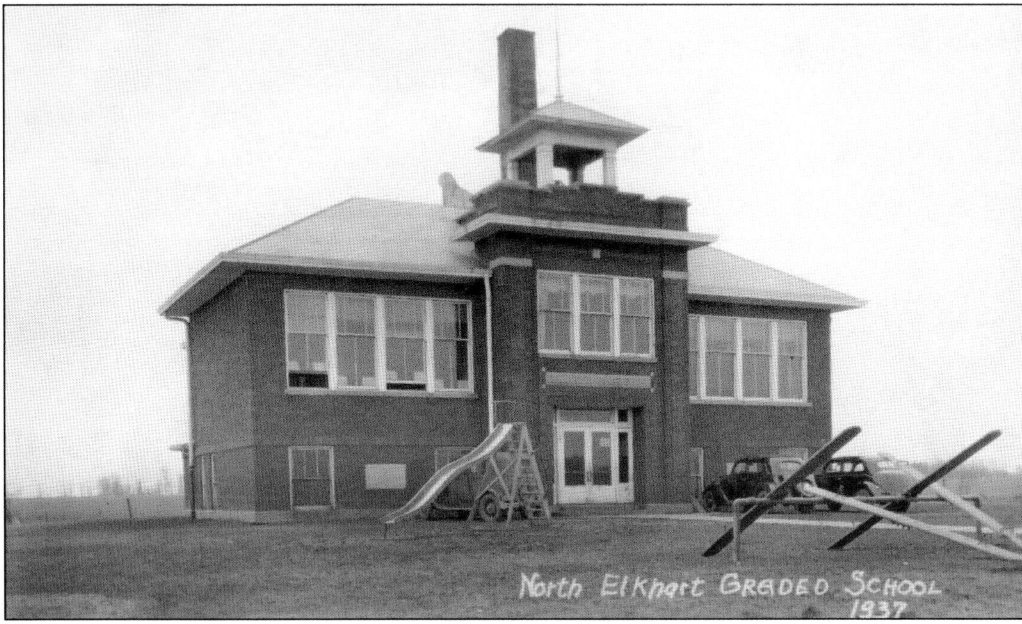

The North Elkhart School, built in 1916, was a step up from the old one-room schools. It would later be one of many schools falling to consolidation in the early 1970s, and for a time Elkhart Township elementary students attended the Wawaka School. The building was near the small village of Cosperville and close to the Elkhart River, in north central Noble County. (NCHS.)

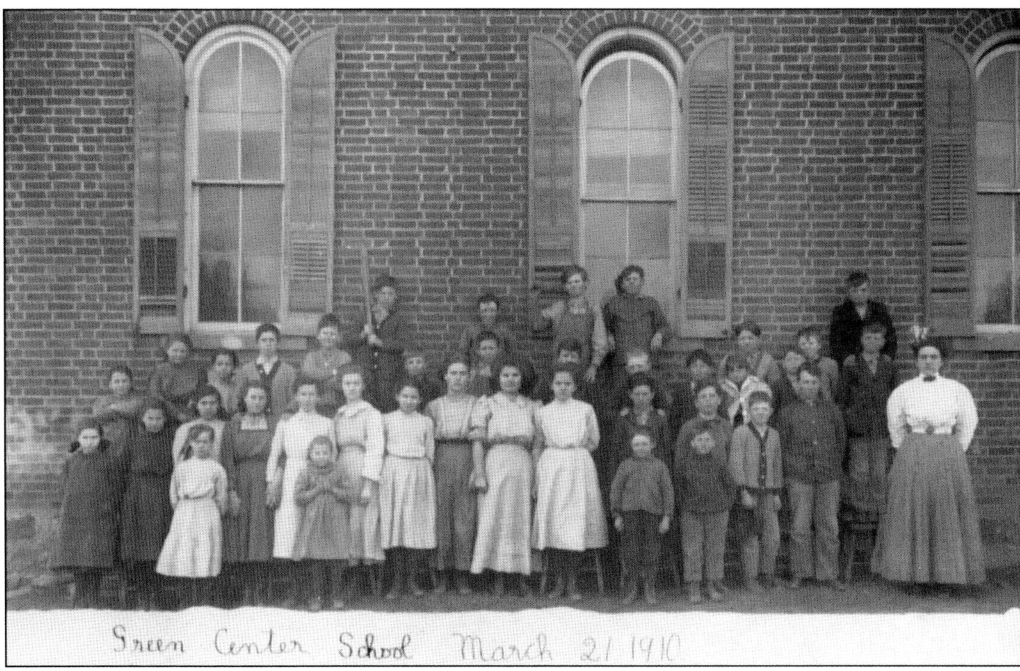

Green Center School students stand outside their south central Noble County school for a 1910 class photo. The last one-room school in Noble County, this building was constructed in the 1870s and replaced by a larger school in 1854. That building was turned into a community center in 1983. (NCHS.)

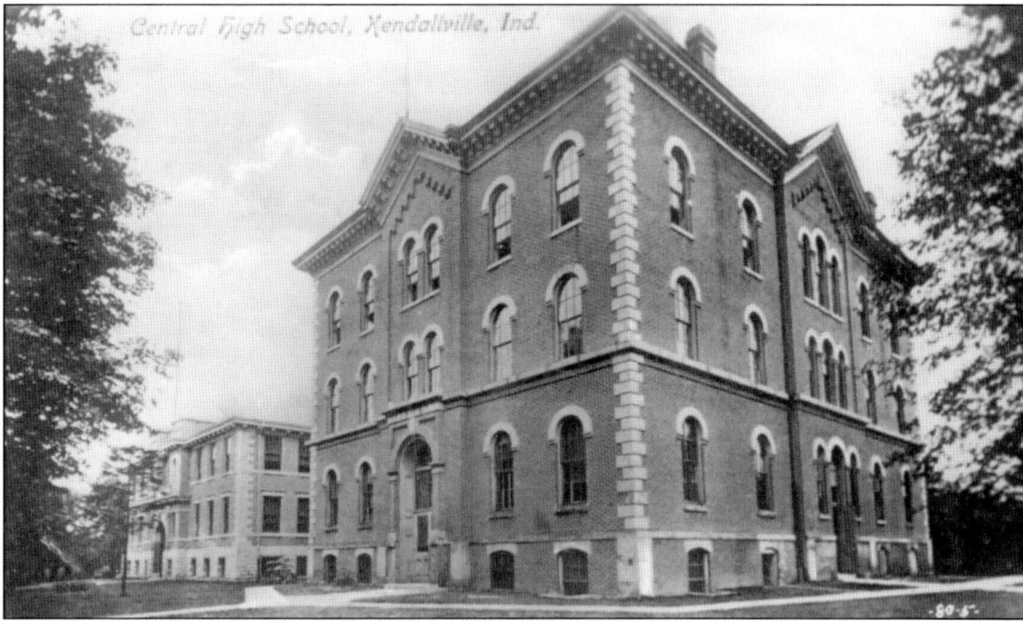

The first school in Kendallville, a three-story frame building at Diamond and Riley Streets, was constructed in 1858, but it was not until 1879 that the first high school class graduated. This 1909 photograph shows Kendallville Central High School, which was renamed in 1966 when the East Noble School District was established. (NCHS.)

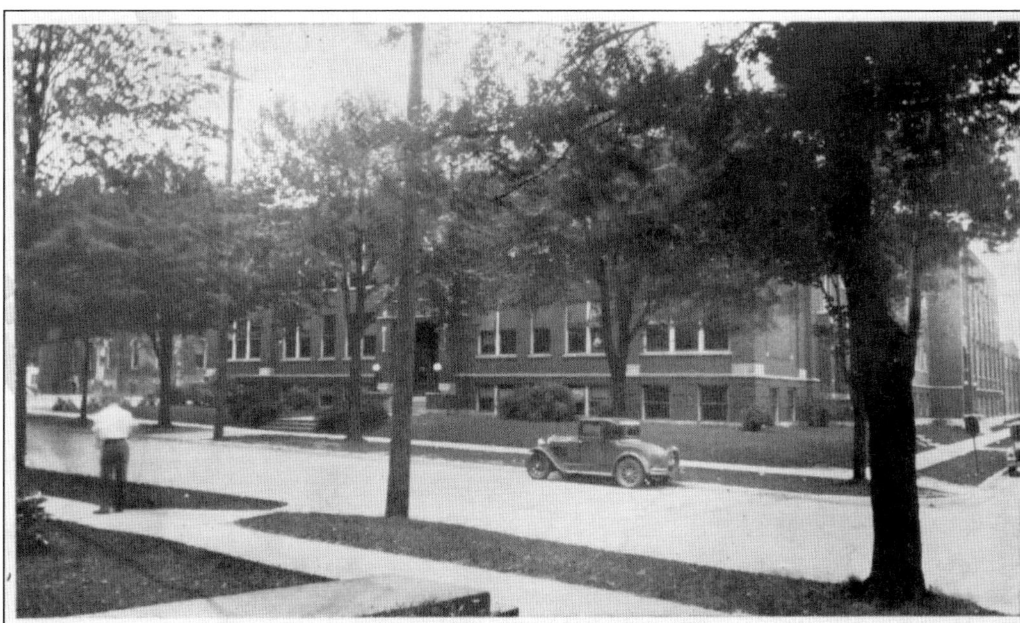

This building at Diamond and Riley Streets served as Kendallville High School until 1966, when the East Noble High School was built on the south side of the city. It then became the Kendallville Middle School and has served in that capacity ever since. (Courtesy Mike Mapes.)

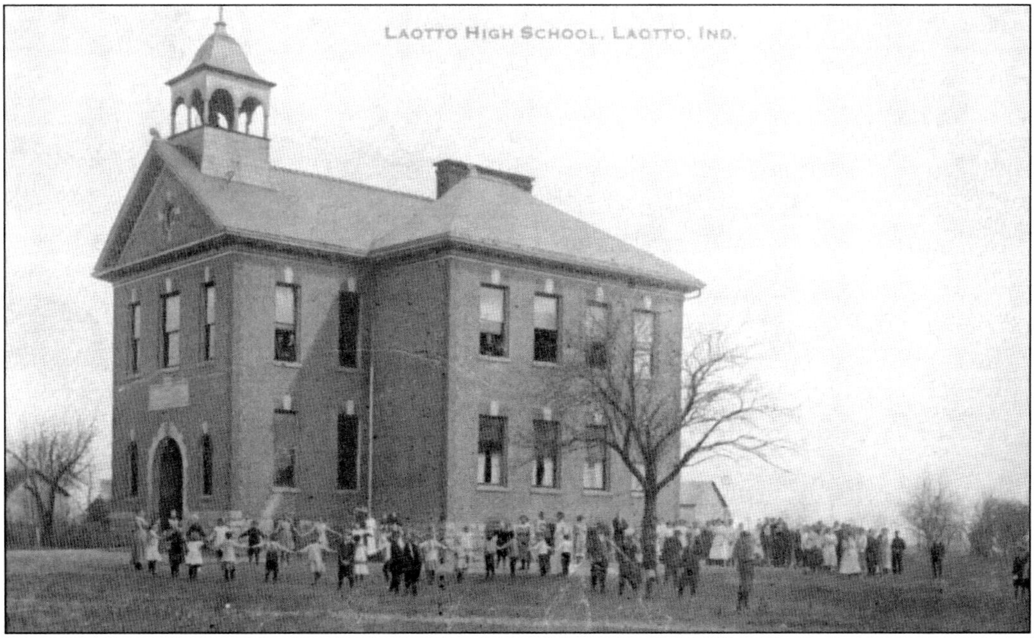

The LaOtto High School served the southeast corner of Noble County from 1902 until 1937 and later was home to elementary school students. The structure was used by the local Wesleyan church after 1965 until it was demolished in 1992. LaOtto students are now part of the East Noble School Corporation. (Courtesy Vern Christlieb.)

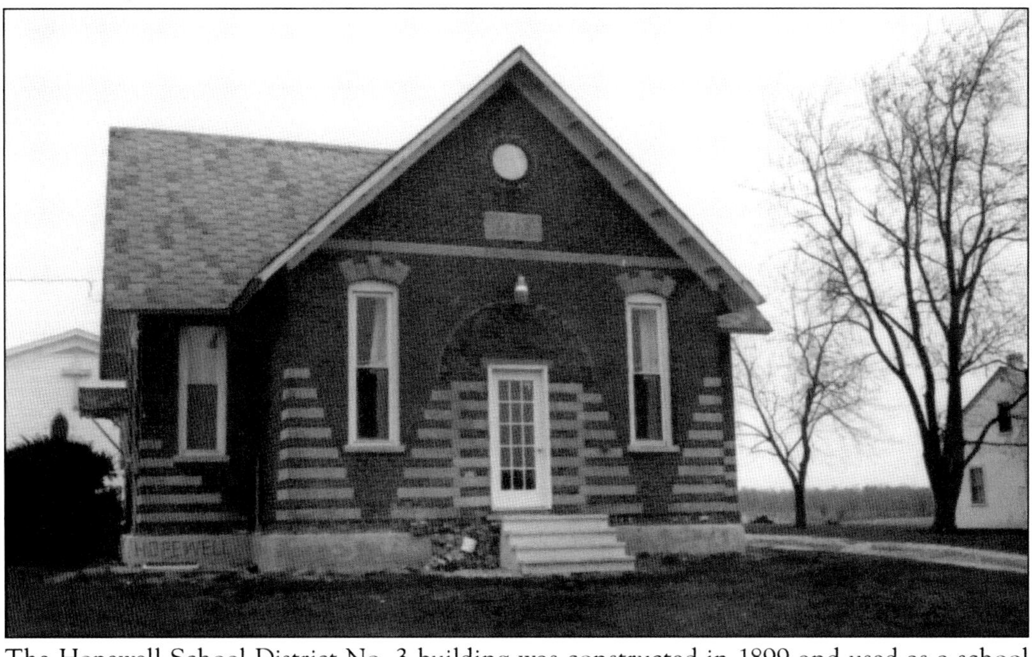

The Hopewell School District No. 3 building was constructed in 1899 and used as a school until 1938, when Hopewell students rode the bus to LaOtto. The town of Hopewell eventually vanished, but as late as 2007 the building was being used by the Hopewell Church as a reception hall. The land for both the church and the school was donated by Jonas Strouss after he settled nearby in 1836. (NCHS.)

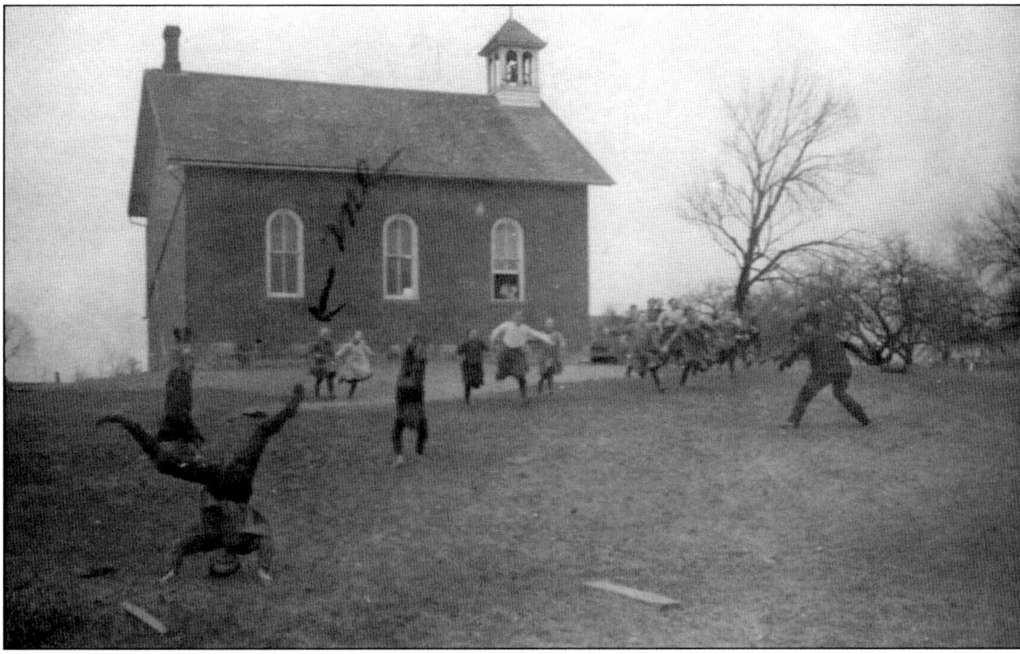

Students play outside a Kendallville area schoolhouse in 1908. John Harker was the teacher in what the photograph identifies as the Pippen Schoolhouse, although it appears to be the Singery School. (Courtesy Mike Mapes.)

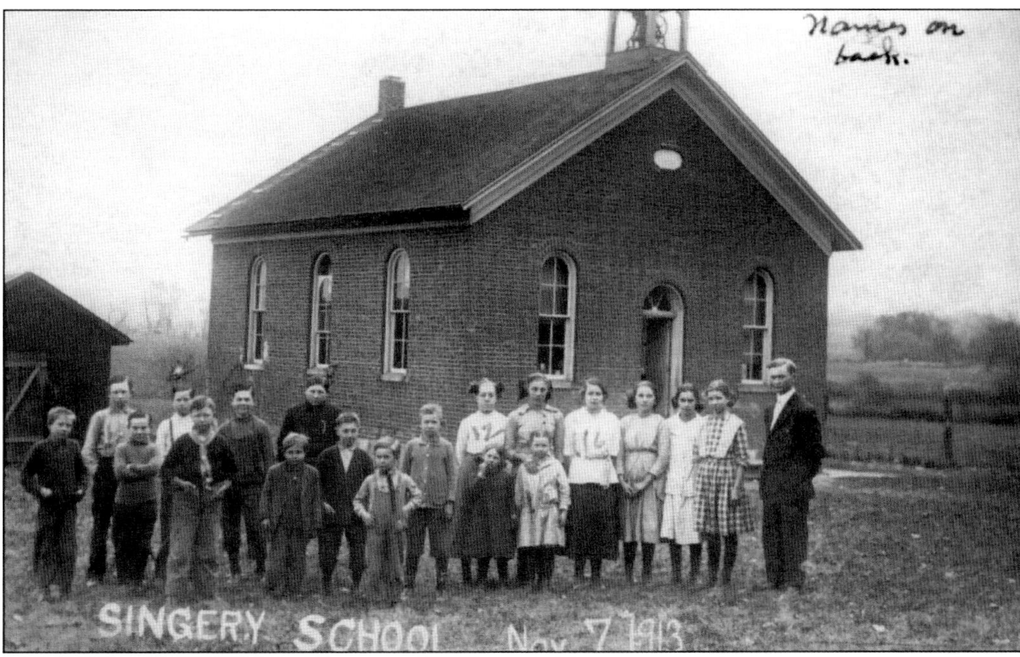

Students stand in front of the Singery School in 1913. The school was in Allen Township in east central Noble County and was typical of dozens of one-room schoolhouses of the time. In 1894 the original Singery School teacher was reportedly Libbie Bortner. (NCHS.)

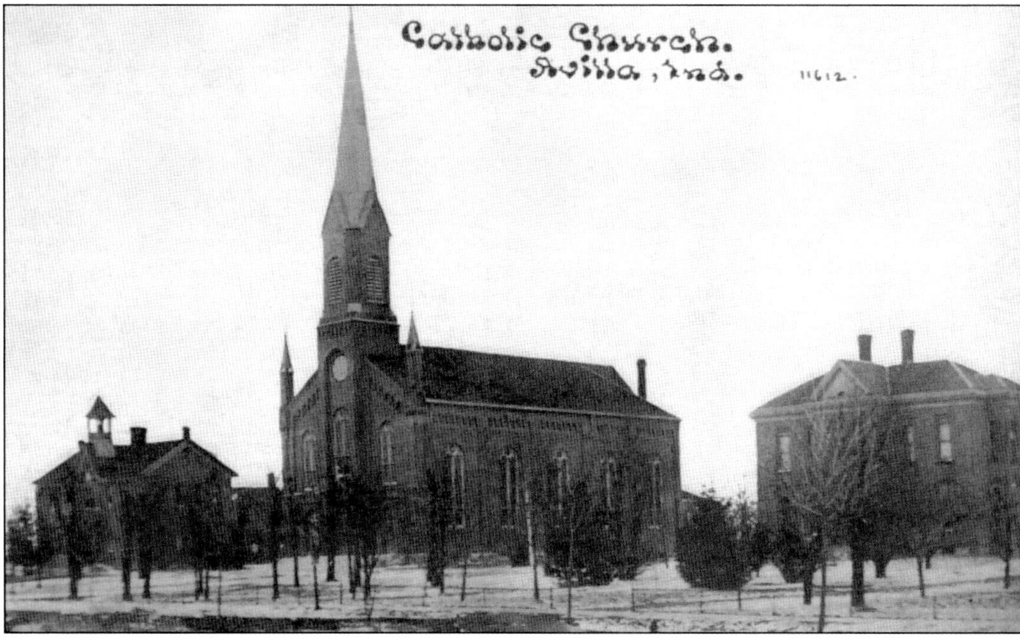

Although most of the spire is no longer on its 1878 church, St. Mary of the Assumption Catholic Church has prospered in its Avilla location. The location now features a Catholic school and a Franciscan convent. (Courtesy Mike Mapes.)

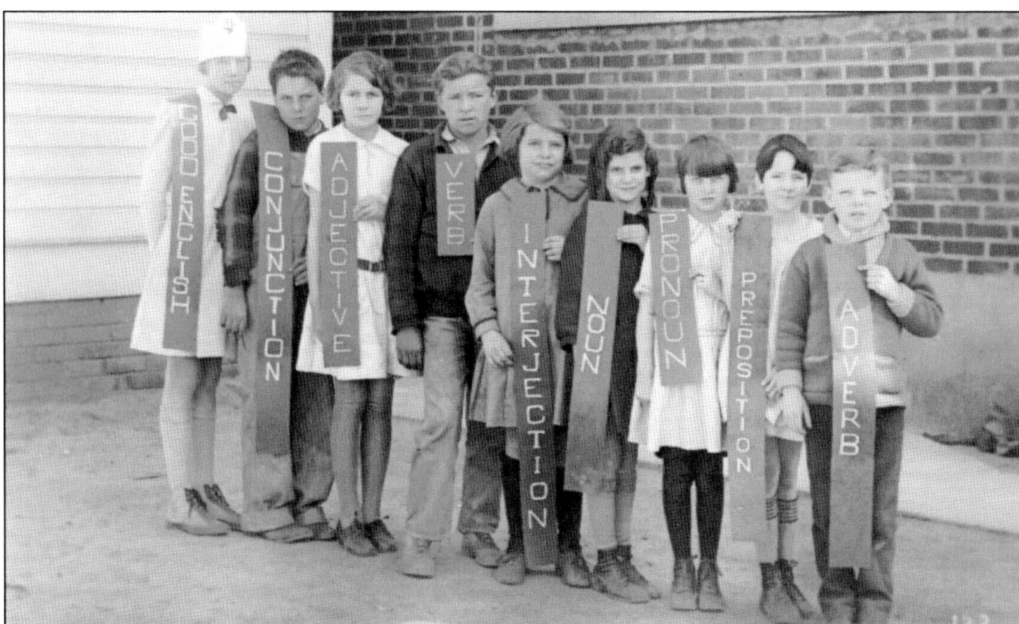

In a Cromwell photograph from the early 1900s, schoolchildren demonstrate their places in a play about the parts of a sentence, presumably for English class. (Courtesy Mike Mapes.)

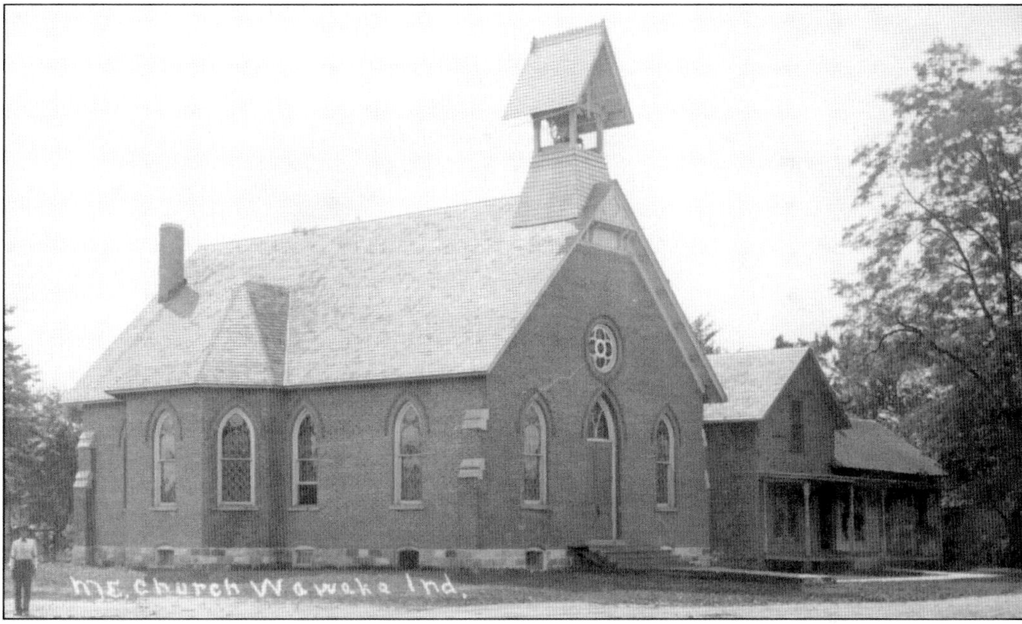

The Wawaka United Methodist Church was founded in 1857; the first minister was reportedly Rev. A.E. Mahin. (Courtesy Mike Mapes.)

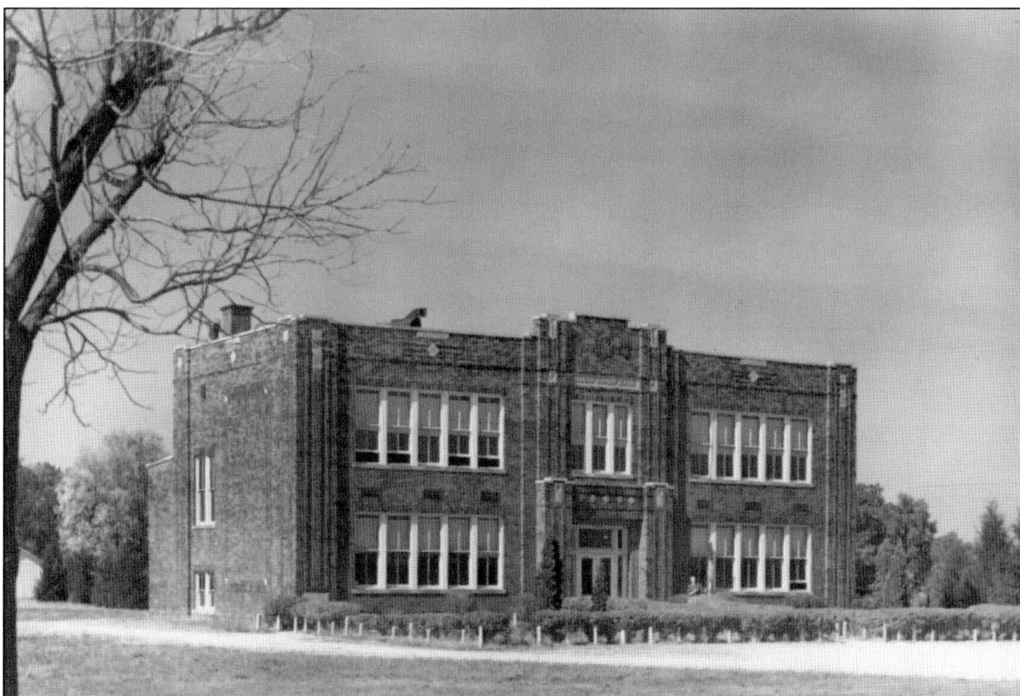

The Washington Center School was built in 1925, south of Knapp Lake, in southwest Noble County. The first schoolhouse in Washington Township was built in 1840, but in 1925 all the schools in the township were consolidated into this two-story brick building, which housed all eight elementary grades. High school students were bused east to Wolf Lake until 1967, when more consolidation created the West Noble School Corporation. (NCHS.)

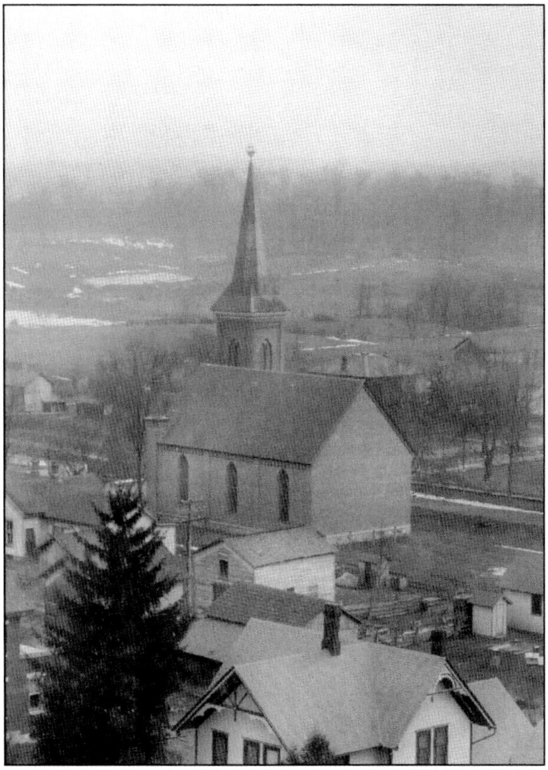

The First Presbyterian Church was organized in Port Mitchell in 1844 but moved to Albion along with the county seat two years later. After the church burned in 1867, services were held in the courthouse, then in the town's Lutheran church, until a new Presbyterian church was put up in 1876. The entire cost of the building project, at Oak and Highland Streets, was $7,100. J.P. Moore was the first minister, with Nelson Prentiss serving as clerk of session. The building was damaged by fire a second time in 1901 and a third time on January 1, 1951. It was remodeled and rededicated both times and is still serving the community today. (Both, NCHS.)

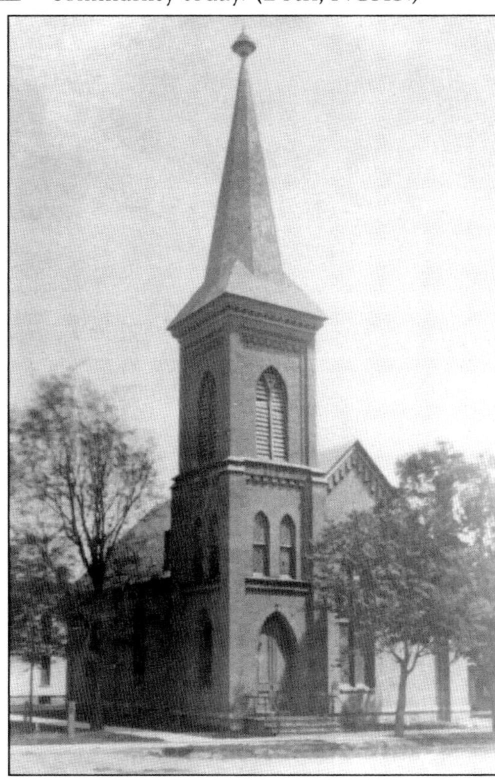

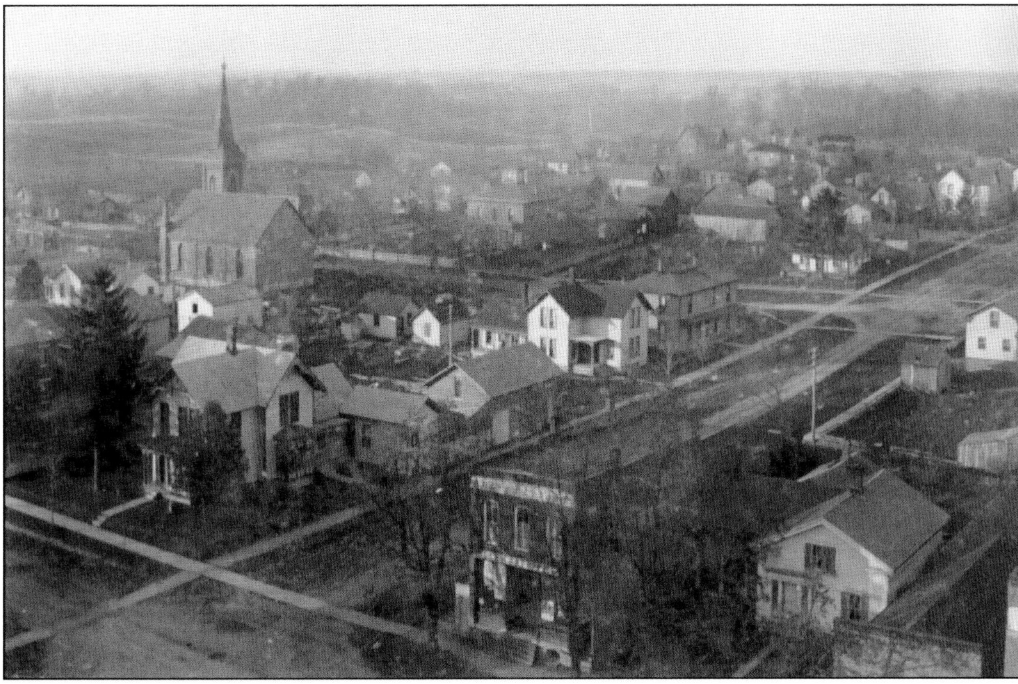

Much of the block on the left of this photograph, taken from the Noble County Courthouse in the spring of 1894, was destroyed or damaged by fire in 1901, including the First Presbyterian Church of Albion. The church was rebuilt and still stands today. The *Noble County Democrat* newspaper office is lower center, across the street from the block that would burn. (Courtesy Noble County historian Sarah Knopp.)

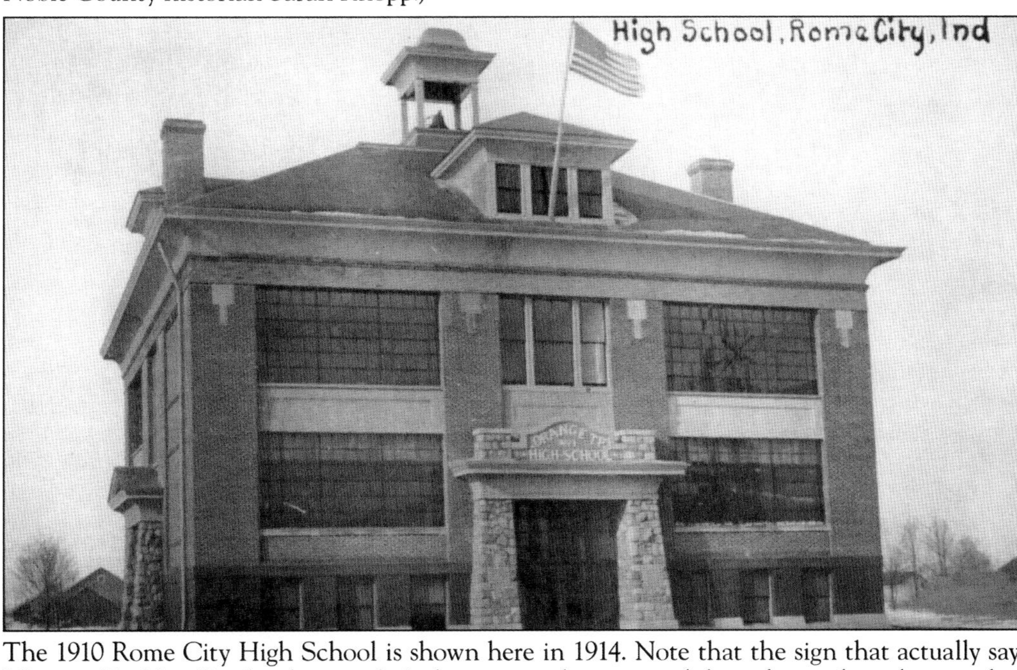

The 1910 Rome City High School is shown here in 1914. Note that the sign that actually says "Orange Tp. No. 1"; schools in early Indiana were the responsibility of townships, by state law. (Courtesy Mike Mapes.)

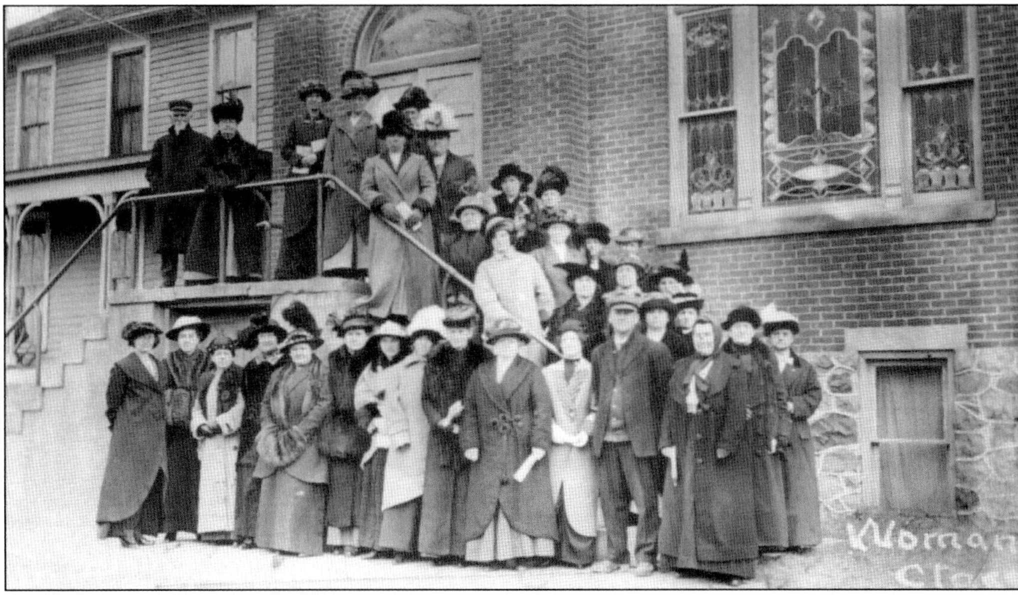

A group poses outside after a "women's class" at the Methodist church on South Orange Street in Albion. Only a historical marker is left to indicate where the once imposing brick building stood. (NCHS.)

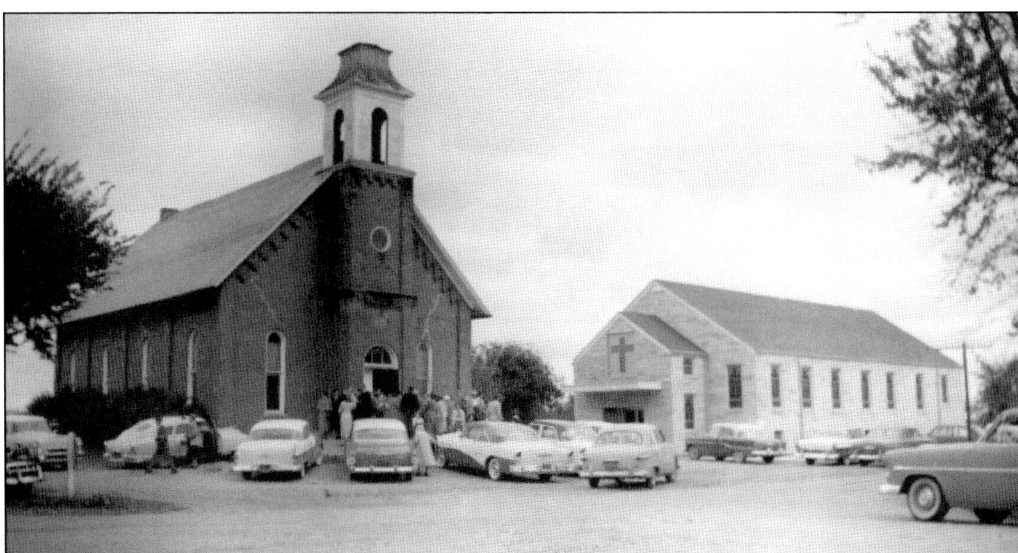

Old and new churches stand together in this mid-1950s photograph of the Merriam Christian Chapel. The church dates to 1843, although it was not until 1852 that the congregation erected a wood-frame structure. In 1881, they dedicated the building on the left, but by 1951 they ran out of space and bought land next door. The new building, constructed with Indiana limestone, was dedicated in 1957 and expanded in 1965. (NCHS.)

Six

Transportation— Roads and Rails

Getting around Noble County was once simple: people didn't. When the county was organized in 1836, there were two main roads—the Fort Wayne–Goshen Road, running northwest to what would become Ligonier, and the Mongoquinong Trail north through the eastern part of the county. That trail would later be lined with oak planks for a toll road, before being made a concrete highway in 1923. The Lima Plan Road also served as a line of the Underground Railroad.

Early settlers built their own roads as they went. Rough wagon trails became impassable in wet weather and had to wind around Noble County's swamps and lakes. After Albion was platted in 1847, roads were built going there from surrounding towns. Even where those roads no longer exist, reminders are seen in the other communities, which still have Albion Streets.

Taking advantage of the water, the State of Indiana planned a system of canals, one of which would have bisected Noble County. But the state overextended itself and abandoned the project. In Noble County, all that remains is a feeder reservoir, Sylvan Lake, and a few cuts where the canals were begun. One of those cuts, ironically, became an overland route called Canal Road.

The railroad was eagerly anticipated. Track locations often guaranteed the success—or failure—of new villages. The first went through the northern tier of townships around 1857, which contributed to the growth of the only two cities in Noble County, Kendallville and Ligonier. The next, north from Fort Wayne, ran through the east part of the county and then cut across the Sylvan Lake dam. In 1874, the Baltimore & Ohio connected Albion with the rest of the world, while a fourth railroad cut through the county's southeast corner.

Today, two of those railroads remain, and trains still sometimes stop locally. Two US highways, five state roads, and a grid of secondary roads provide access. In addition to an airport in Kendallville, airstrips dot the area. Once difficult and dangerous, transportation is now routine.

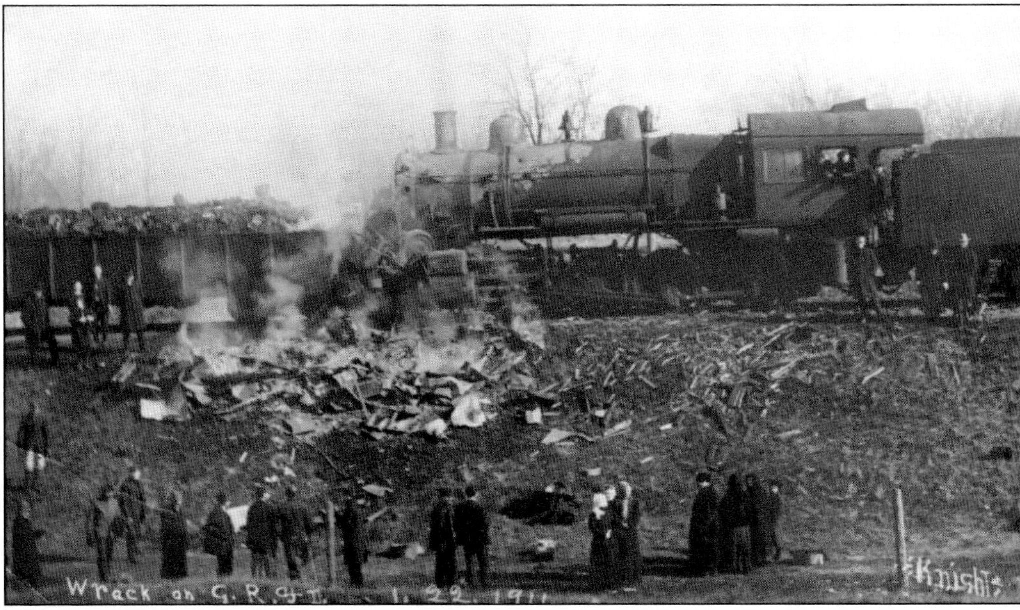

Crowds examine the aftermath of a 1911 wreck on the Grand Rapids & Indiana Railroad, which passed from Fort Wayne north into Michigan. At the time, there were about 77 miles of railroad tracks in Noble County, so wrecks and derailments were not uncommon. (Courtesy Mike Mapes.)

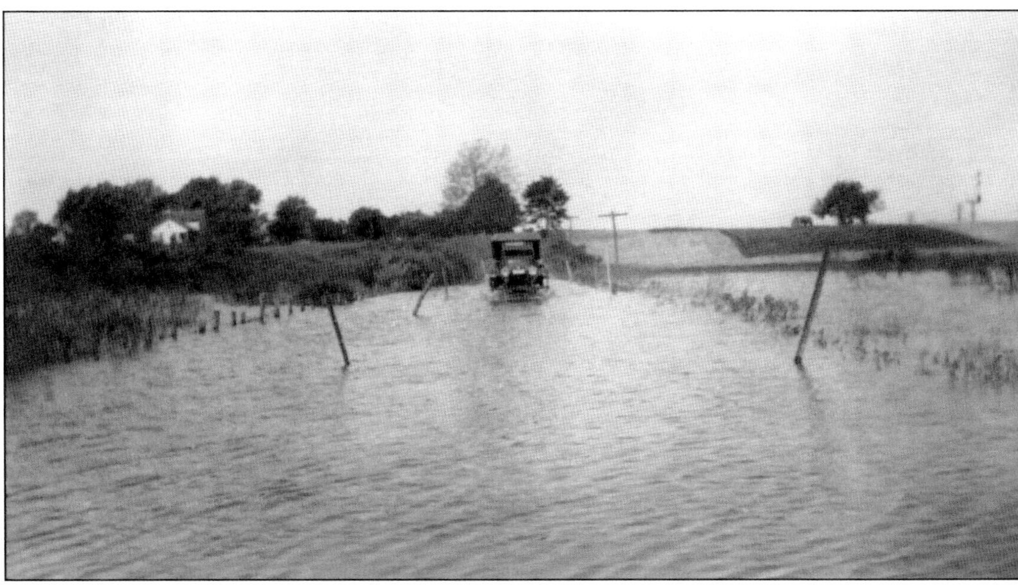

A driver makes his way through a flooded area near Brimfield. With much of Noble County originally swamps, flooding was a problem. The original dirt roads could quickly become impassable. In 1847, an attempt was made to solve the problem by lining an entire road from Fort Wayne past Kendallville with oak planks. Before it became SR 3, it was known as the Lima Plank Road. (Courtesy Marcia Garrett.)

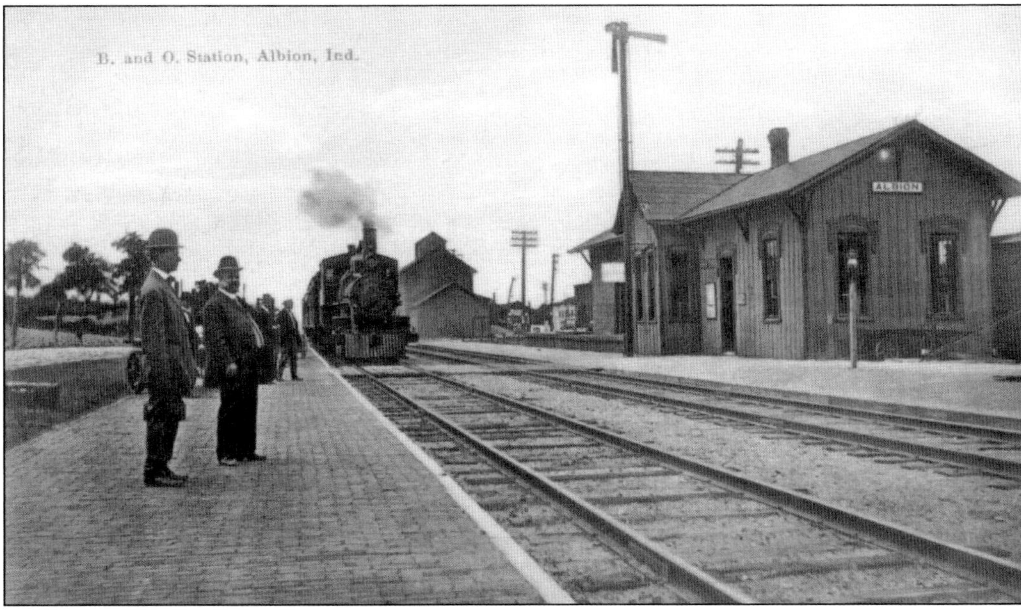

A train arrives at the Baltimore & Ohio Railroad depot on the south side of Albion in this 1909 photograph. Beyond the train is the B&O grain elevator, which burned down in a spectacular fire in the late 1980s. The railroad line through Albion, Avilla, and Kimmell was completed in 1873, after delays caused by an 18-foot-deep, muck-filled sinkhole found just west of Albion. (Courtesy Mike Mapes.)

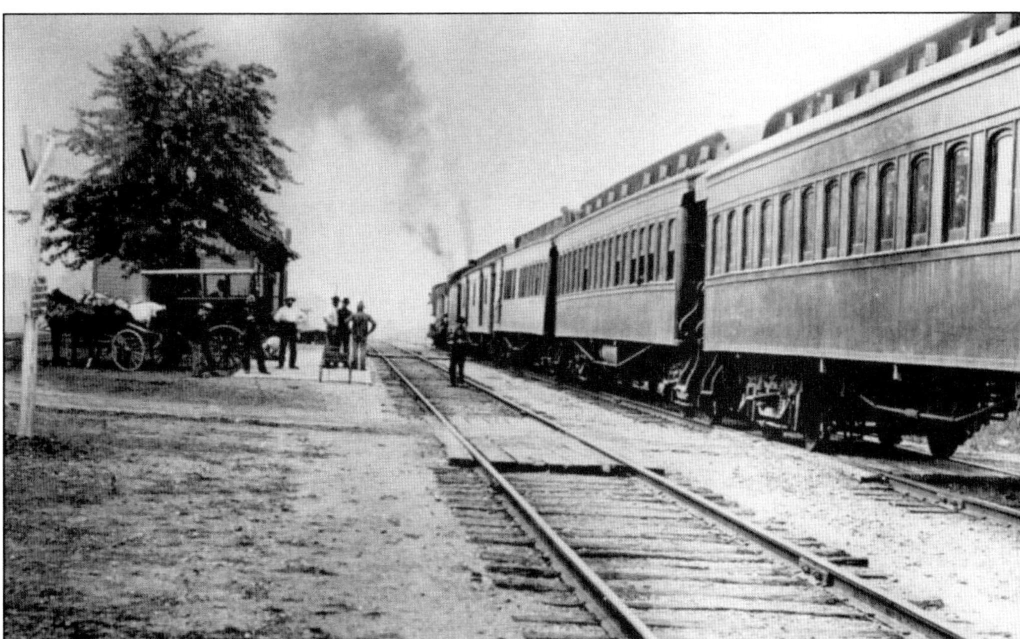

Horses are among those waiting more or less patiently as a passenger train stops at the Baltimore & Ohio Railroad depot in Cromwell. (STHS.)

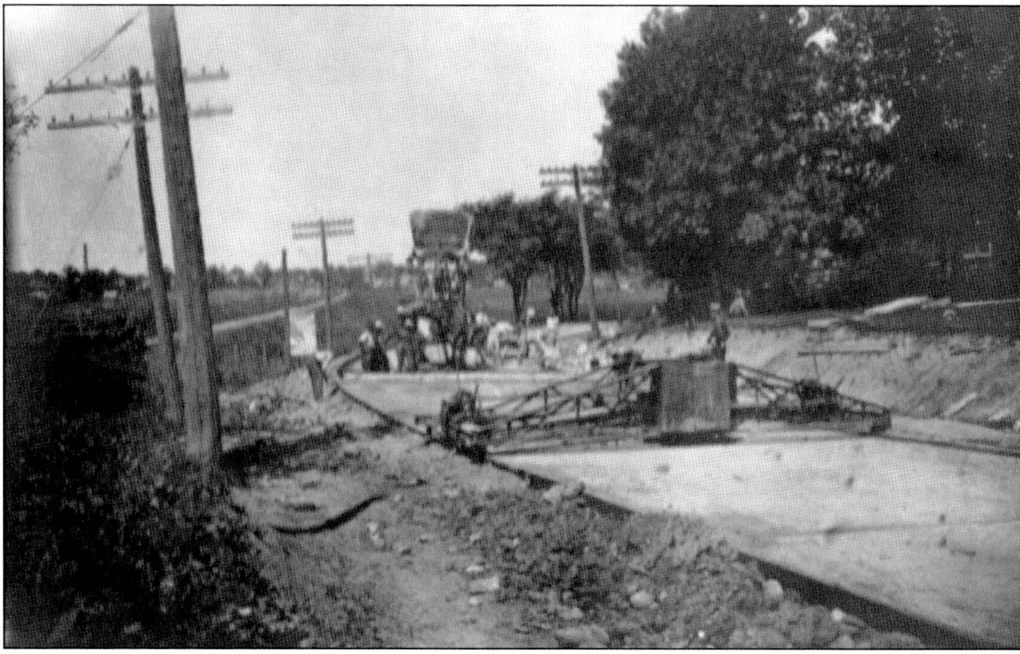

A construction crew builds US Highway 6 near the Ralph Riddle farm, near Kendallville. Originally the Sauk Indian Trail in Indiana, the route became a gravel road and was designated State Road 17 in 1918, then SR 6. In 1932, it became part of the 3,198-mile-long US 6, now also known as the Grand Army of the Republic Highway, to honor Civil War veterans. (NCHS.)

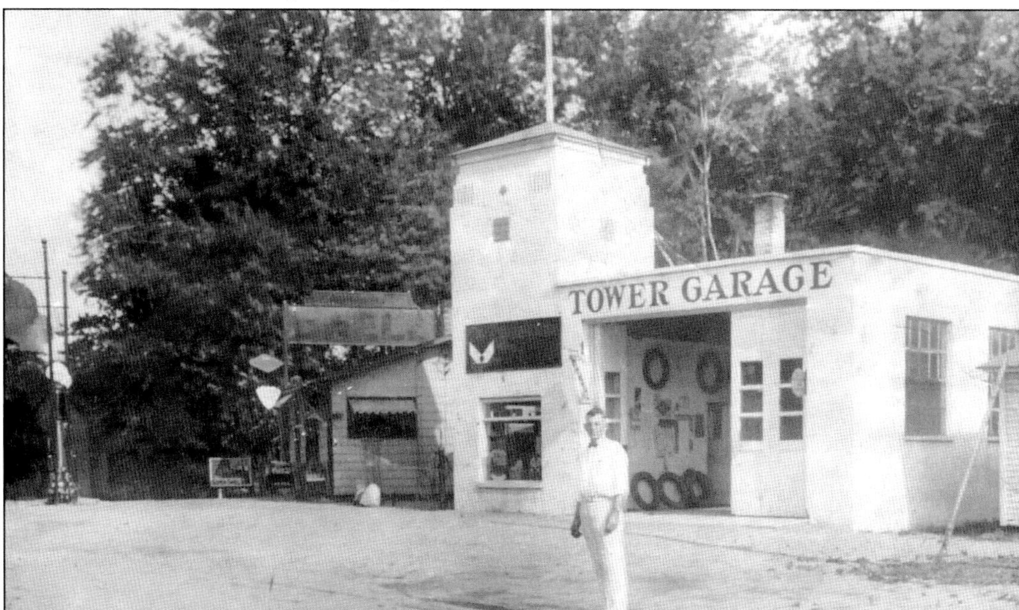

Tower Garage stood ready to help motorists speeding by Brimfield on US 6. It was accompanied by the Tower Place Restaurant and Cabins, run by William and Mildred Gess from 1947 to 1968. At one time, Brimfield had blacksmiths, a doctor, a hotel, a sawmill, and a literary society, in addition to a school. Although the federal highway and railroad remain, most businesses gradually died out. (NCHS.)

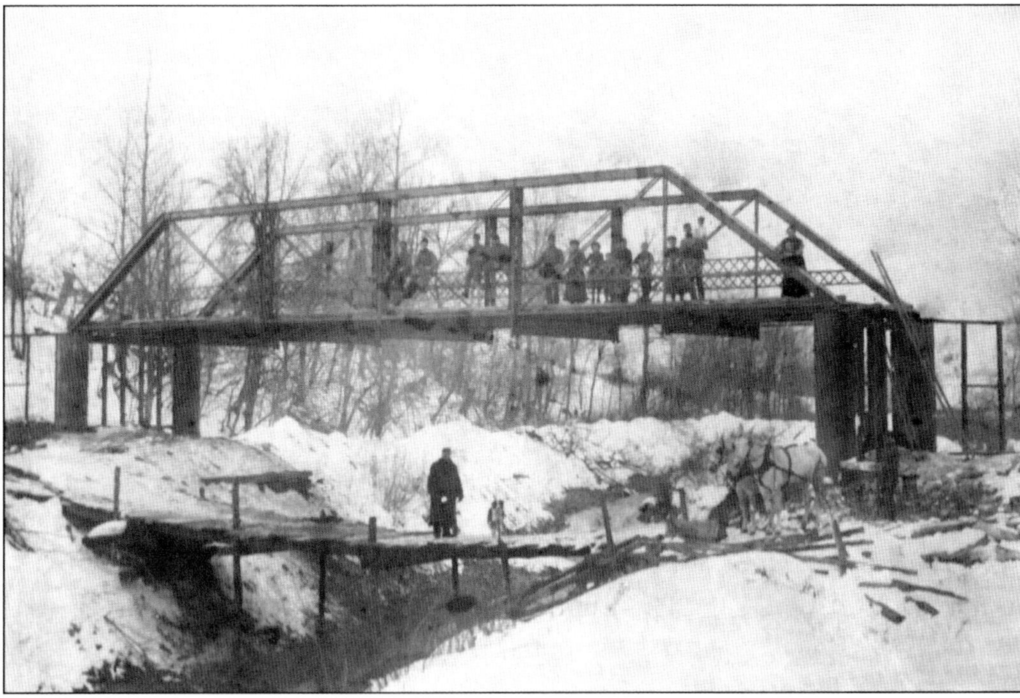

A new bridge crosses Forker Creek, west of the present Chain O' Lakes State Park, in this 1902 photograph. Water from the park's many lakes drains into the creek, which in turn empties into more of Noble County's 117 lakes. In 1927, the bridge was replaced with a culvert. (NCHS.)

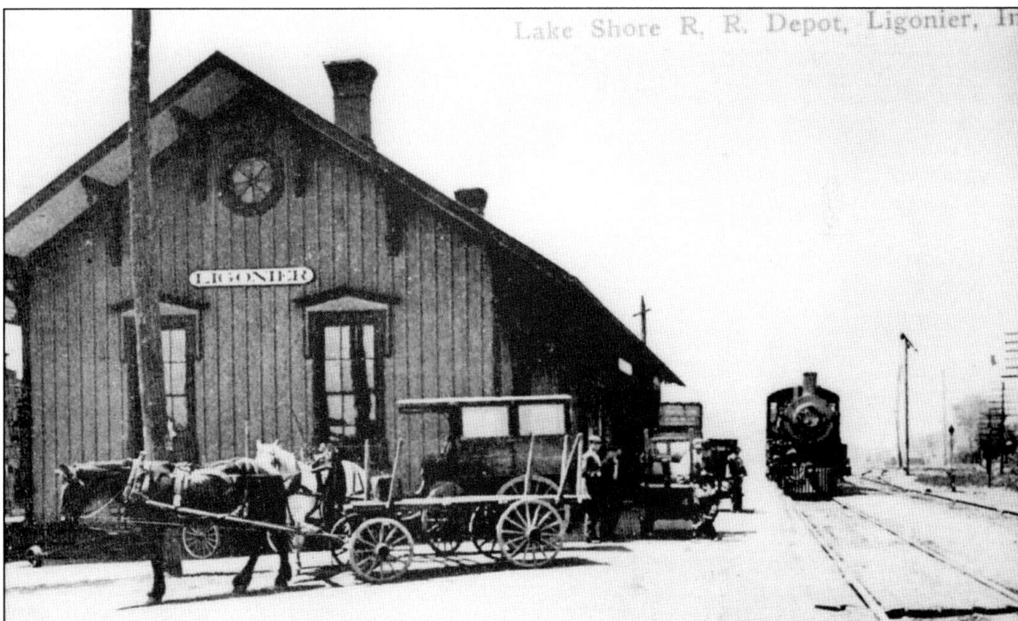

When the Lake Shore & Michigan Southern Railway came through Ligonier around 1857, it attracted early businessmen like Solomon Mier and Issac Straus, guaranteeing the town's survival. The railroad missed Rochester, which was a stone's throw away, and that community eventually vanished. (STHS.)

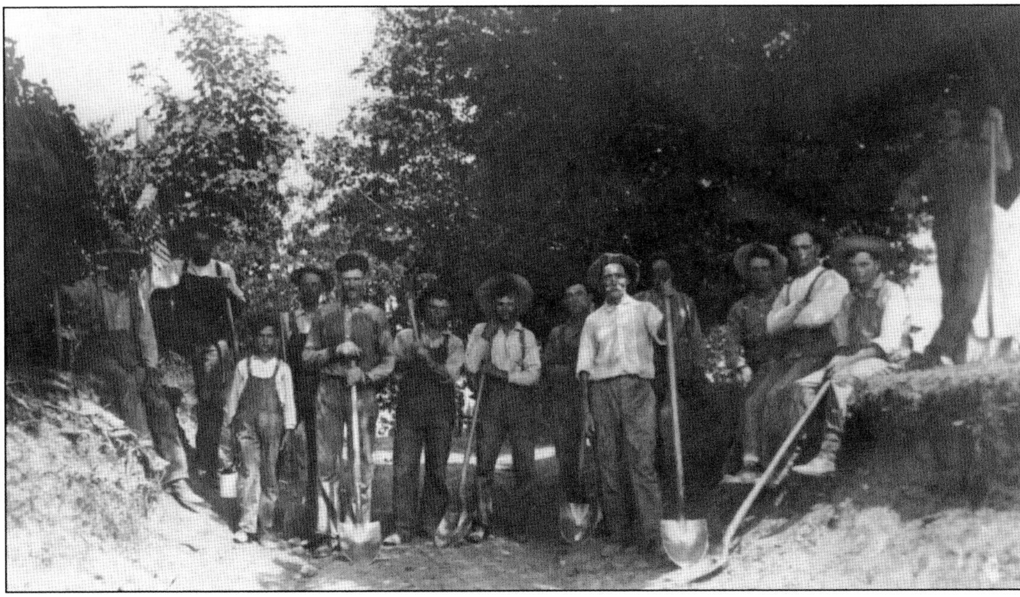

Workers pause while constructing a road that later became State Route 9, passing north and south through central Noble County. The highway's route through southern Noble County was later shifted a short distance to the east. The only local people known to be in the work crew are Albion residents Fletcher "Vinegar" Butler and Burl "Bunny" Butler, who directed teams of horses, and Todd Weeks. (NCHS.)

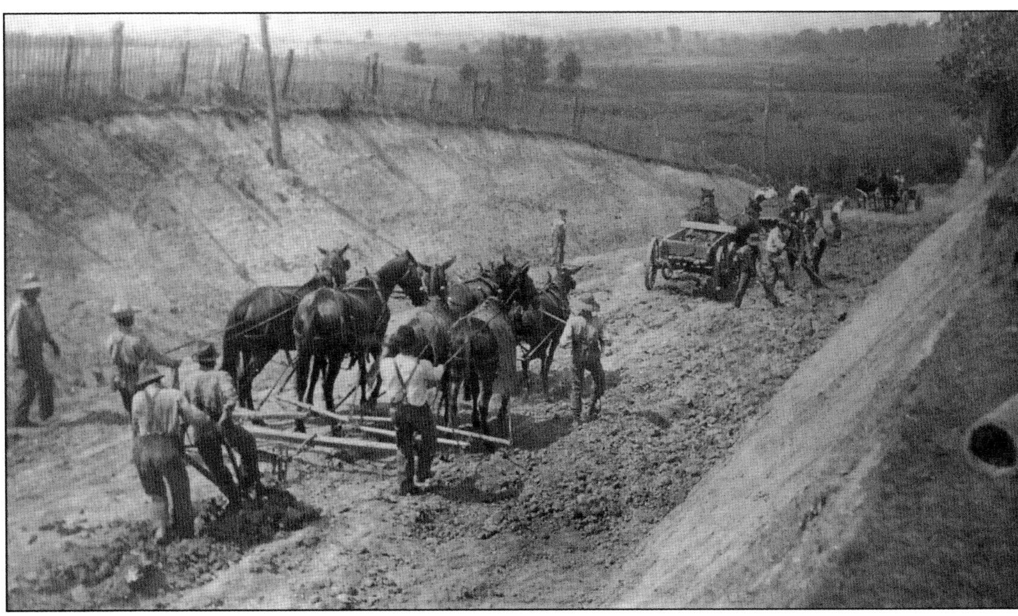

Horsepower provides the earth moving as workers put in a new road through central Noble County. In 1926, that route became State Route 9, one of five state highways that pass through the county. Two of the horse teams were directed by Albion residents Fletcher "Vinegar" Butler and Burl "Bunny" Butler. (NCHS.)

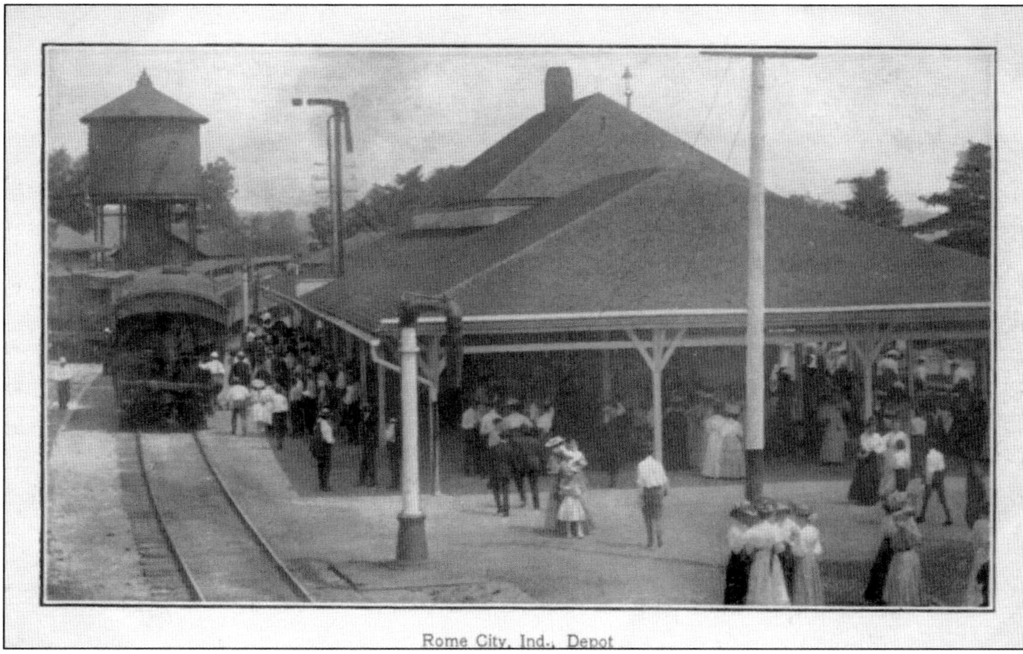

Passengers get ready to embark at the Grand Rapids & Indiana Railroad depot in Rome City. For a time, products produced in Rome City were shipped from the railroad station in Brimfield, until the GR&I came through in the early 1870s. (Courtesy Mike Mapes.)

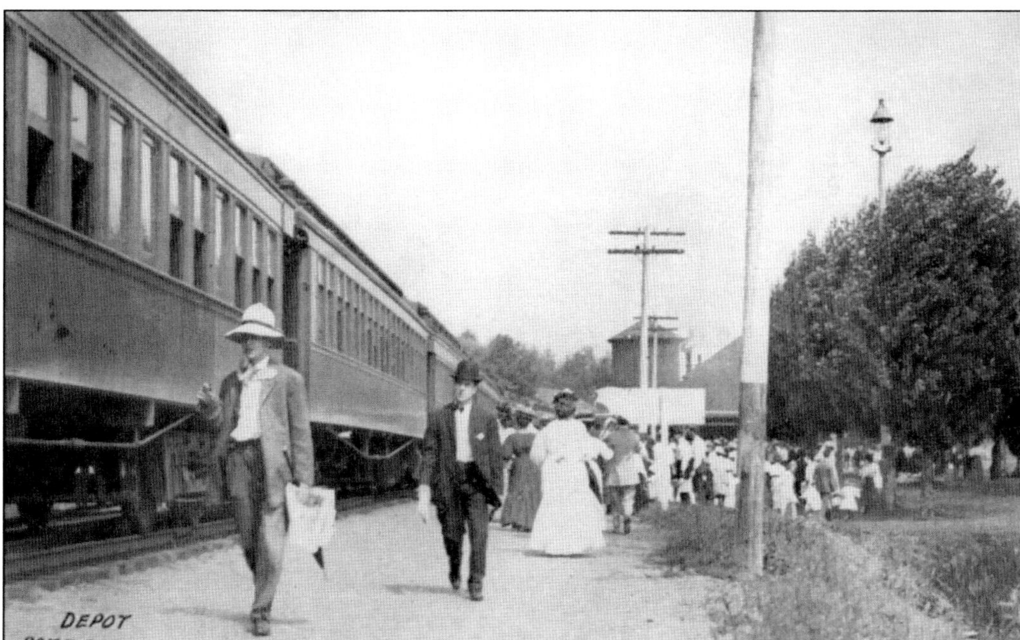

A 1908 photograph shows passengers at the Grand Rapids & Indiana Railroad depot in Rome City. (Courtesy Mike Mapes.)

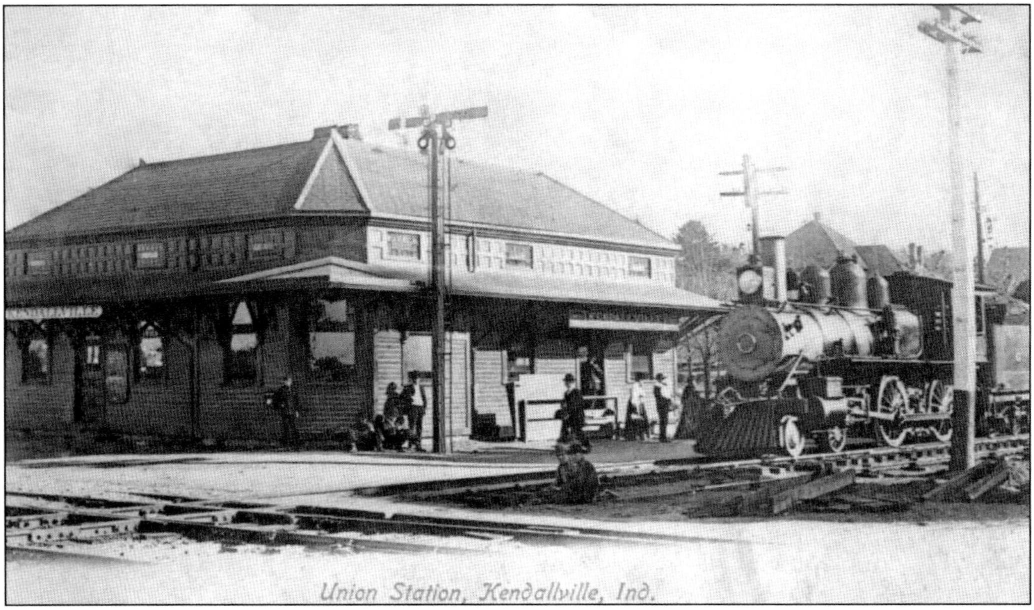

Lake Shore train no. 23 arrives at Union Station in Kendallville, in northeast Noble County. One of the two railroads running through Kendallville was the Lake Shore & Michigan Southern Railway, which was consolidated from other railroad companies in 1869 and ran from Buffalo, New York, to Chicago. The building was still standing as of 1975 but was later torn down. (Courtesy Mike Mapes.)

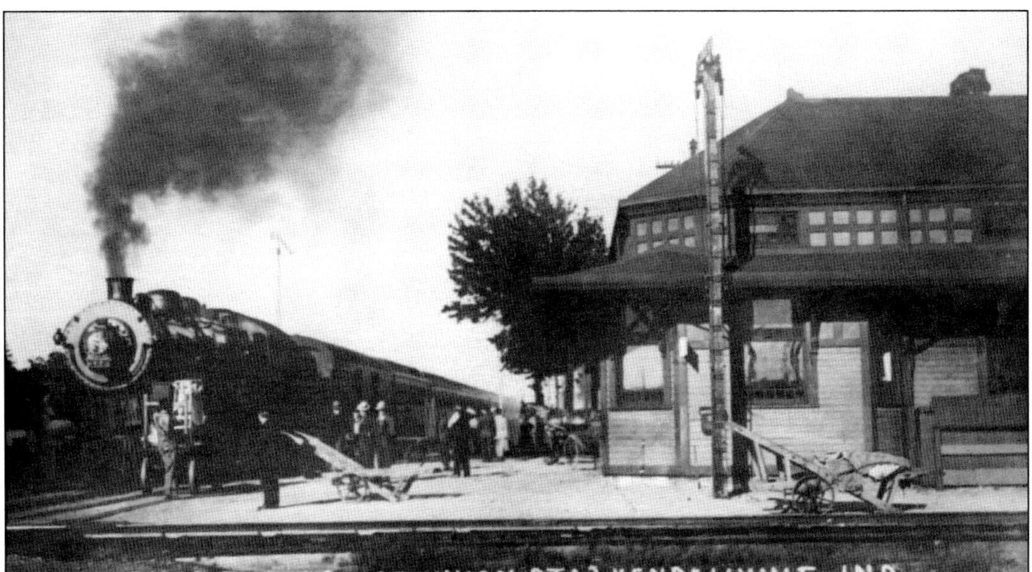

A train pulls into Kendallville's Union Station in 1870. (Courtesy Mike Mapes.)

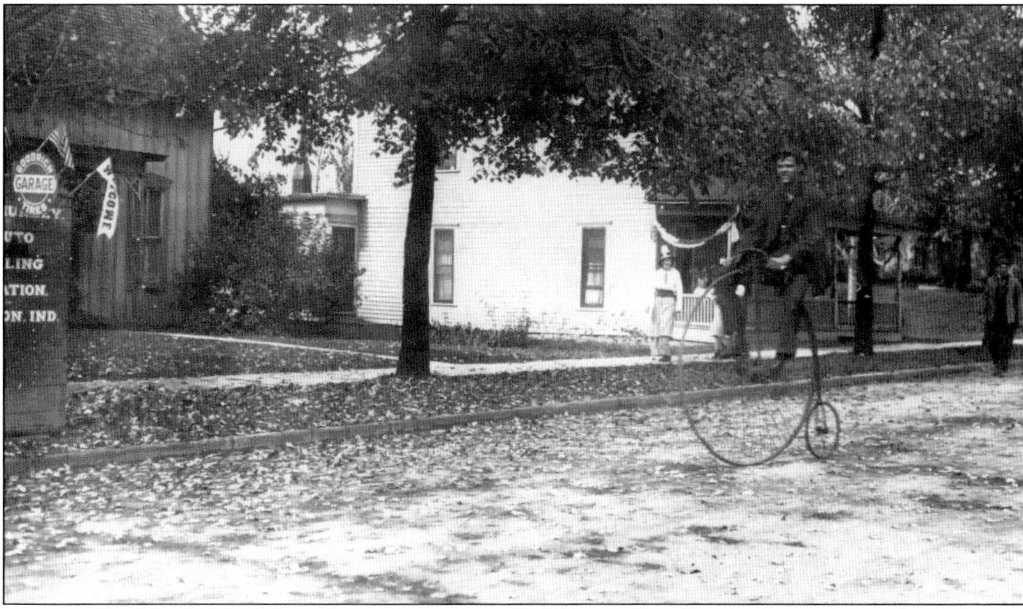

"Slim" Cropper shows off his bike-riding skills near his South Orange Street garage, which he opened in Albion in 1914. Signs for the business, in a building formerly owned by C.M. Eagles, can be seen on the left edge of the photograph. Cropper was a mechanic at the Ford garage that later became the Albion Fire Department, and he worked at dealerships run by Logan Winebrenner and Ross Zimmerman. (NCHS.)

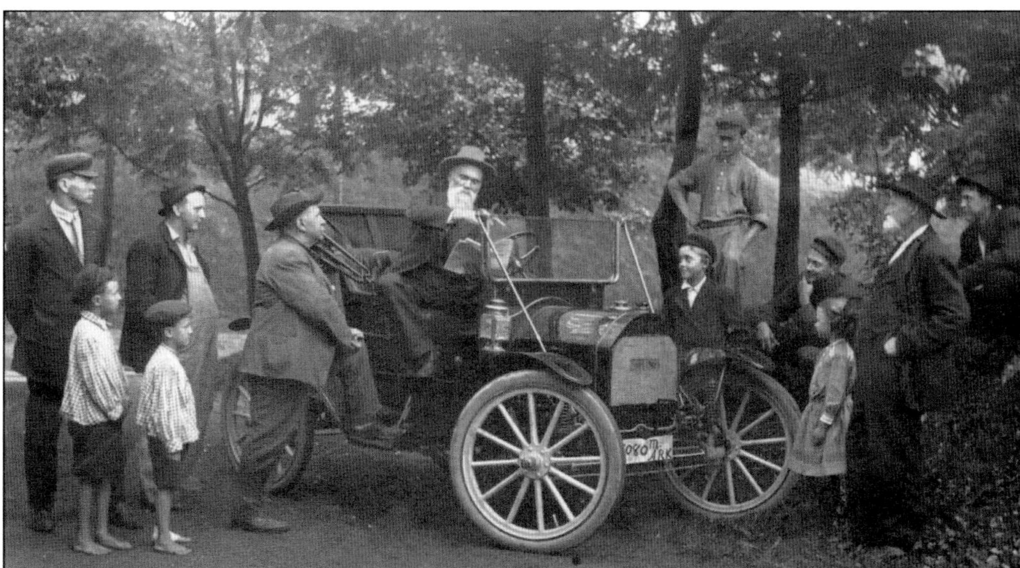

One of the first horseless carriages to make the two-hour trip from Fort Wayne immediately attracted the town's attention. John Savoie, an owner of the Albion Hotel, is behind the wheel of the fire-engine-red Brush Motor Car. The Detroit company began operations in 1907 and went out of business in 1913. (NCHS.)

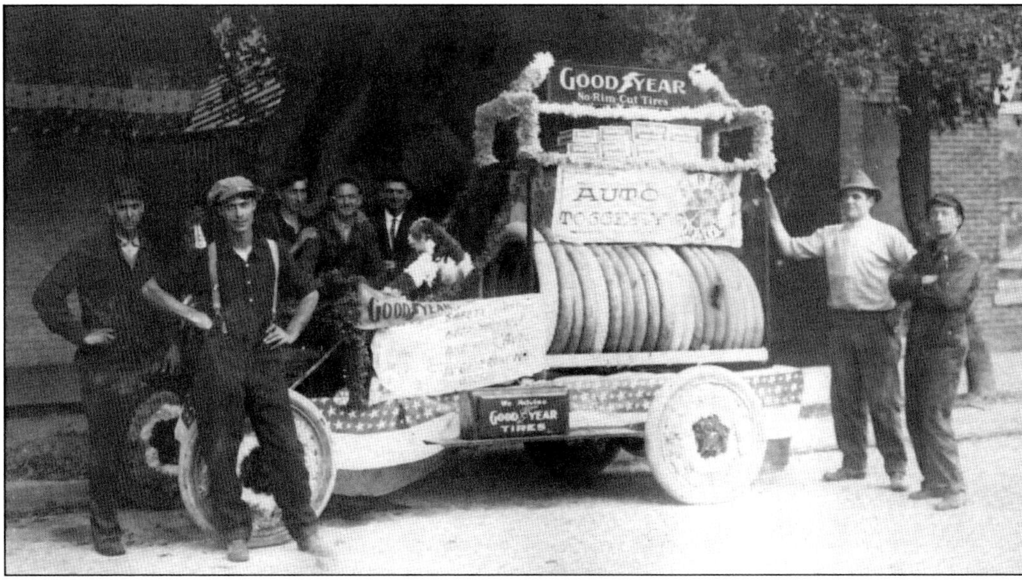

With new modes of transportation came the need for maintenance and new parts. The Albion Garage was one of the first businesses to meet that need, and it only made sense to advertise their tires during the Albion Street Fair, on what amounted to a rolling billboard. Pictured from left to right are Homer Ohlwine, Harlen Rosen, Bill Todd, Lex Ward, John "Tug" Wilson, Sam Kuhns, and Al "Pug" Kunkle. (NCHS.)

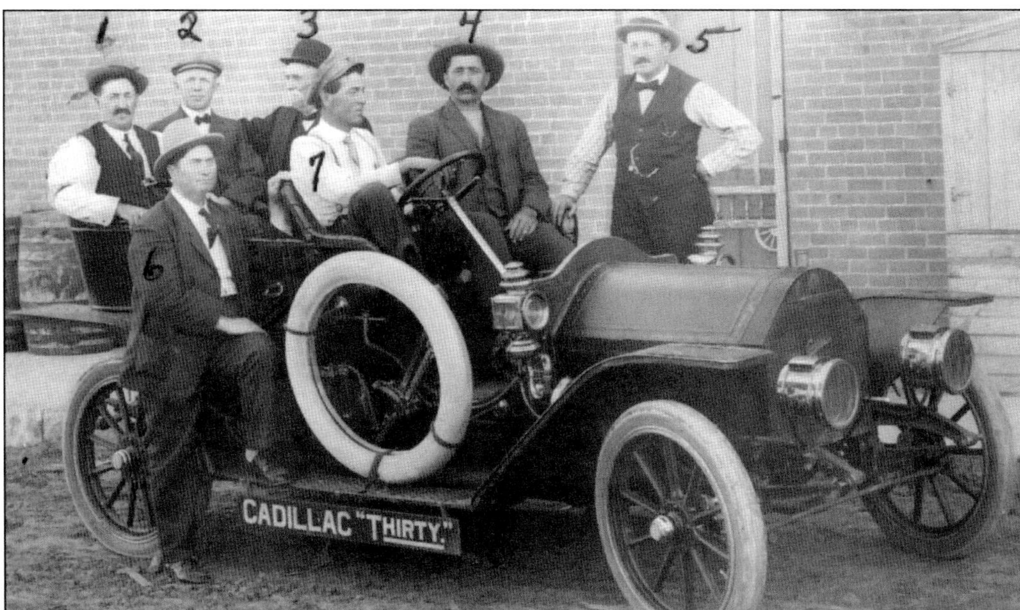

A Fort Wayne land agent was so anxious to sell Texas land to Albionites that he came to Albion, along with a man who drove all the way from Texas itself. It was a testimony to the toughness of the Cadillac 30, Cadillac's only car produced from 1908 to 1914. In addition to making that drive before paved roads were common, the 30 was the first car to feature an electric starter. (NCHS.)

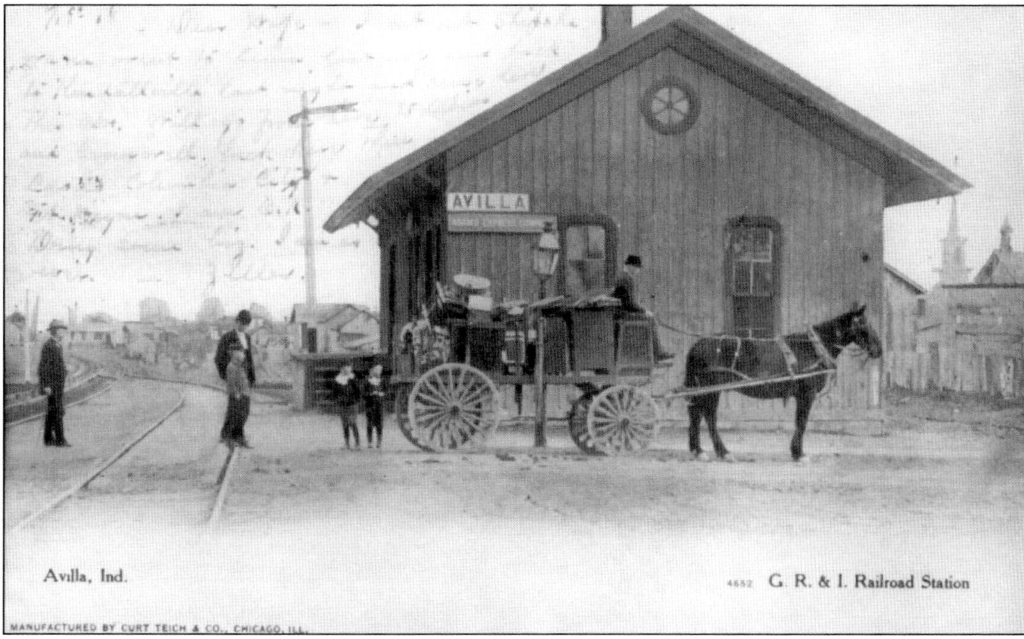

The Grand Rapids & Indiana Railroad station in Avilla was near downtown, just east of the well-located St. James Hotel. Although the depot and tracks are now gone, the hotel has been turned into the still popular St. James Restaurant. (Courtesy Mike Mapes.)

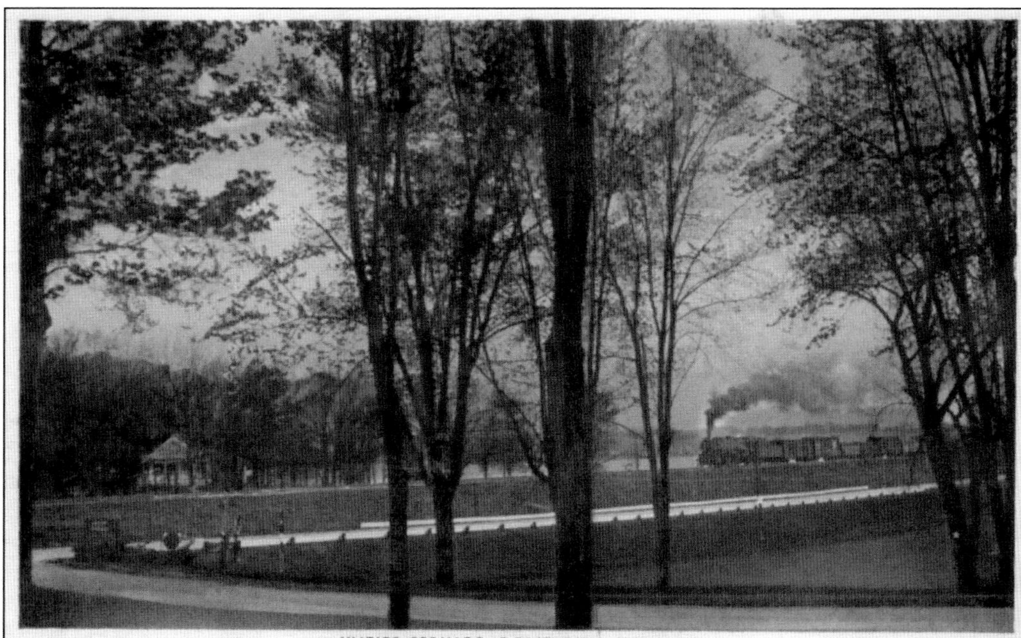

A train goes by Kneipp Springs, on the north edge of Rome City. The property, originally owned by the Grand Rapids & Indiana Railroad, was named after springs that reportedly had healing properties and has since had several owners. (Courtesy Mike Mapes.)

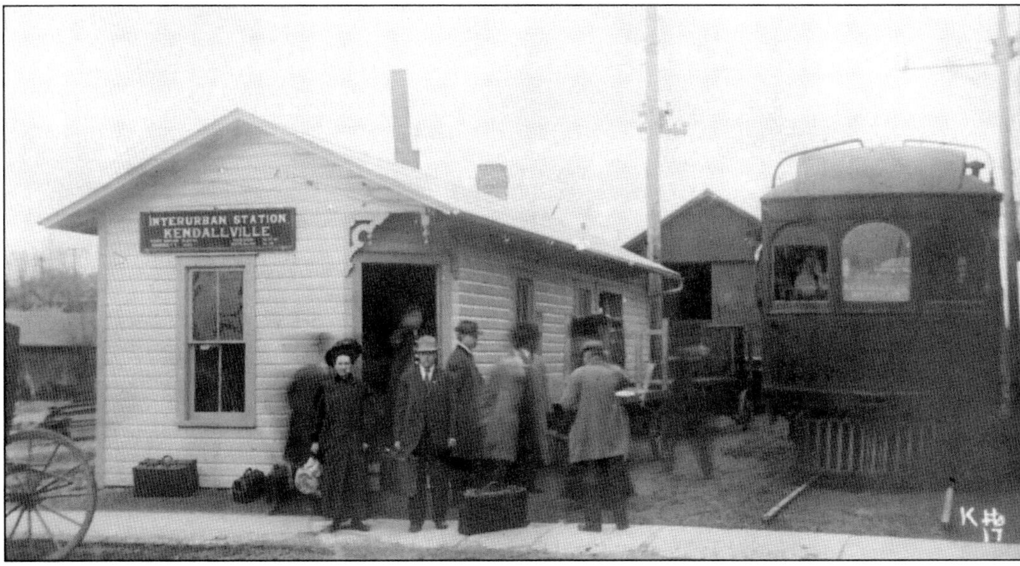

In the above photograph, passengers wait at the interurban station in Kendallville. From 1907 to 1937, the interurban electric railway operated on the former Grand Rapids & Indiana Railroad line, taking passengers and freight from Fort Wayne to Avilla and Kendallville. Below, the interurban stops in Avilla to take passengers to the Kendallville Fair for a fee of 10¢. (Both, courtesy Mike Mapes.)

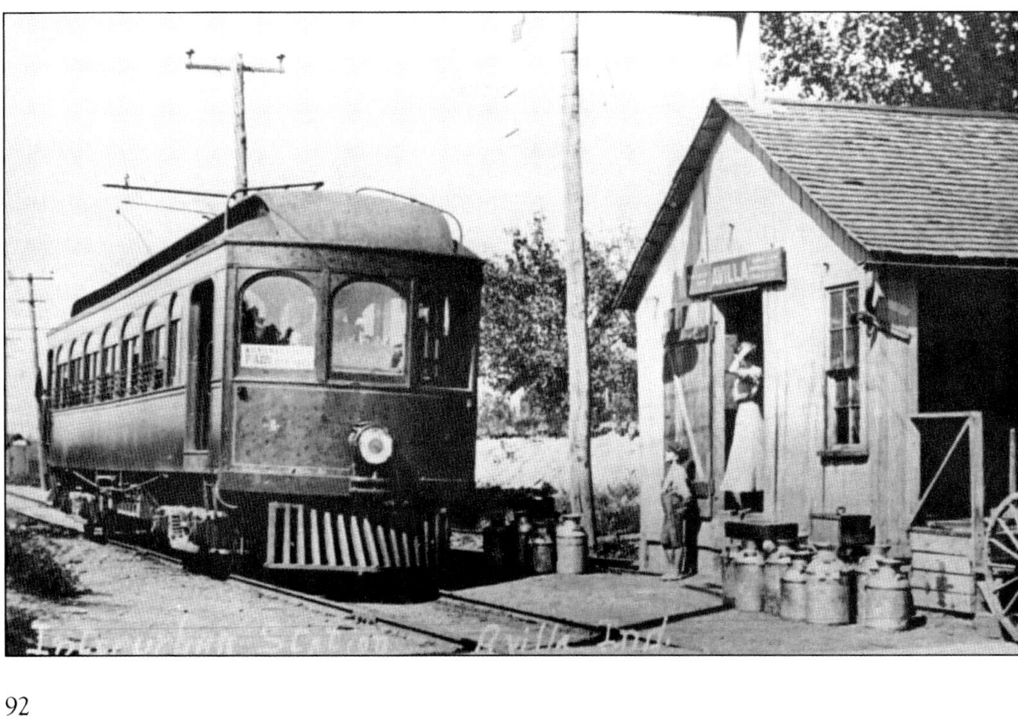

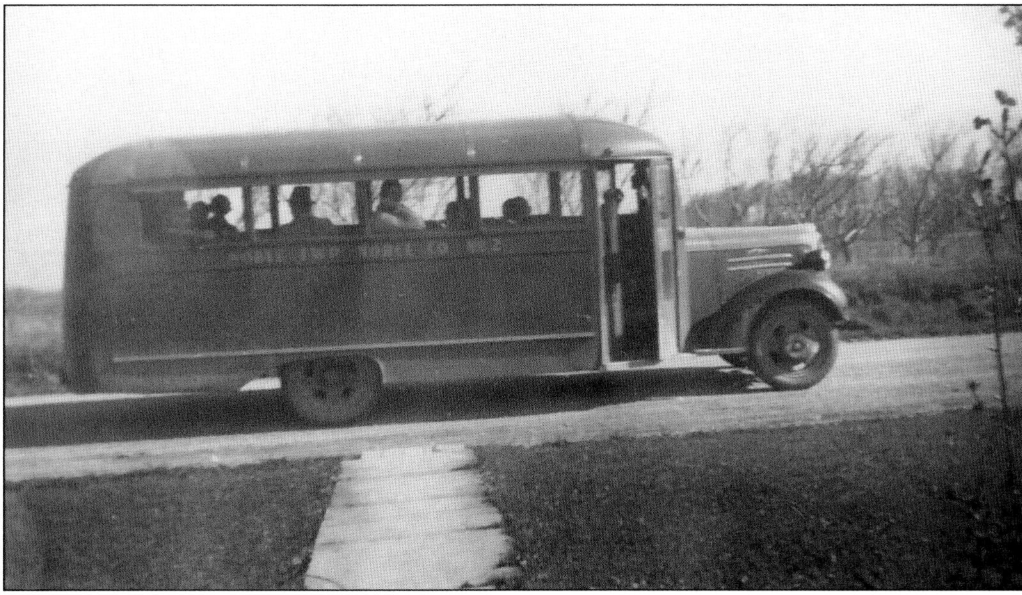

A school bus transports Noble Township students in this photograph from around 1940. In the 1820s, land was set aside in each township for a school. Although there were often several schools in individual townships, township officials were responsible for schools until consolidation began in the 1960s. (Courtesy Ellen McBride.)

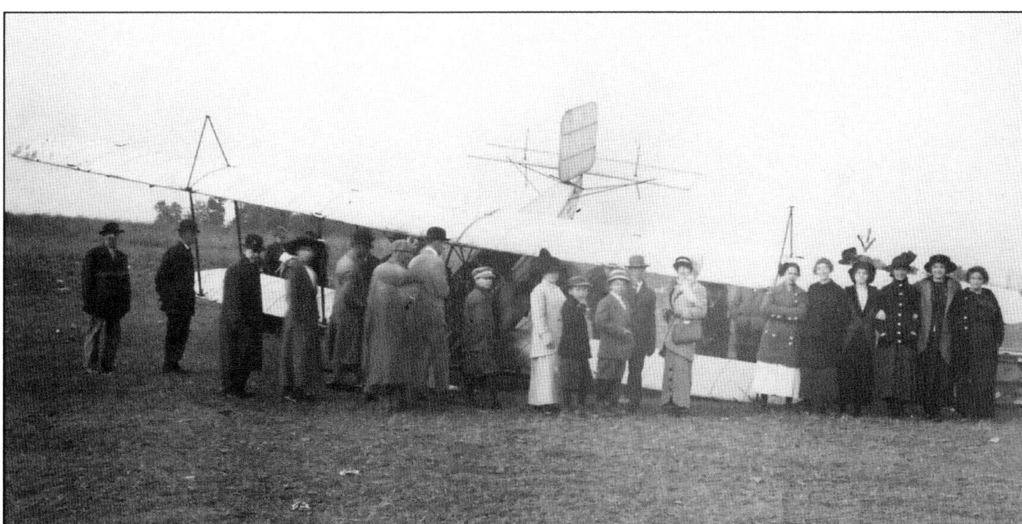

Albion residents gather around an airplane that made a rough landing on the east edge of town. Many Albionites had probably never seen an airplane up close at that point. At around the same time, in 1913, another plane appeared and circled over the W.H. Favinger home in Albion, alerting residents to an overheated chimney that set the home's roof on fire. (NCHS.)

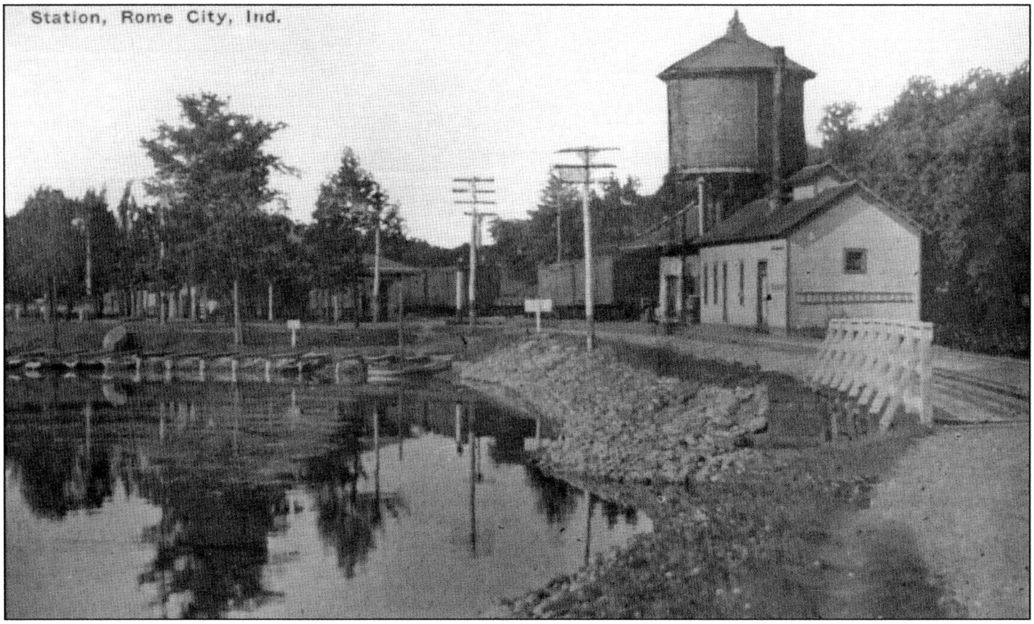

There is some irony in the fact that the Sylvan Lake dam was originally built to provide a feeder dam for a canal project, intended to provide easy, cheap transportation through Northeast Indiana. After the project failed, the Grand Rapids & Indiana Railroad passed over the dam to provide that transportation. In this 1912 photograph, a train stops at a station near the water. (Courtesy Mike Mapes.)

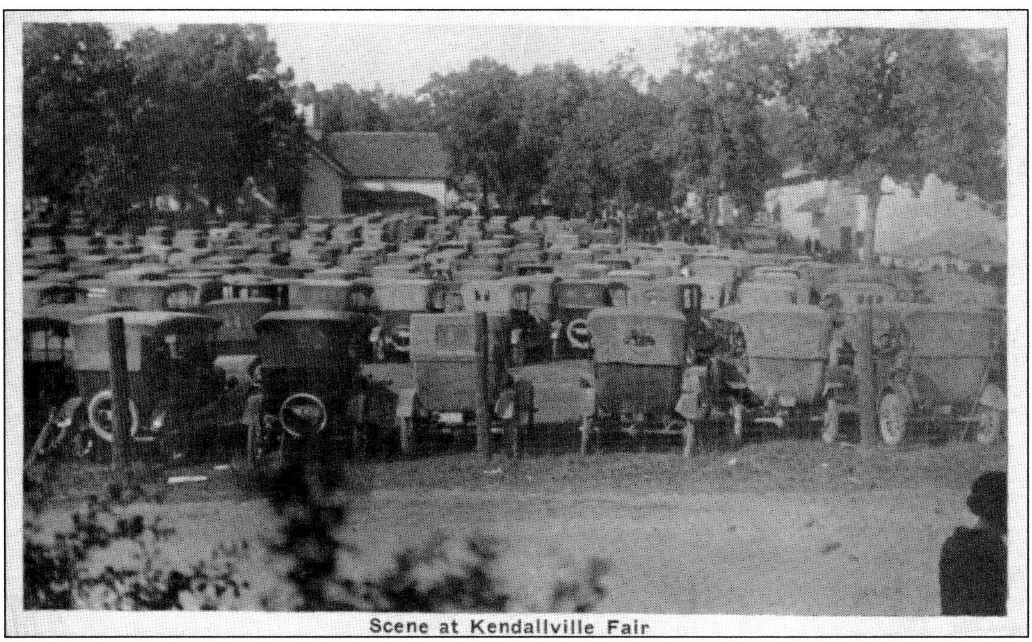

Automobiles jam the parking lot during the Kendallville Fair in the early 1900s. Beyond them is Floral Hall, built in 1883 and still standing despite two close calls with fires. It is one of the oldest buildings on the Noble County Fairgrounds. (Courtesy Mike Mapes.)

Seven

Starting Services

As self-sufficient as early settlers were, some basic services followed them—with others much delayed. Northeast Indiana was infested early on by criminals called blacklegs, who terrorized Noble County for 25 years. There was even a plan to rob a train near Brimfield, although it apparently never came to fruition.

In 1852, the state approved regulators, volunteers dedicated to restoring law and order. About 500 men in Noble County set out to stop the blacklegs, who soon found themselves behind bars. One, Gregory McDougal, admitted to having stolen 34 horses, robbed four stores, passed counterfeit money, and broken out of two jails. He boasted that no jail could hold him. When the jury learned that McDougal had killed two people, they were done taking chances. McDougal was hanged, and the blacklegs' power was broken.

From then on, law enforcement became more traditional—from the Noble County sheriff and town marshals. Albion had a hoosegow (a small jail), which became unnecessary when the Noble County Jail was built.

Fire protection lagged behind, despite fires that devastated almost every downtown in the county at least once. Larger towns began forming fire departments in the late 1870s, with Albion's coming in 1888. This was one of three fire departments that traveled to Wawaka in 1929, when part of its unprotected downtown burned.

Firefighters took water from cisterns, and pipes were later buried underground to feed both fire hydrants and the water needs of the citizens. Albion, like most towns of its size, formed its own water and electric works and later added sewer lines.

Hospitals also sprang up, such as the Luckey Hospital in Wolf Lake that is now a museum. Albion's first hospital, New Hope, was a block south of downtown, and the structure was later a dentist office for many years.

Another service was poor relief, and the Noble County Poor House was established to help take care of the destitute and infirm. The occupants helped take care of themselves by working a small farm on the property; later, the second (and last) poorhouse was turned into a nursing home.

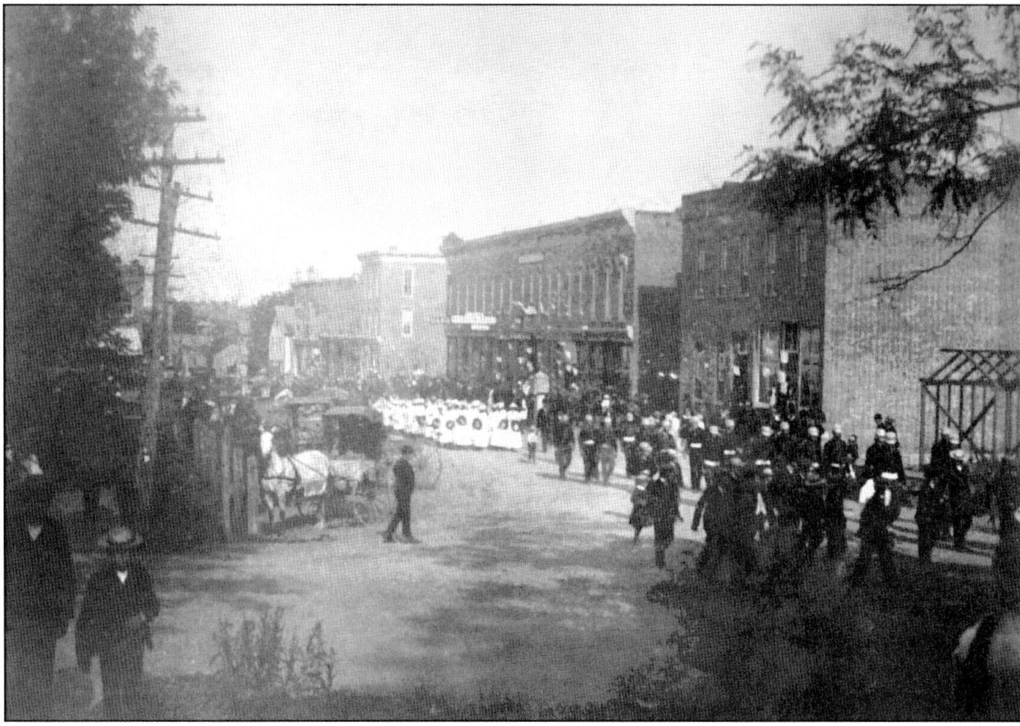

A parade winds its way down Albion's West Main Street in 1887. The unfinished frame building at the far right is Albion's first firehouse, still under construction. (Courtesy Linda Shultz.)

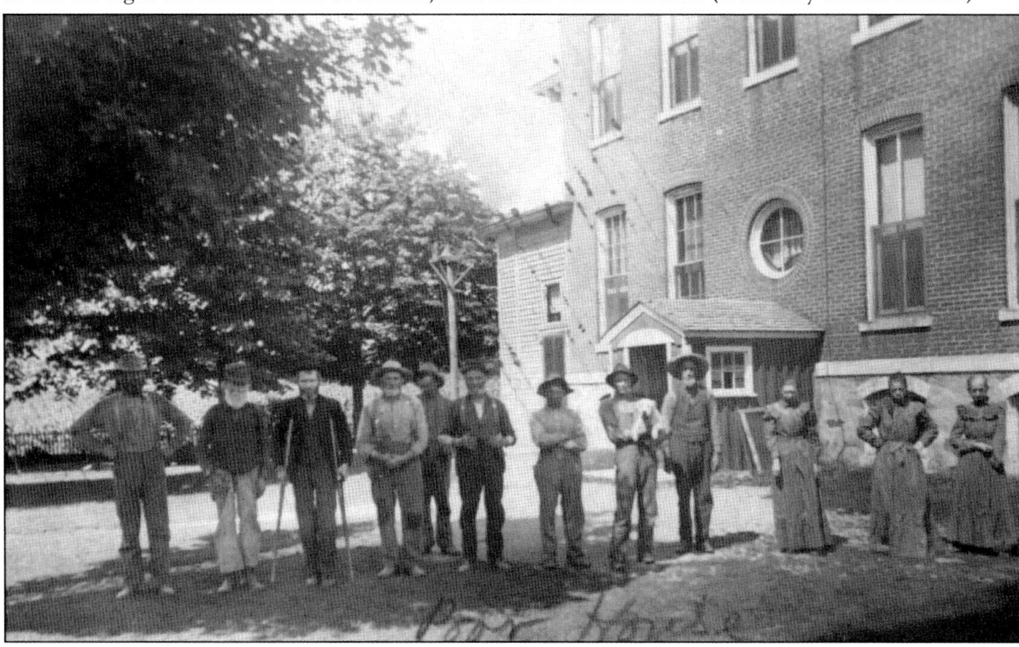

On the far left in this 1909 photograph, Henry Kirkpatrick was superintendent of the Noble County Poor House, northwest of Albion. A new two-story brick building was erected in 1870, in the center of a 160-acre farm that the "inmates" worked. The facility housed the superintendent's family and as many as 100 residents, who grew crops and cared for a herd of dairy cows. (NCHS.)

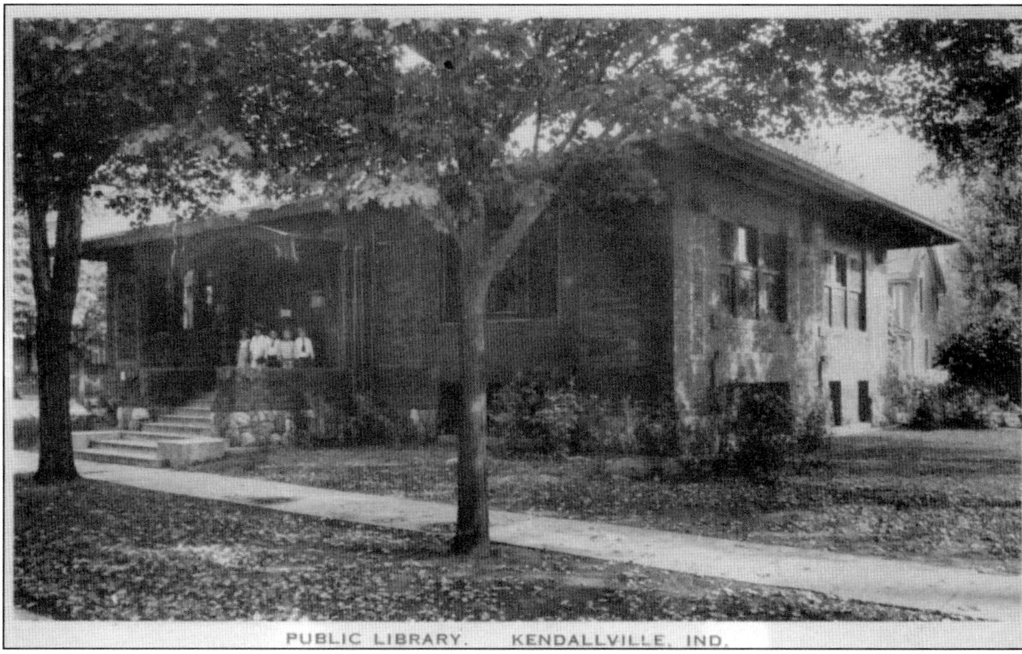

In 1902, the Kendallville Civic Club helped establish a library in the basement of the public school. It was not until 1913 that, with the assistance of a $12,500 Carnegie Corporation grant, this library was begun at Rush and State Streets. It was replaced in 1968 by a new library. In 2007, the present library was built on the former site of McCray Hospital. (Courtesy Mike Mapes.)

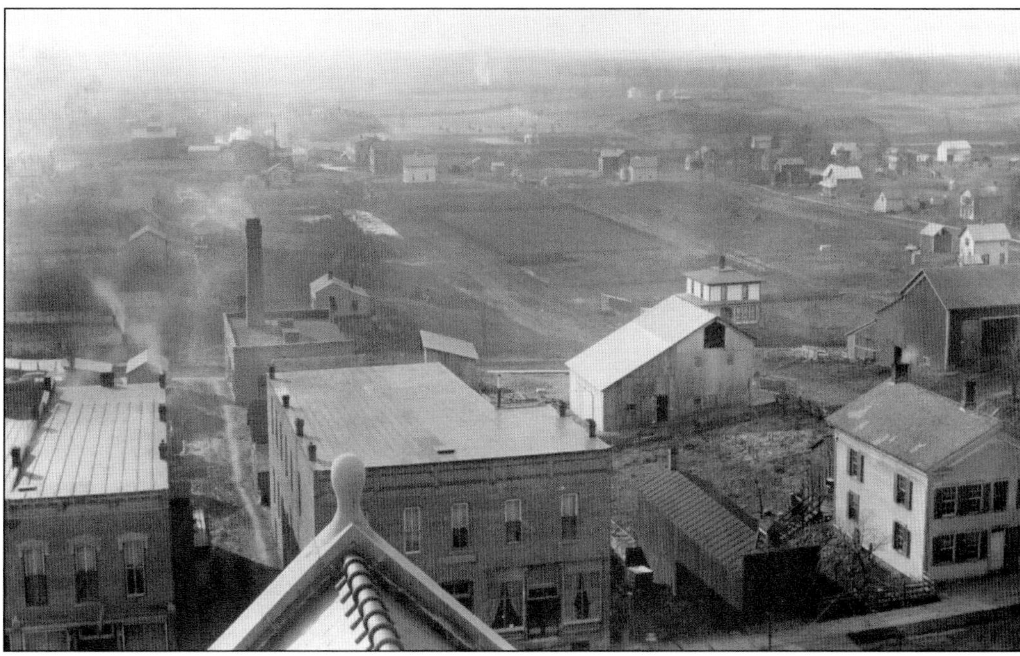

Albion's first firehouse is visible at lower right in this view looking south from the courthouse tower. The long, narrow, one-story building held three hand-drawn apparatuses—a hand-pumped engine, a hose cart, and a hook-and-ladder wagon. Although an attorney's office now occupies the space, the buildings on either side still exist. (Courtesy Noble County historian Sarah Knopp.)

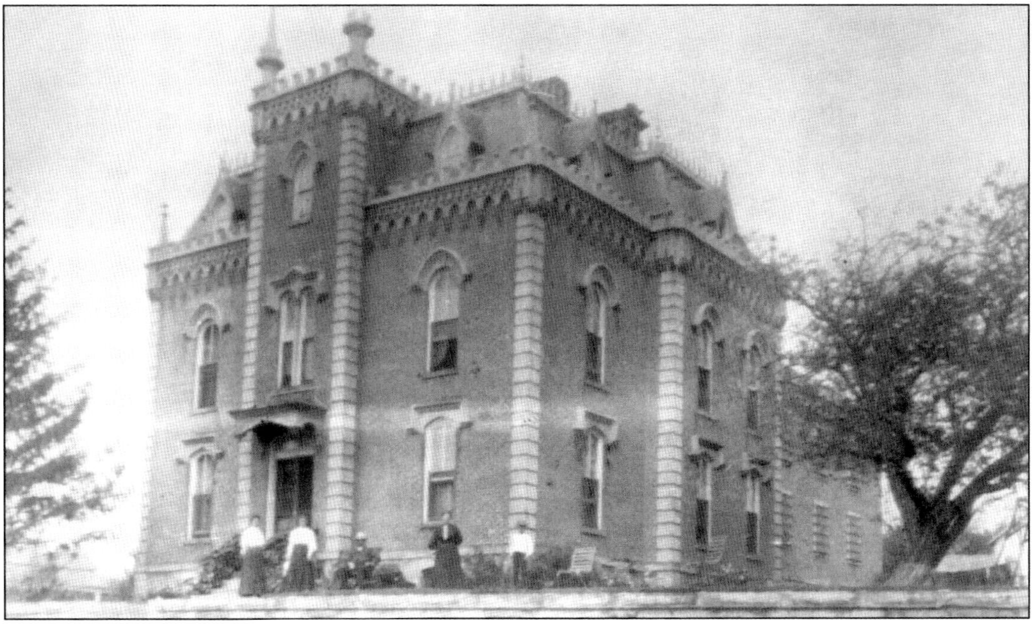

The sheriff and his family pose in front of the Noble County Jail in Albion. Built in 1876 for $27,000, the jail held not only the inmates but also the sheriff's family in a separated front part. After a new jail was completed in 1967, the Noble County Historical Society took over the older structure and opened the Old Jail Museum, which is now on the Indiana Historical Registry. (NCHS.)

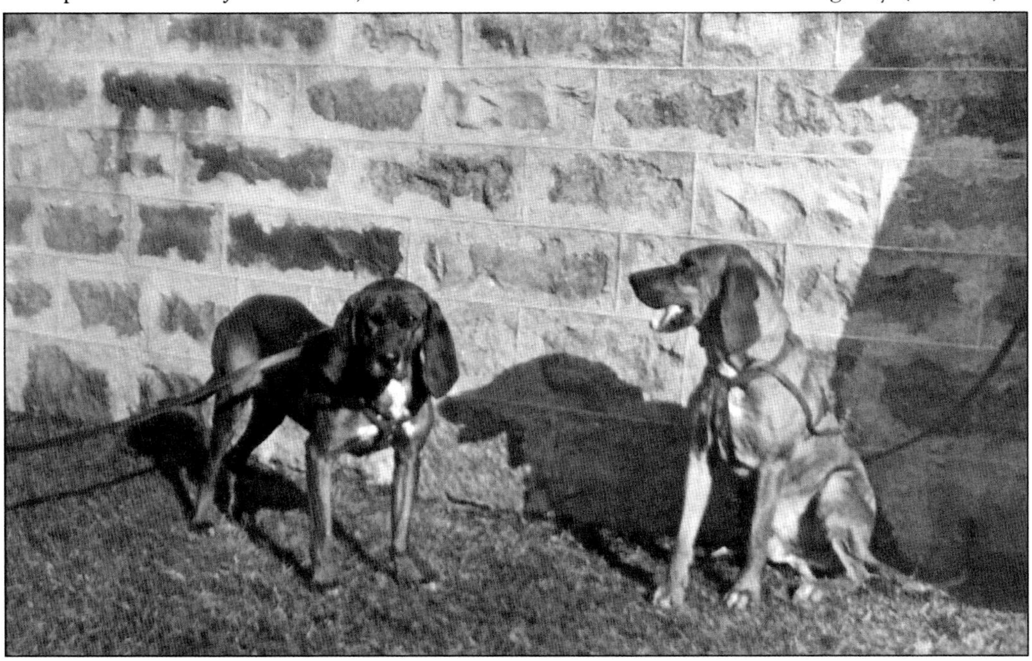

As sheriff, Albert D. Sawyer had secret weapons—bloodhounds, pictured here guarding the Noble County Jail. Sawyer, whose family had been in the area for 80 years, was sheriff from 1914 to 1918. Despite the extra help, four prisoners did manage to break out of the jail. Early on January 11, 1917, they pried open an air shaft register, dug out a stone in the outer basement wall, and stole Sawyer's Ford. (NCHS.)

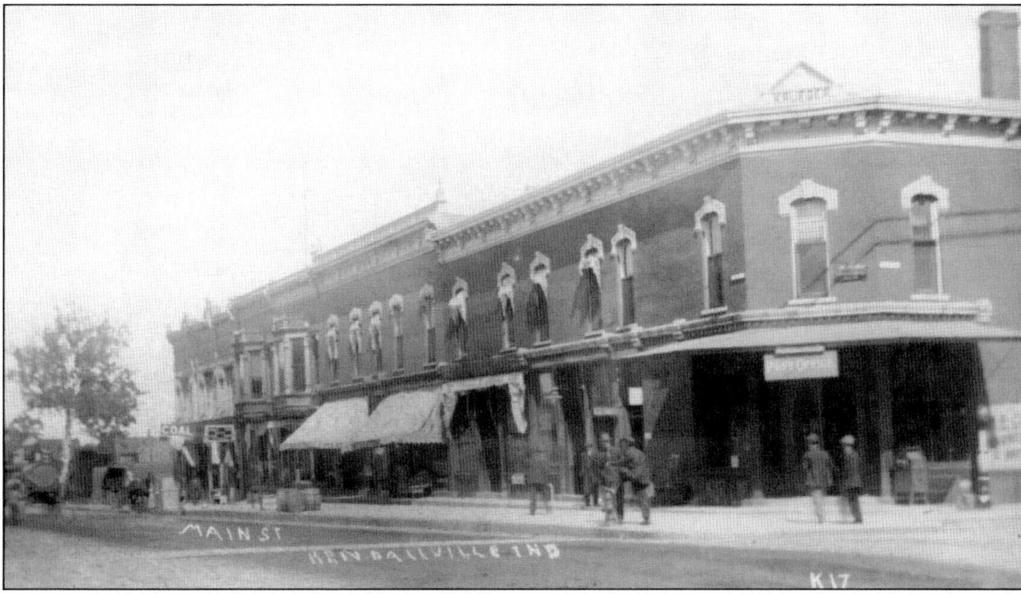

The Kendallville Post Office stood for a time in a building now occupied by KPC Media, publisher of several local newspapers. William Mitchell, who has not one but two city streets named after him, convinced federal officials to establish Kendallville's first post office in his cabin, in 1849. Many villagers thought the town should be named after Mitchell—perhaps Mitchelltown or Mitchellville. But since it was the post office that required a name, Mitchell picked the name of the US postmaster general, Amos Kendall, of Tennessee. The town was incorporated in 1863 and became a city three years later. Sometime after that, the post office seen below was built. It was later replaced with another building. (Both, courtesy Mike Mapes.)

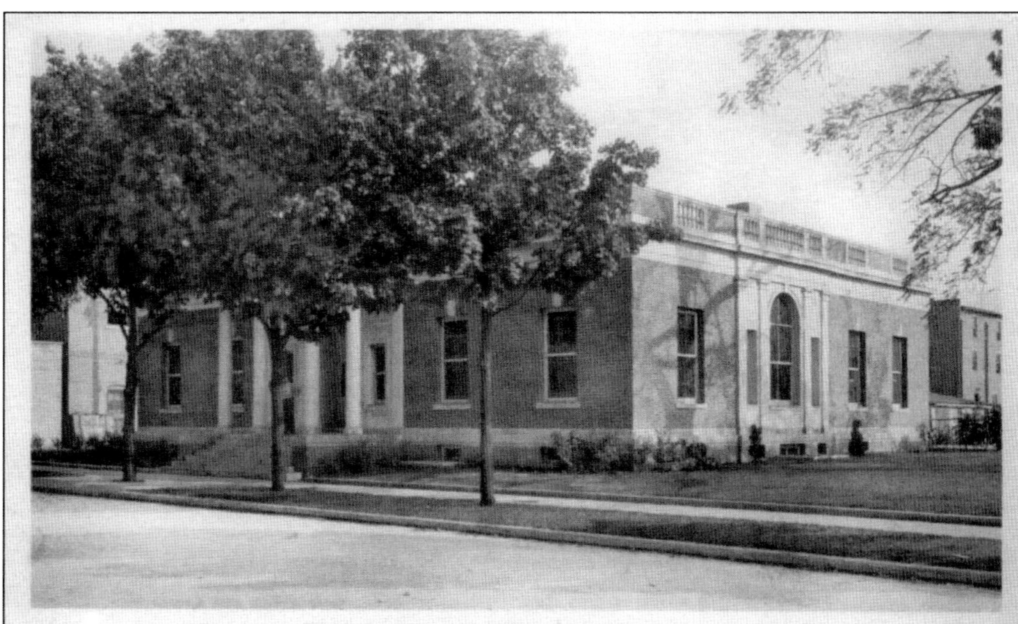

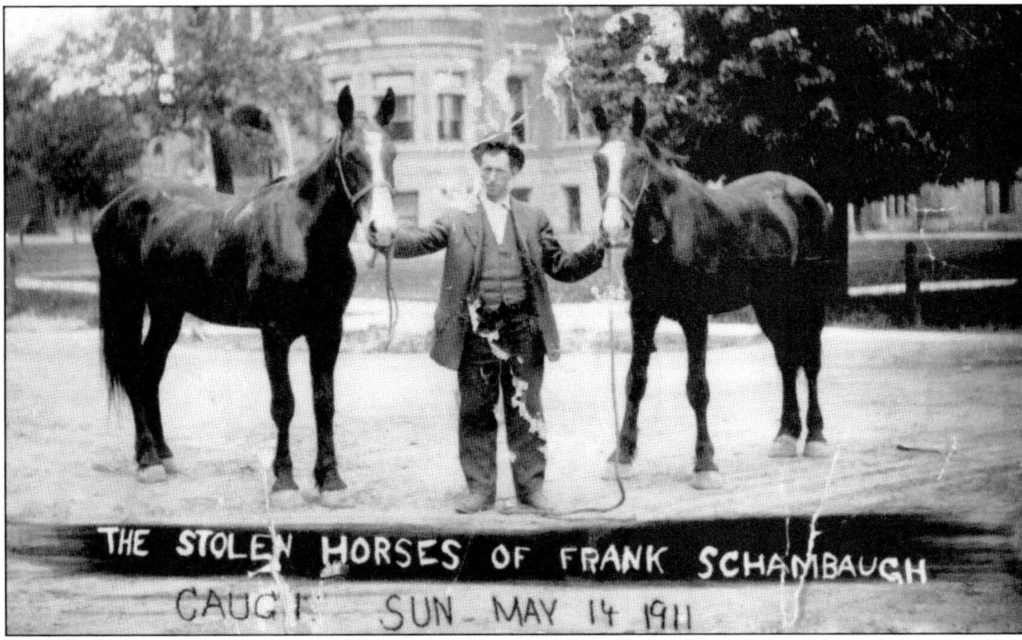

Horse thieves remained a problem well into the 20th century, as in this case from May 14, 1911. The animals were soon back in the possession of their owner, Frank Schambaugh, who showed them off in front of the Noble County Courthouse. The blacklegs were known for stealing horses years before, but that gang was broken up in 1858 by vigilantes known as the Committee of Noble County Invincibles. (NCHS.)

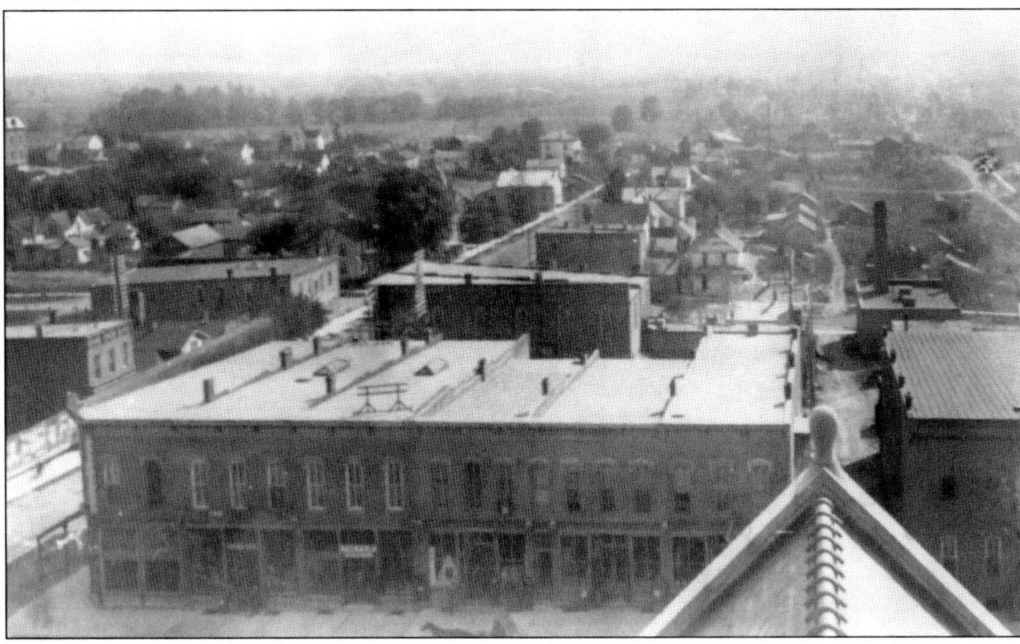

Albion's first hospital is visible near the center of this photograph, behind the south side courthouse square businesses. Dr. John W. Morr established the New Hope Hospital in the building, which at other times contained a hotel, the dentist office of Dr. John P. Hayes, Lily of the Valley flower shop, and later a photography studio. (NCHS.)

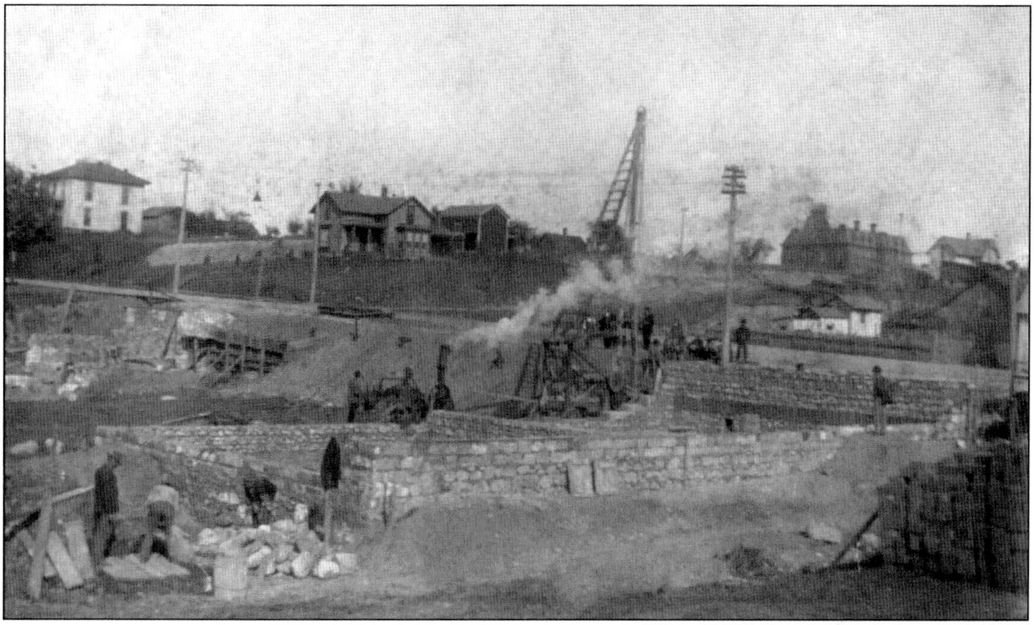

Crews work to construct the Albion Water and Electric works on South Orange Street, near the present site of the water department building, around 1895. The Albion High School is visible at center right. The top of the hill, near the middle of the photograph, would be the eventual site of Albion's first water tower. (Courtesy Noble County historian Sarah Knopp.)

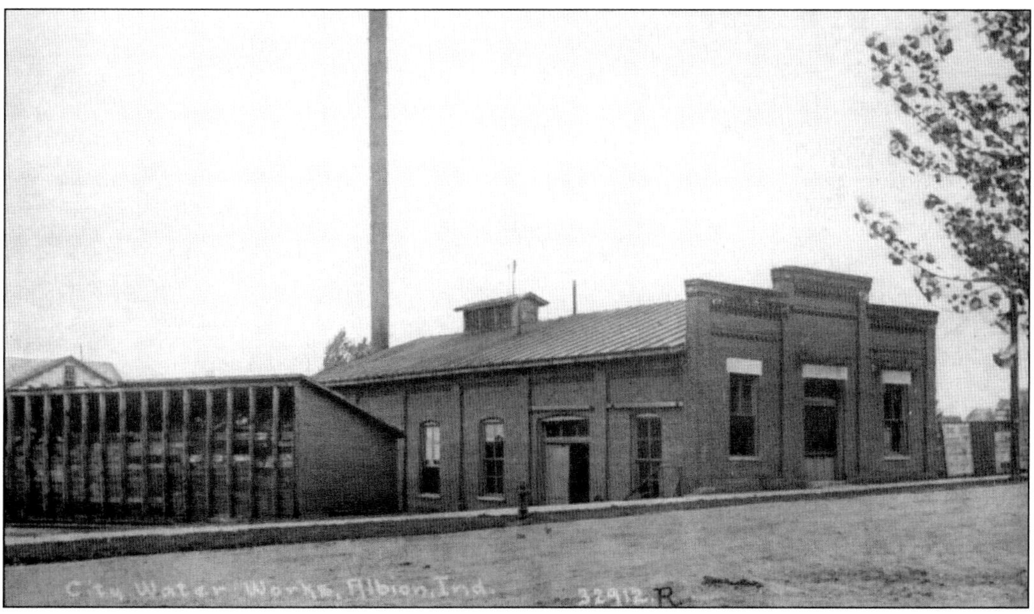

The Albion Water and Electric works were in the same plant for a time, on South Orange Street near the present site of the water department building. Water mains were first installed in 1895. By the turn of the 20th century, two dozen hydrants (like the one in front of this building) protected the town. (NCHS.)

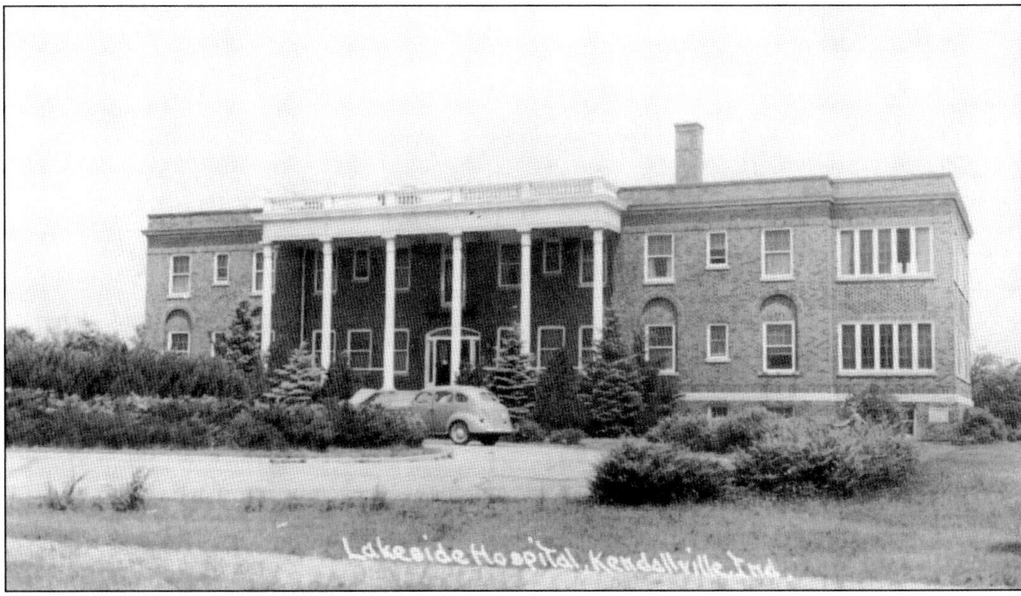

The above photograph of Lakeside Hospital in Kendallville was mailed in 1943, in the midst of World War II. The cancellation stamp urges the buying of war bonds. Half the money for the 1912 construction of a hospital was donated by Elmer E. McCray, who organized the McCray Refrigerator Company in the city in 1890. At one time, a third of Kendallville's population reportedly worked for the company in one way or another. The hospital was named after him in 1952, as seen in the newer photograph below. It became Parkview Noble Hospital and was moved just west of Kendallville in 2004; the old hospital was demolished to make room for the new main branch of the Kendallville Public Library. (Both, courtesy Mike Mapes.)

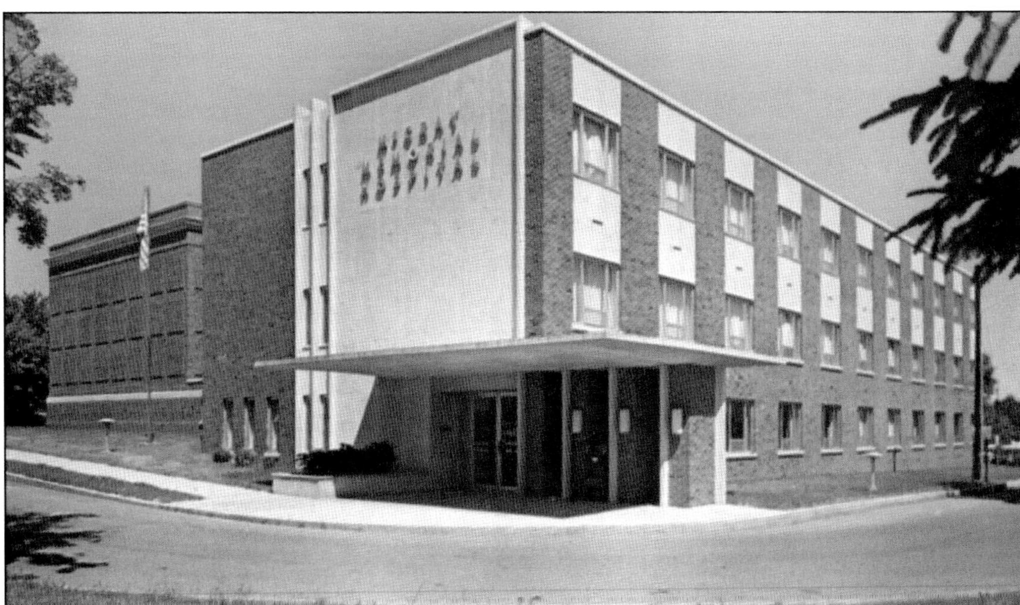

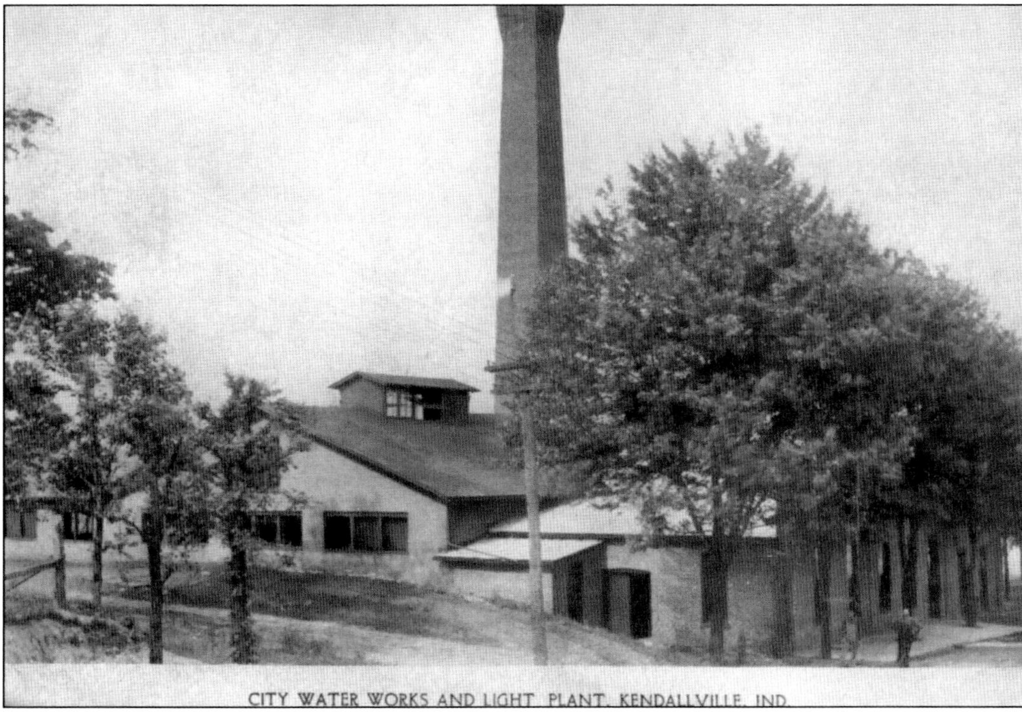

In the early 1900s, Kendallville got its water and power from a facility along the west side of Bixler Lake. To this day, that remains the location of the city's water department. (Courtesy Mike Mapes.)

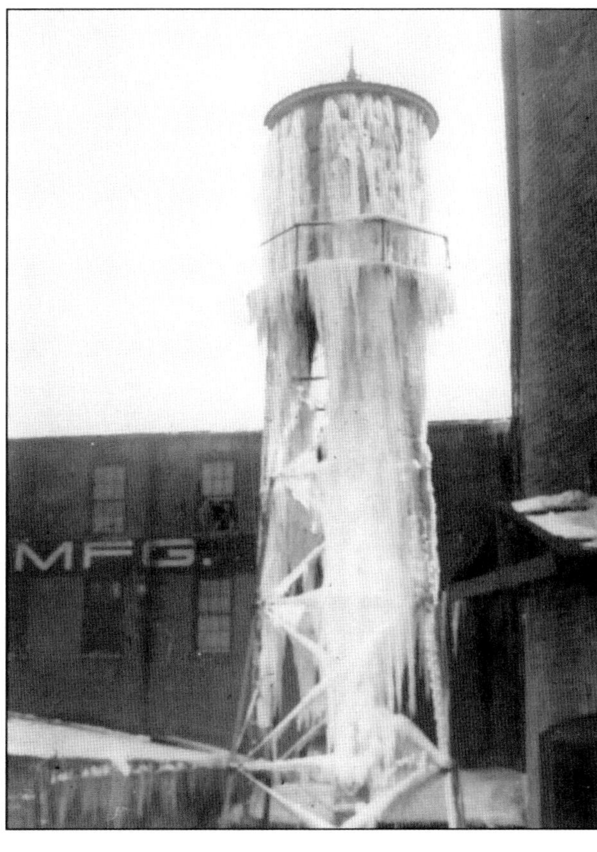

When it overflowed in the early 1900s, the Flint and Walling water tower in Kendallville demonstrated just how cold Indiana winters can get. (Courtesy Mike Mapes.)

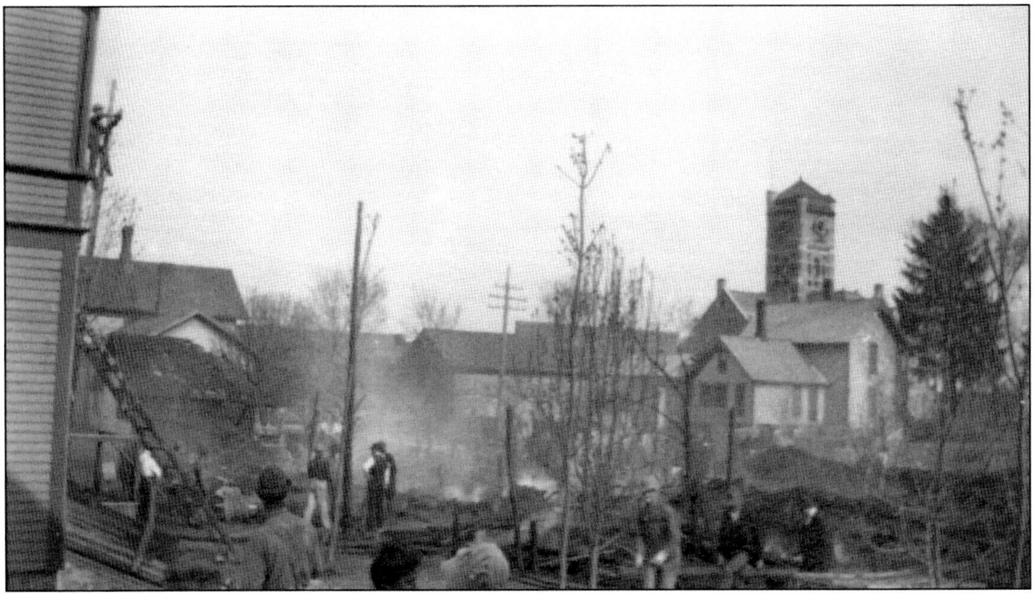

Volunteer firefighters finish extinguishing a blaze that leveled part of a block northwest of the courthouse square in May 1901. High winds fanned the flames, which started in the barn of drayman B.F. Easly and spread to two other barns and a cooper shop, before heavily damaging the United Presbyterian Church nearby. Easly suffered burns while trying to rescue horses from his building. (Courtesy Linda Shultz.)

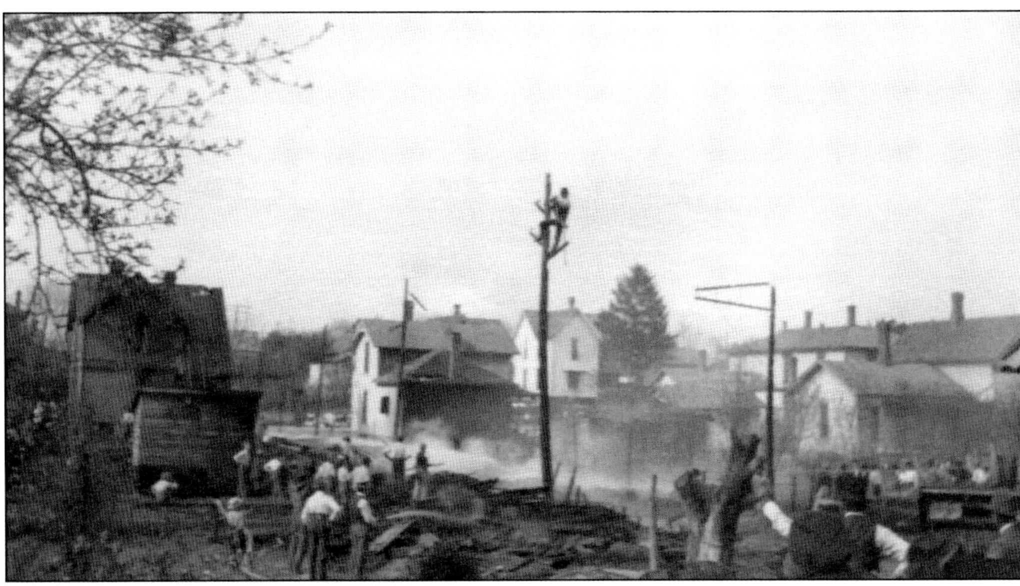

Albion volunteers overhaul at a fire that destroyed three barns, a cooper shop, and the United Presbyterian Church on the northwest side of Albion on May 2, 1901. Damaged homes and buildings, saved by the hard work of the firefighters, can be seen nearby. (Courtesy Linda Shultz.)

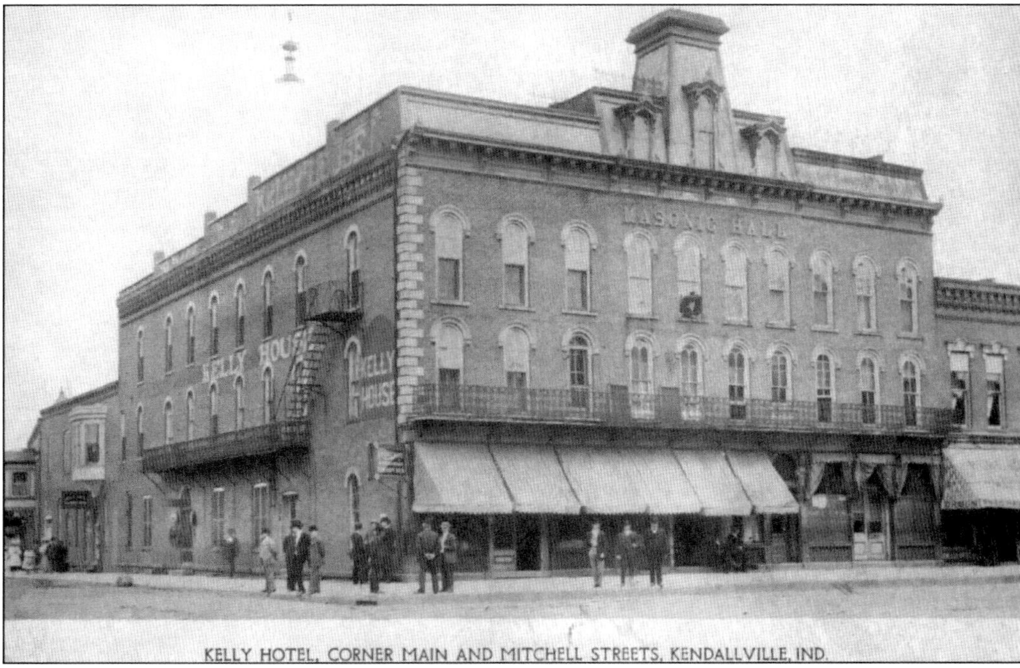

The Masonic lodge used the upper rooms of the Kelly House Hotel, at Main and Mitchell Streets in Kendallville. It was not unusual for lodges to build large buildings, then rent storefronts and lower floors for other purposes. This photograph was taken around 1908. (Courtesy Mike Mapes.)

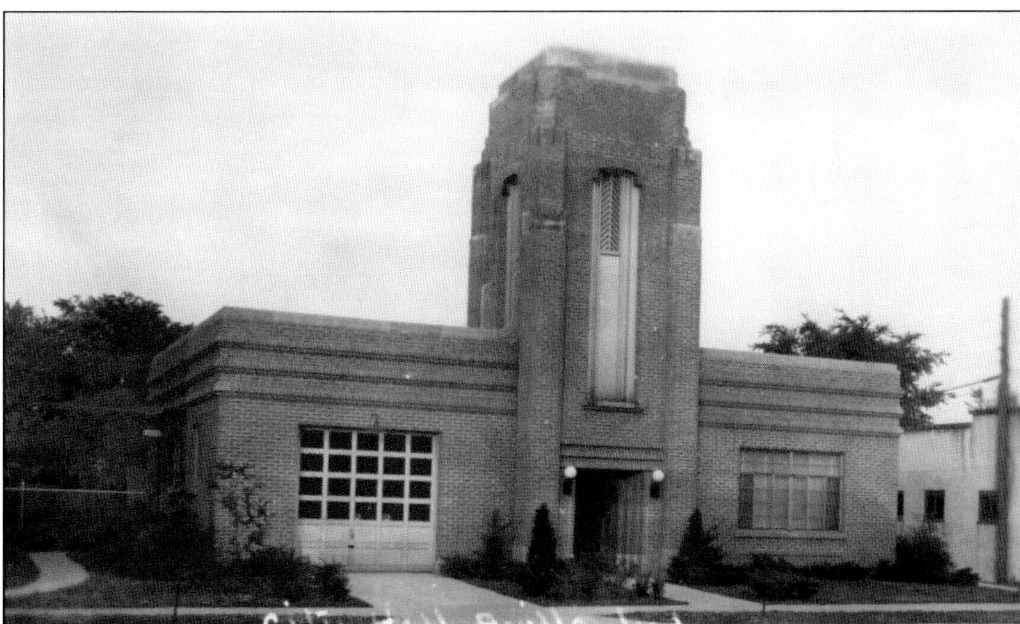

Avilla's town hall still exists but is much changed. Over the years, the tower was removed and the garage door walled in to provide more office space. (Courtesy Mike Mapes.)

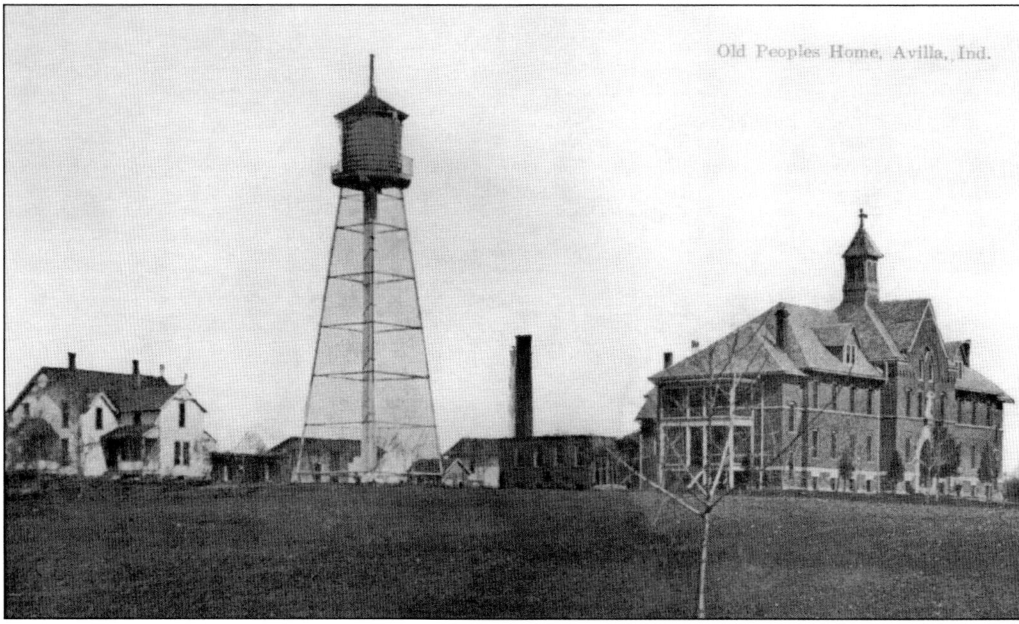

Sacred Heart Home in Avilla, seen here around 1915, was designed by Wing and Mahurin, a Fort Wayne architectural firm, and built in 1896. These buildings were later razed and replaced with a newer facility. (Courtesy Mike Mapes.)

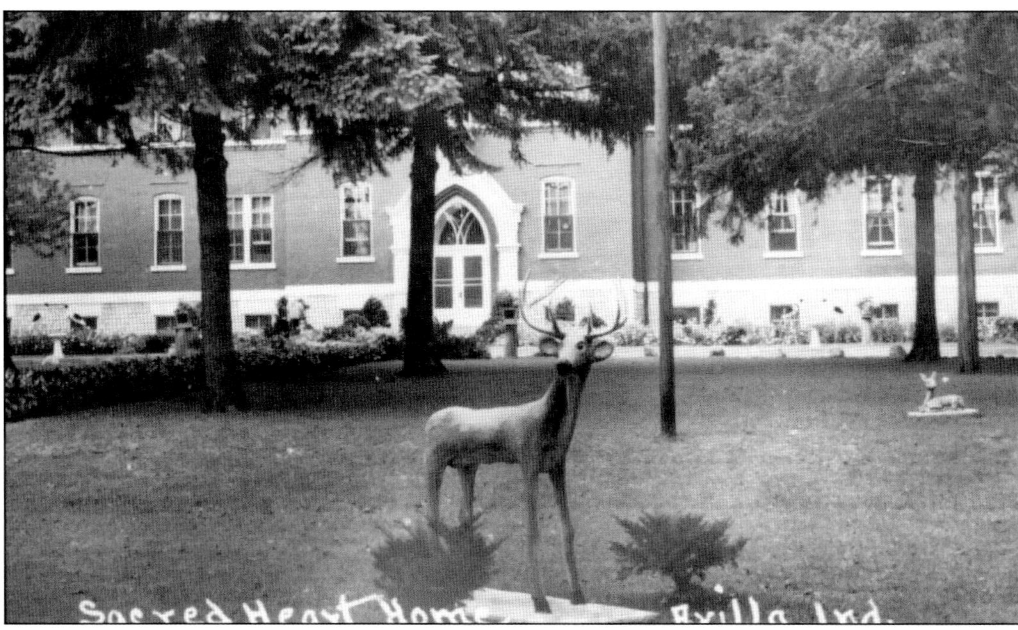

Deer statues adorn the Sacred Heart Home lawn in the mid-1940s. In 1976, the retirement home was moved to a new location just north of Avilla. (Courtesy Mike Mapes.)

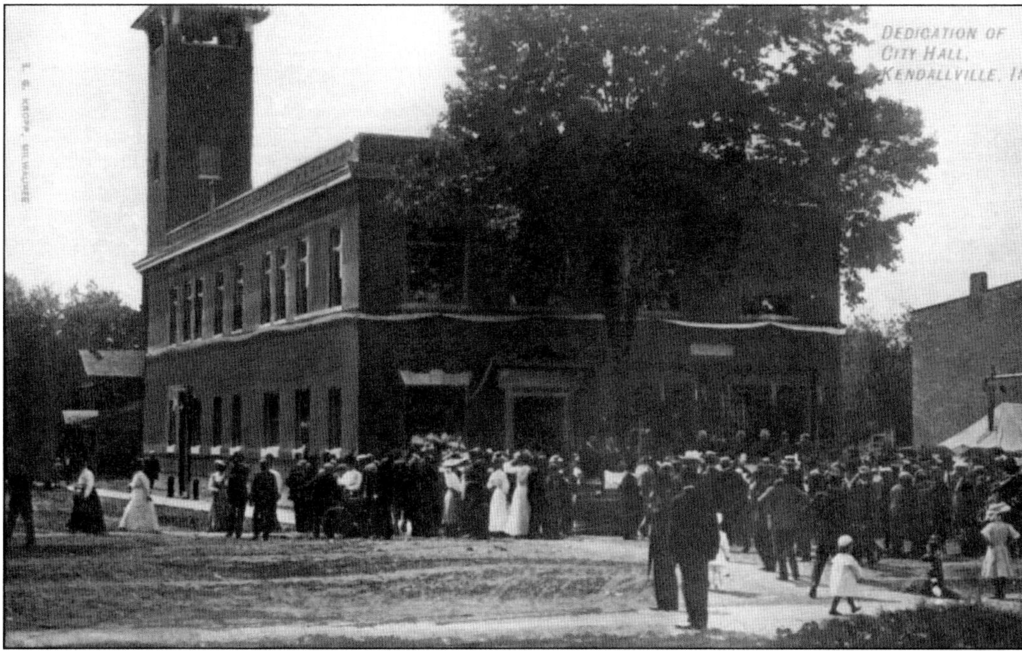

A crowd gathers for the dedication of Kendallville City Hall in 1907. The police and fire departments also occupied the building at Main and Rush Streets until 1913, when fire gutted the structure. (Courtesy Mike Mapes.)

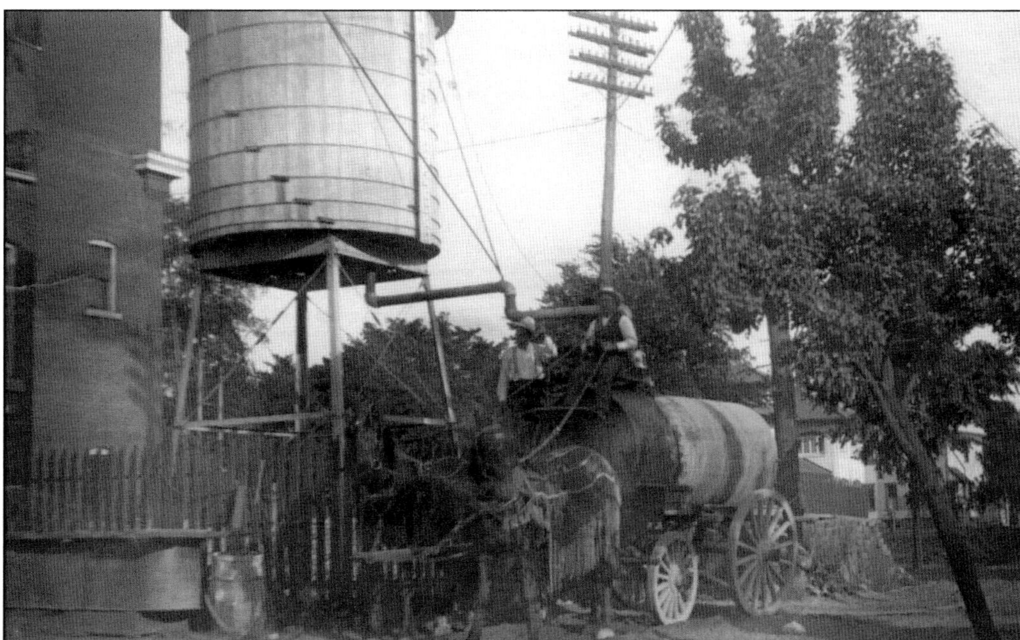

Water wagons, like this one being refilled in Kendallville, were used to dampen the community's dirt streets and keep the dust down. (Courtesy Mike Mapes.)

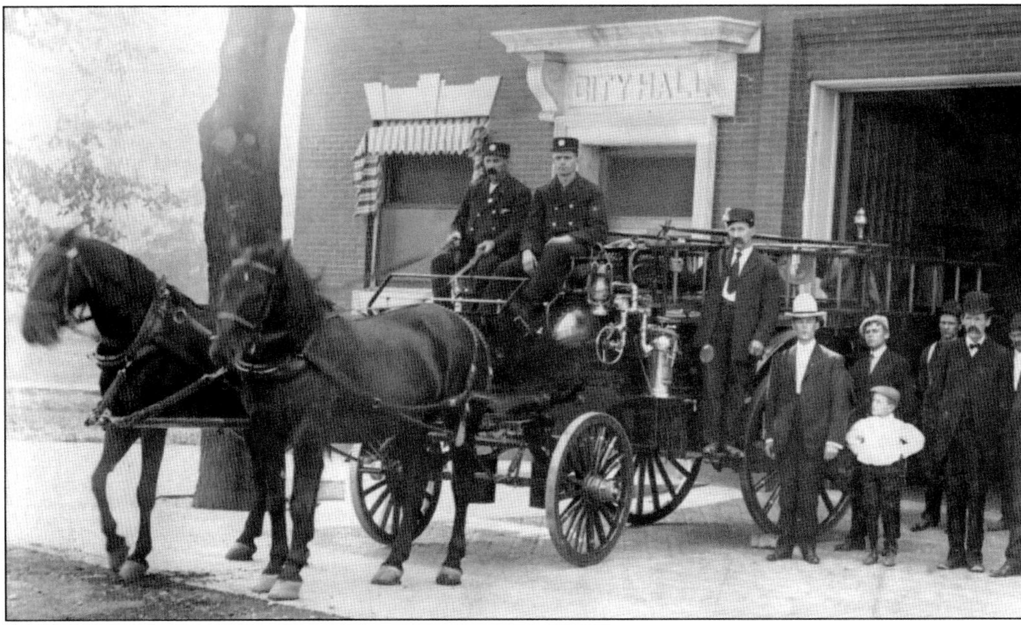

Kendallville firefighters pose with their horse-drawn apparatus around 1910. At the time, Kendallville's fire department consisted of a two-wheeled, hand-drawn hose cart and the combination hose, chemical, and ladder wagon. Chemicals in the wagon's tank could be mixed to provide pressure for fighting small fires. The KFD was made up of two full-timers, 17 volunteer firefighters, and two horses. (Courtesy Mike Mapes.)

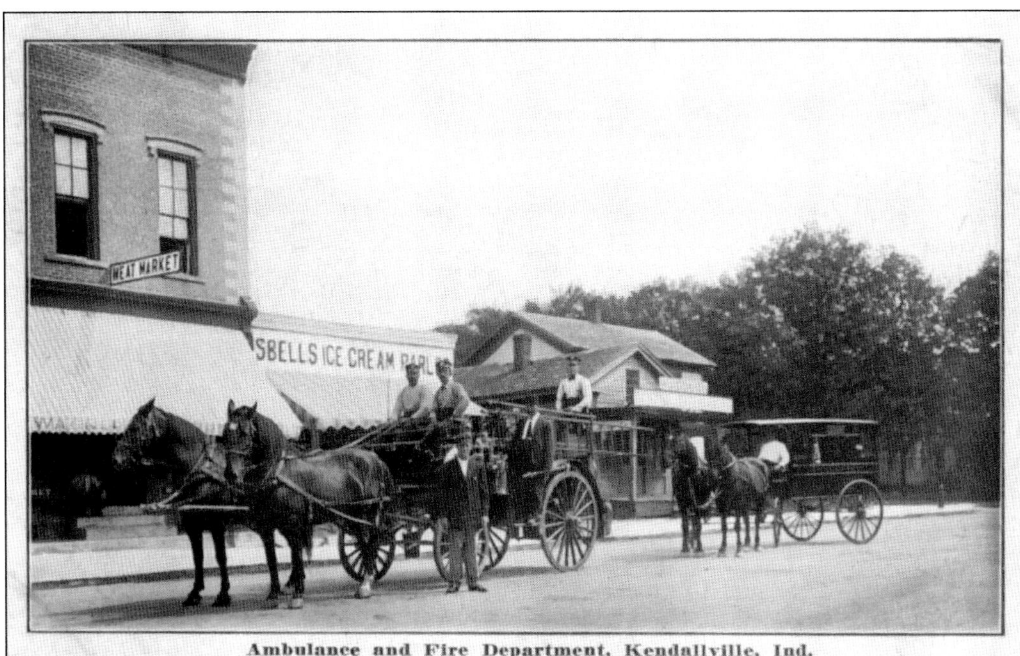

By 1915, Kendallville's services included an ambulance, seen here behind the horse-drawn fire wagon. Through much of the first half of the 20th century, funeral homes provided ambulance service in many communities. (Courtesy Mike Mapes.)

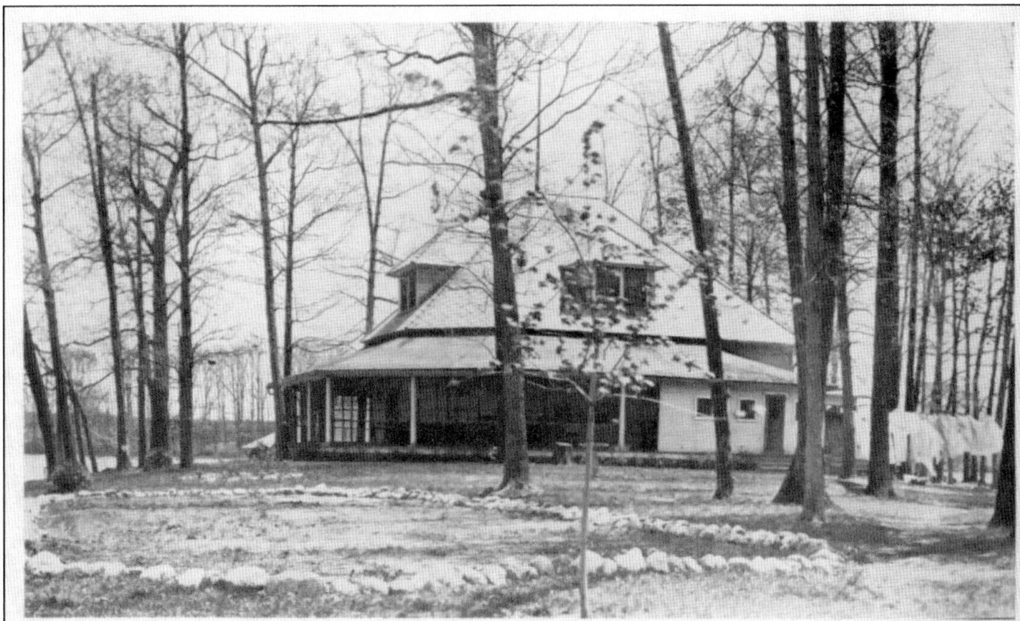

THE ANTLER'S CLUB, KENDALLVILLE, IND. C-654

The Benevolent and Protective Order of Elks, known generally as the Elks Lodge, ran the Antler's Club, northwest of Kendallville. The Elks were established as a private New York club around 1867, called the "Jolly Corks." They were mostly concerned with avoiding the New York excise tax. But the members decided they wanted to be more helpful to the community, and they went on to become one of the leading fraternal orders in the United States. Today, the Kendallville Elks Country Club has a nine-hole golf course that started in 1910 and a ballroom that hosts events, as well as weekly dinners. The 1940s photograph below shows the Elks Temple in Kendallville. (Both, courtesy Mike Mapes.)

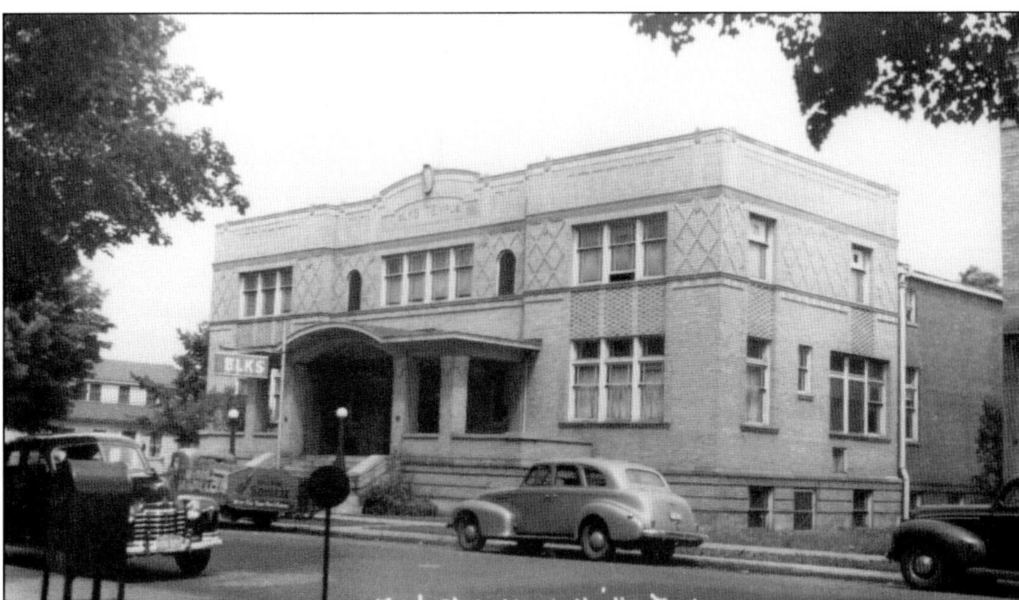

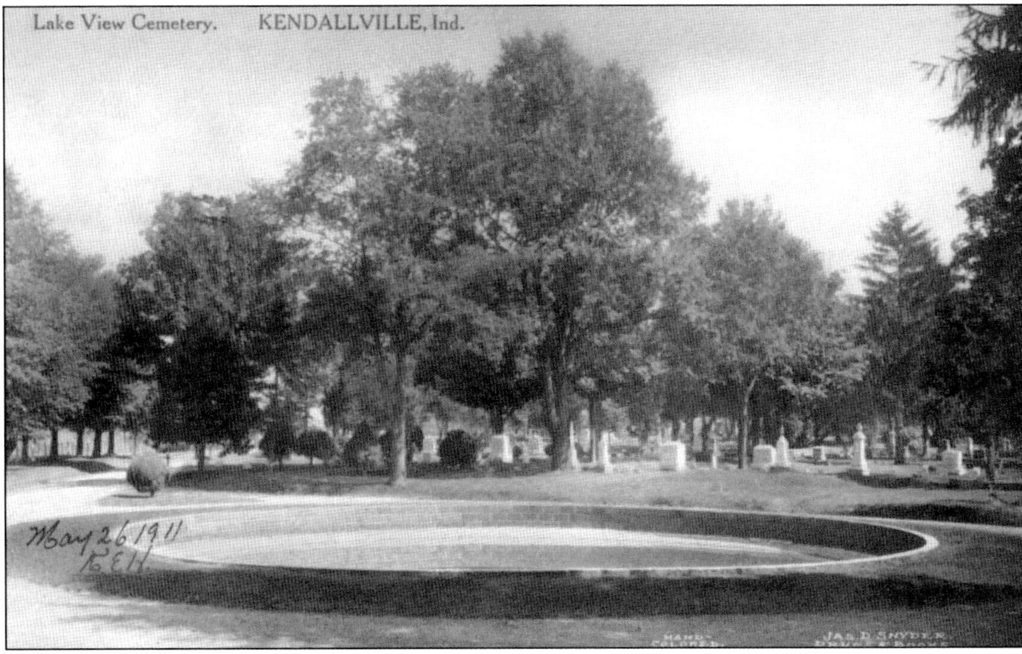

Established in 1867, Lake View Cemetery is one of the larger cemeteries in Noble County. The area rests on either side of Riley Road, just north of Kendallville. (Courtesy Mike Mapes.)

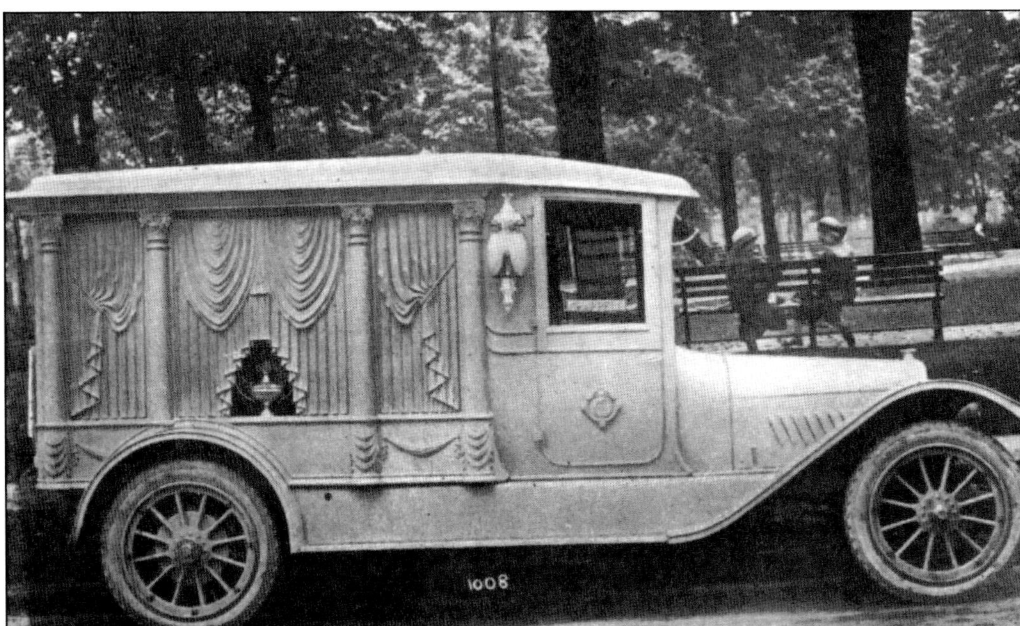

J.M. and F.M. Chappells' hearse was a bit more decorative than modern counterparts. The vehicle was also used as a private ambulance in Kendallville, where the Chappell Funeral Home operated. J.M. was president of the Indiana Funeral Directors Association in 1920. (Courtesy Mike Mapes.)

Eight

Recreation and Celebration

Early Hoosiers worked hard; when they had time for recreation, they made the most of it. With no television or radio to keep people home, whenever they gathered it tended to be a community-wide affair.

Festivals were a favorite, especially after the long hours of planting and harvesting seasons. Albion had a street fair every year, now named after the nearby Chain O' Lakes State Park. Wolf Lake's Onion Days seems oddly named, but the town was famous across the country for the amount and quality of onions grown around the community. Similarly, Ligonier had a strawberry festival, renamed after Noble County became one of the top marshmallow producers in the country.

Festivals continue to be popular today, with gatherings such as the Stone's Trace celebration near Ligonier, Chautauqua Days in Rome City, Avilla Days, Cromwell Days, and Kendallville's Apple Festival, which has become hugely popular.

But in the early days an entire town would turn out for just about anything—parades, weddings, graduations, or anything else of note. Touring plays came to opera houses, and the opera houses themselves hosted a variety of activities. Albion's opera house on the courthouse square was the setting for, among other things, roller-skating, bowling, theater, political rallies, school graduations, and even basketball games.

Outdoor activities were popular and remain so, not only at Chain O' Lakes State Park but at many of Noble County's 117 lakes. Sylvan Lake near Rome City is the largest, but fishing, hunting, boating, and swimming are within reach of just about everyone. Two branches of the Elkhart River also meander through the county. Nature areas now attract tourists to the type of swamps and wilderness that were once a hindrance to early settlers.

Small towns were not without modern entertainment, however. Movie theaters sprang up here and there, with Albion having two over the years.

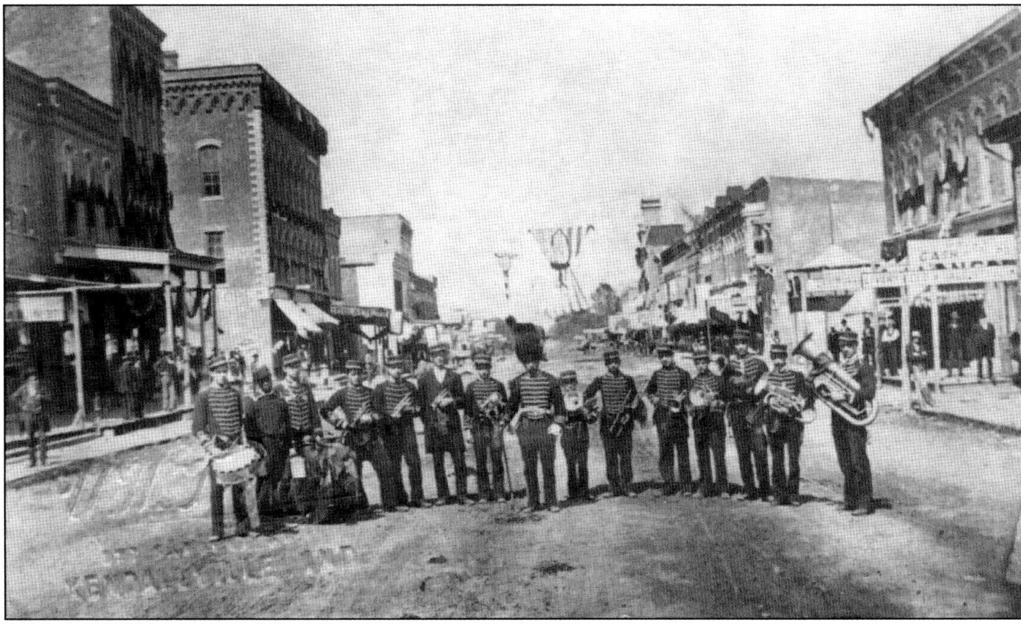

The Kendallville Juvenile Band entertains downtown Kendallville visitors in 1881. John L. Gallup was listed as the group's drum major, while Milo Calkins was the leader. (Courtesy Mike Mapes.)

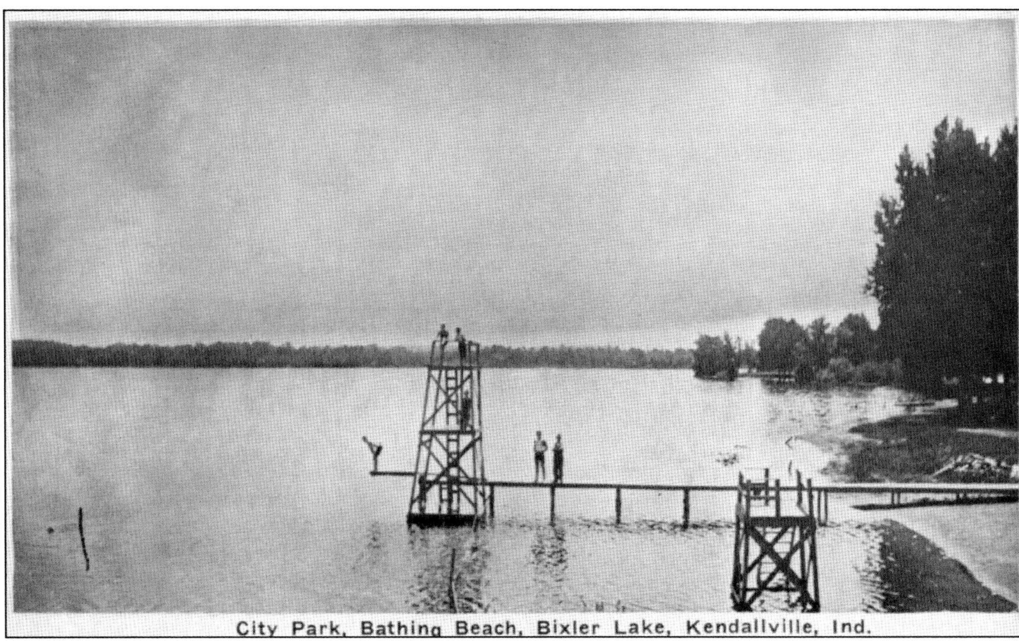

Kids cool off at the Bixler Lake beach, on the east edge of Kendallville, in 1924. The diving board was later replaced by a floating platform, and later the platform itself was taken down. The beach is still a popular summer location, within walking distance for most city residents. (Courtesy Mike Mapes.)

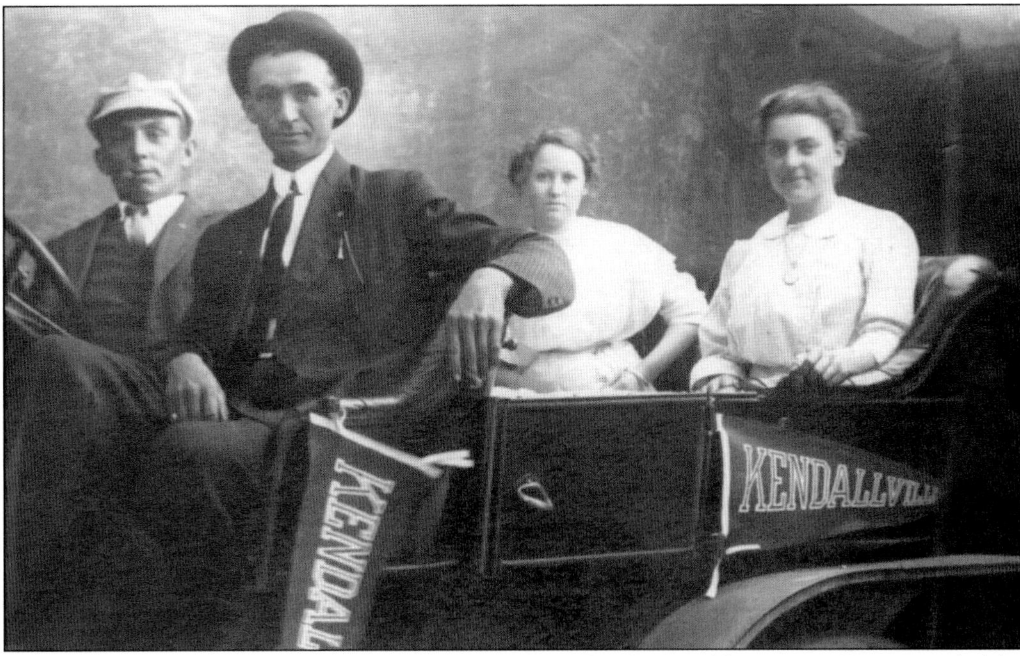

Fairgoers pose for a photograph in the early 1900s. The first Noble County Fairs were held at the Bassett farm northwest of Albion, but in 1882 a fairgrounds was built in Kendallville. After being moved several times, the Noble County Fair eventually settled there. The fair celebrated its 119th anniversary in 2015. Pictured, from left to right, are Sherm Keister, Virgil Spann, Lucy Winebrenner, and Eve (Winebrenner) Egolf. (Courtesy Joy LeCount.)

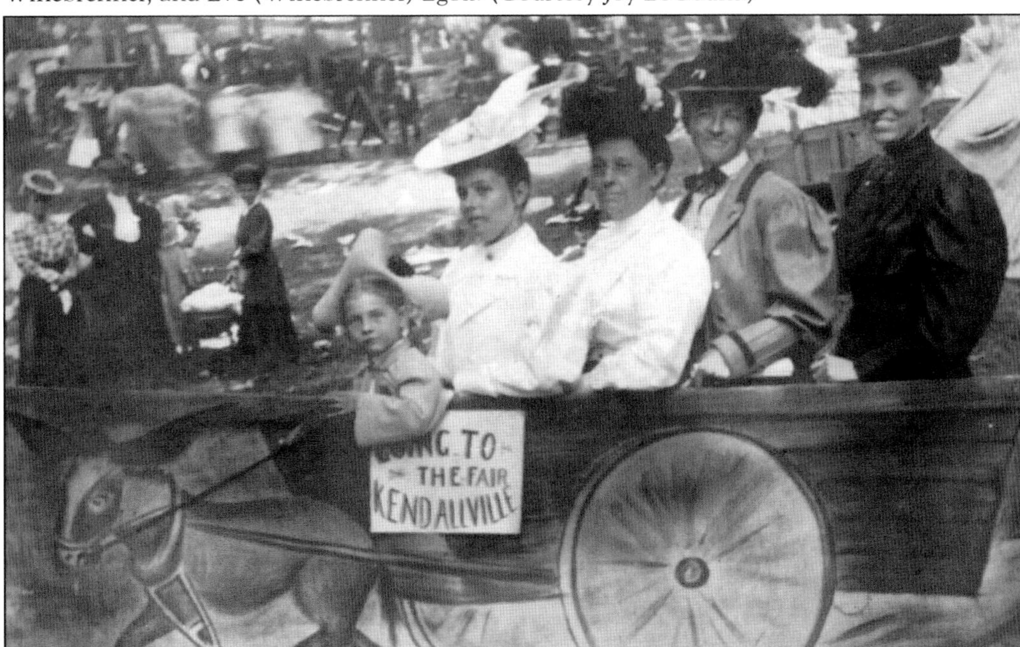

Unidentified Kendallville fairgoers received this novelty photograph as a remembrance of their trip in the early 1900s. The fair was a huge event at the time, drawing people from all across the area. (Courtesy Mike Mapes.)

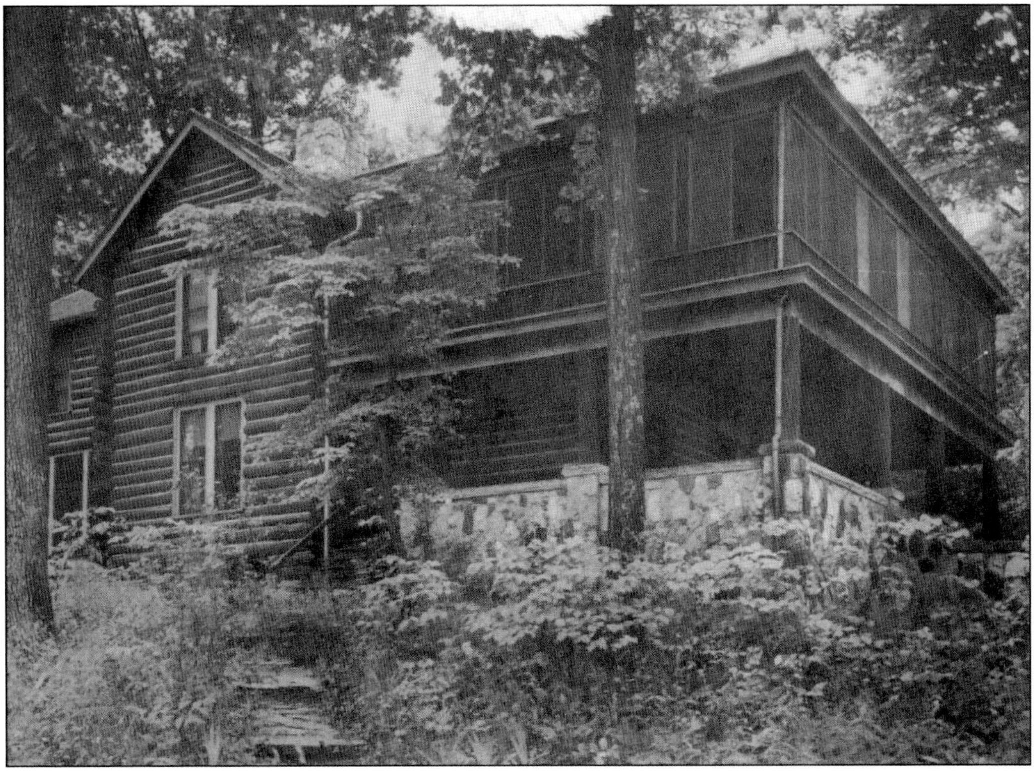

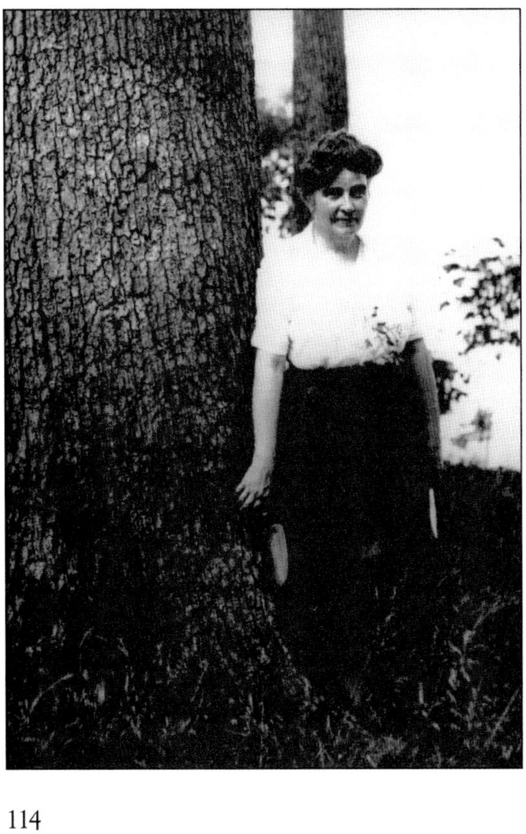

Gene Stratton-Porter's Sylvan Lake Cabin at Wildflower Woods highlights a state historic site on the banks of Sylvan Lake. Stratton-Porter, Indiana's most widely read female author, finished the cabin in 1914 and lived there for several years. She later moved to California, where she died in 1924. The cabin is now the centerpiece of a 150-acre area of shoreline, woods, and formal gardens. (NCHS.)

Gene Stratton-Porter's first book written at her cabin overlooking Sylvan Lake was *Michael O'Halloran* in 1915. She wrote 12 novels, three poetry books, children's books, seven nature studies, and numerous magazine articles. She was the first woman to form a movie studio and production company. Eight of her novels were turned into movies; one, *A Girl of the Limberlost*, was filmed four times. (Courtesy Joy LeCount.)

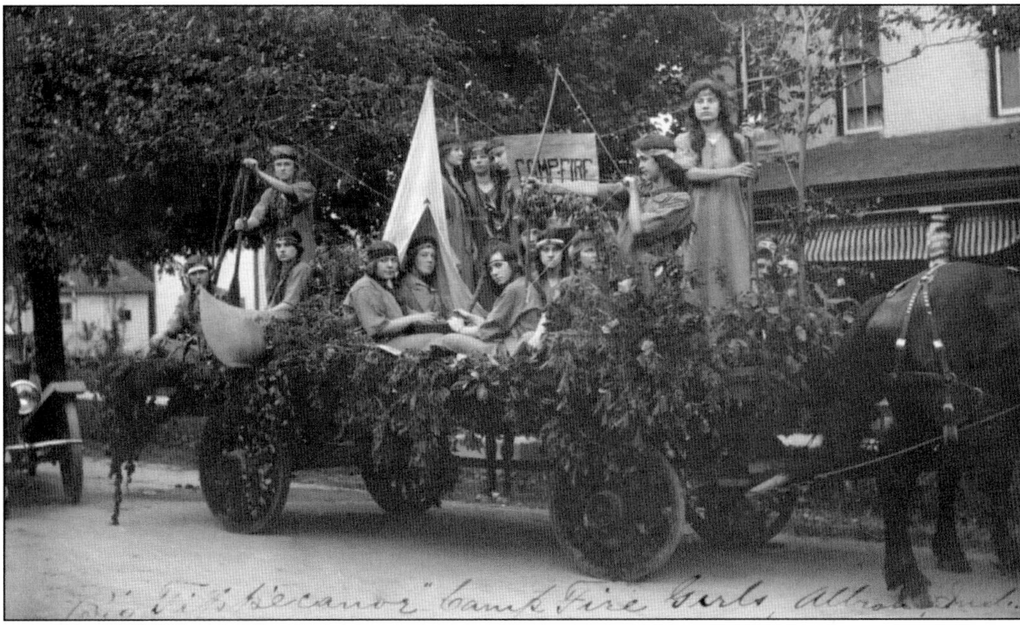

The "Big Tippecanoe" Camp Fire Girls participate in the Albion street fair parade on September 16, 1915. After a state park was founded nearby, the fair became the Chain O' Lakes Festival, which now takes place during the first full week of June. (NCHS.)

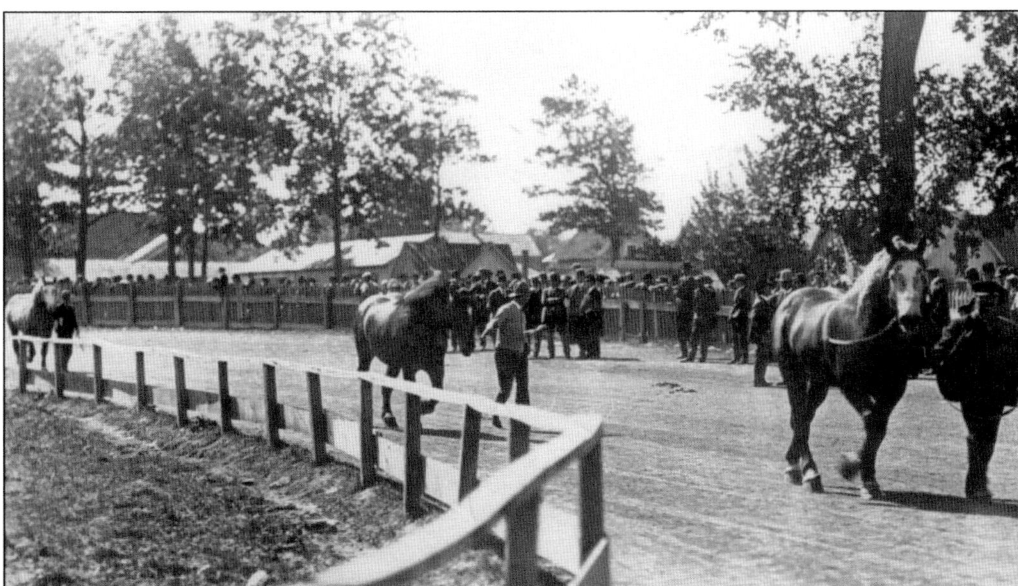

The scene around the track at the Kendallville fairground seems serene. But a week before this 1909 fair, a tragic fire killed a horse and destroyed a horse cart. (Courtesy Mike Mapes.)

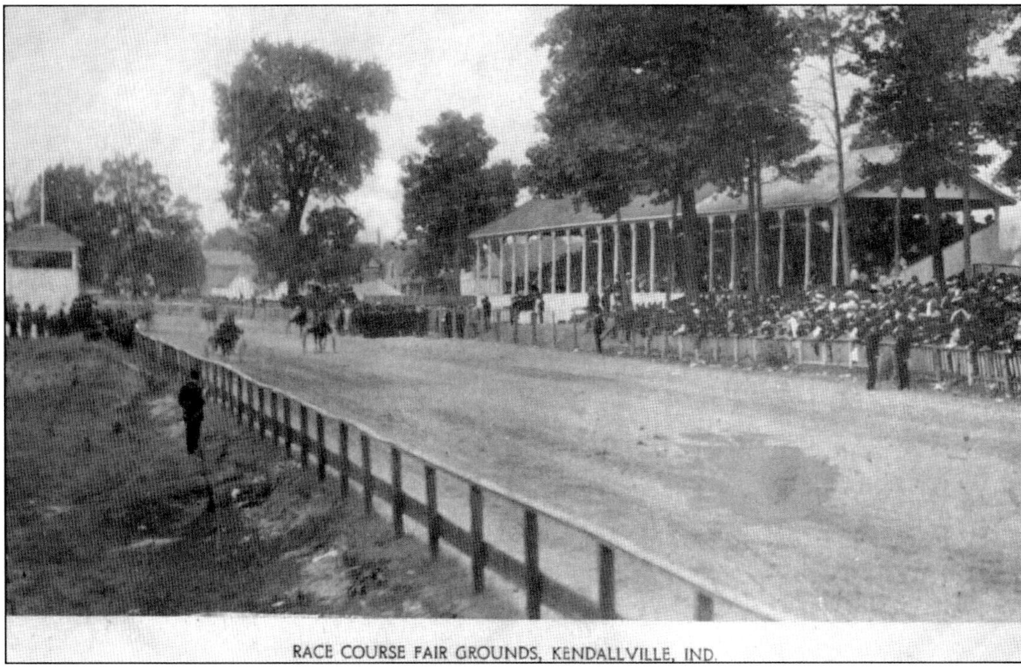

Horses race by the grandstand, built in 1883 at what is now the Noble County Fairgrounds. In 1995, a spectacular fire leveled the wooden grandstand, which originally seated 1,000 but had additions added that brought capacity up to 2,100. After the fire, a fundraising campaign raised $400,000 to replace it with a steel structure. (Courtesy Mike Mapes.)

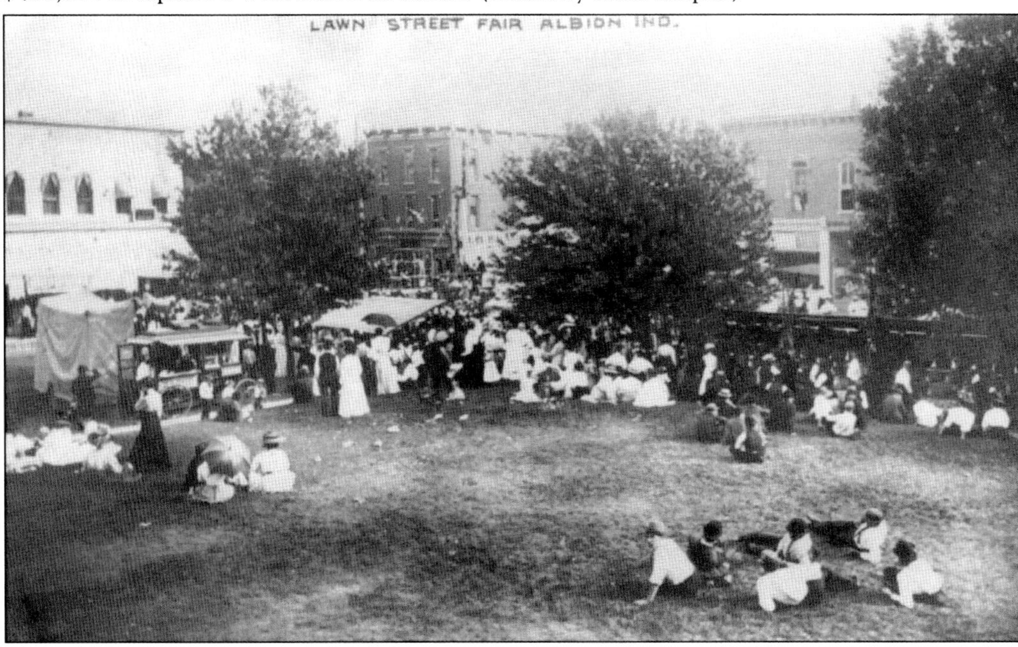

Fairgoers watch the stage or relax on the courthouse lawn during the October 1908 Albion Street Fair. The stage shut off Albion's main intersection at Orange and Main Streets. Almost everyone in town headed for the fair anyway, though, so it did not cause any more traffic problems than already existed. (NCHS.)

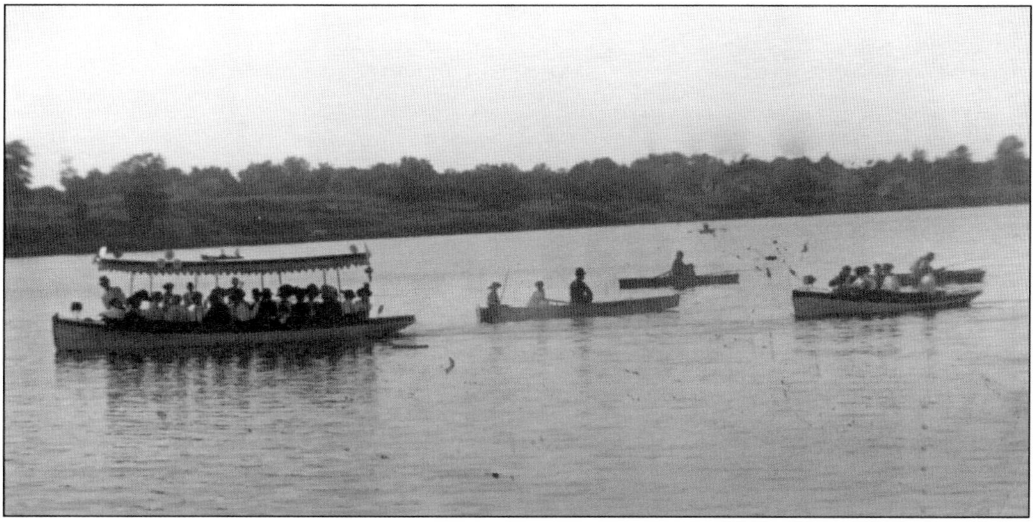

Boaters take an excursion on Bixler Lake, on the east edge of Kendallville. The city purchased 6.4 acres of lakefront property, known as Boy Scout Field, in 1916. It became a popular beach, and over time the Kendallville Park Board opened large park areas all around the lake. Boating, fishing, swimming, camping, hiking, and just about any other type of outdoor activity now take place there. (Courtesy Mike Mapes.)

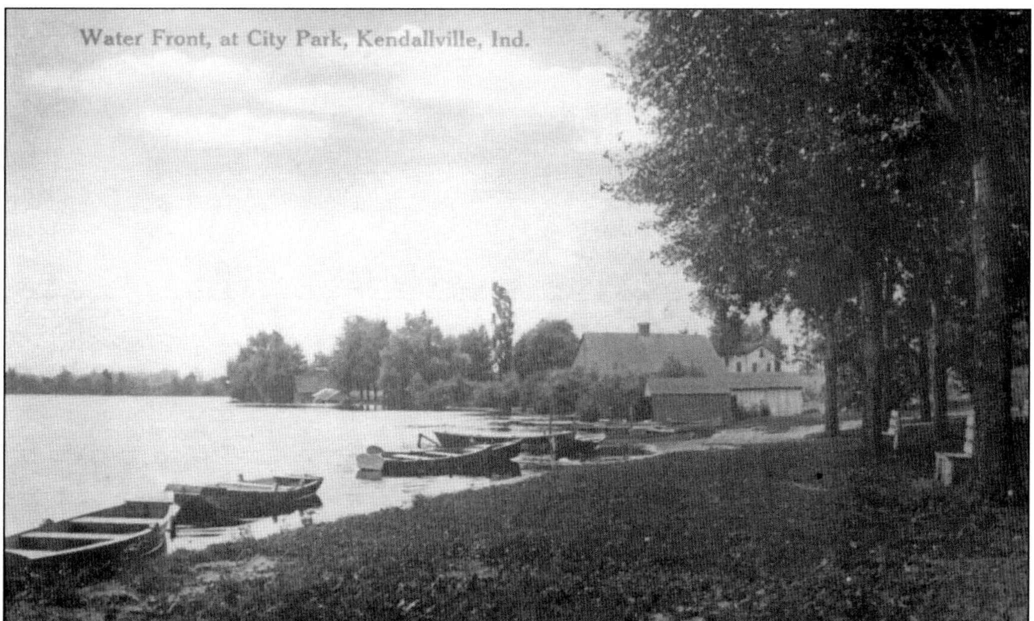

Boats wait along the shoreline of Bixler Lake in 1914. With Kendallville edging right up to the lake, many citizens could walk to the shore for swimming, fishing, or boating. (Courtesy Mike Mapes.)

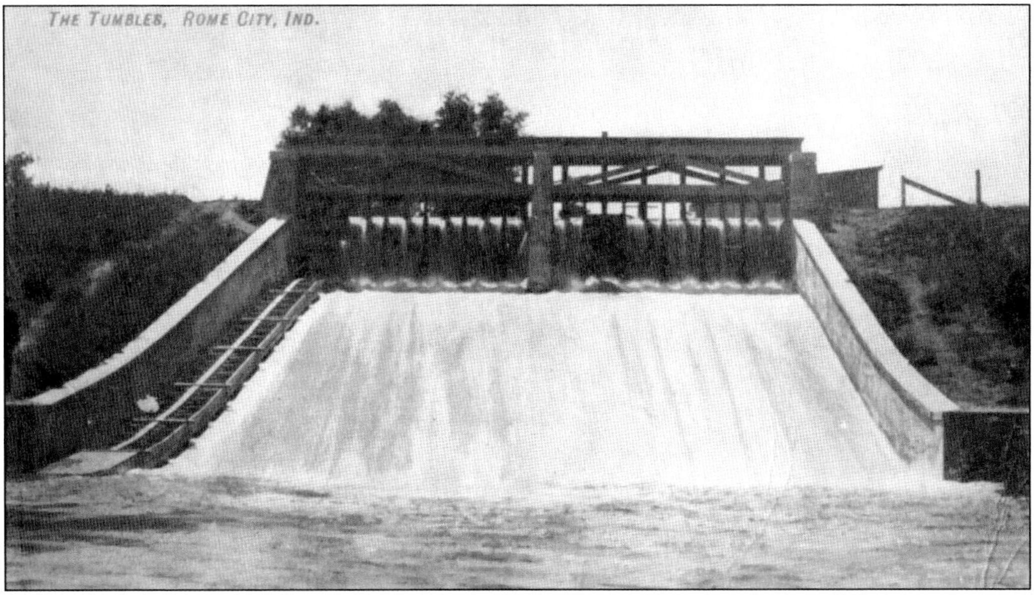

Seen here around 1908, the Sylvan Lake dam had a huge effect on all of Noble County. Work began in 1837 to capture water as a feeder for a canal that was never completed. That led to the establishment of two towns—Northport in 1838 and Rome a little ways south, about six months later. Northport eventually faded away, while Rome City became a tourist attraction. (NCHS.)

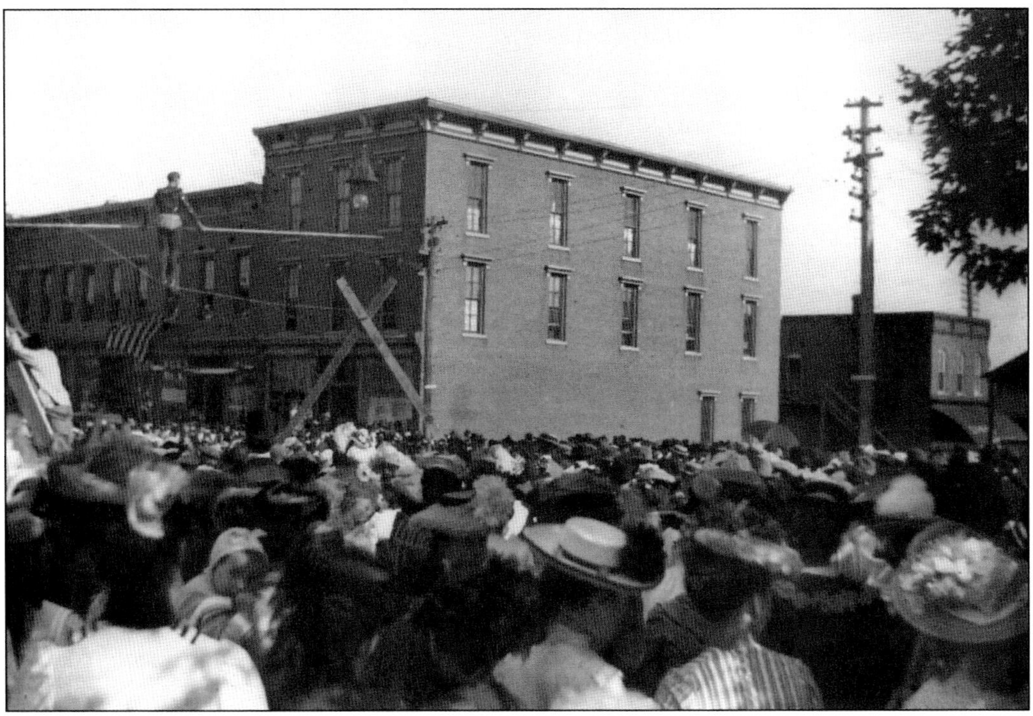

A tightrope walker entertains the crowd during a summer fair in this early 1900s photograph taken from the area of the Courthouse Square. The three-story Black Building, constructed after one of a series of fires that leveled the downtown area's original wooden business blocks, stands in the background. (Courtesy Beth Shellman.)

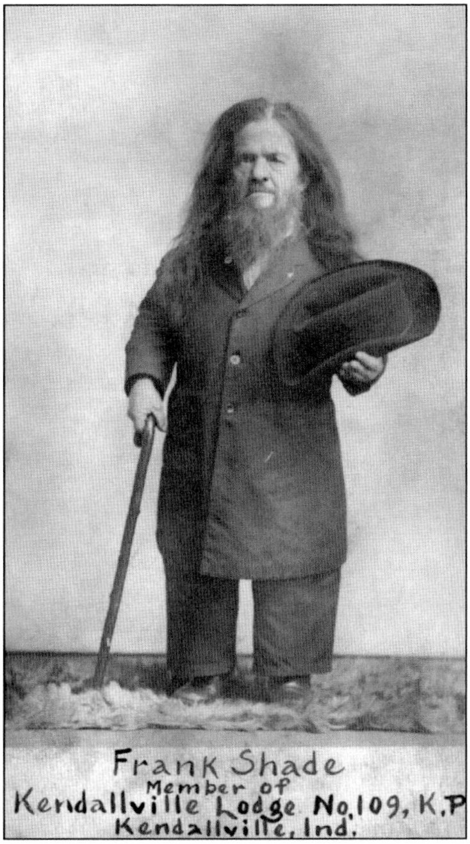

Frank Shade stood a little under three feet tall, as did his wife, but they were big-time local celebrities. Shade was born in 1850 in Indiana but traveled with the Mighty Haag Circus before retiring to Kendallville, where he died in 1924. (Courtesy Mike Mapes.)

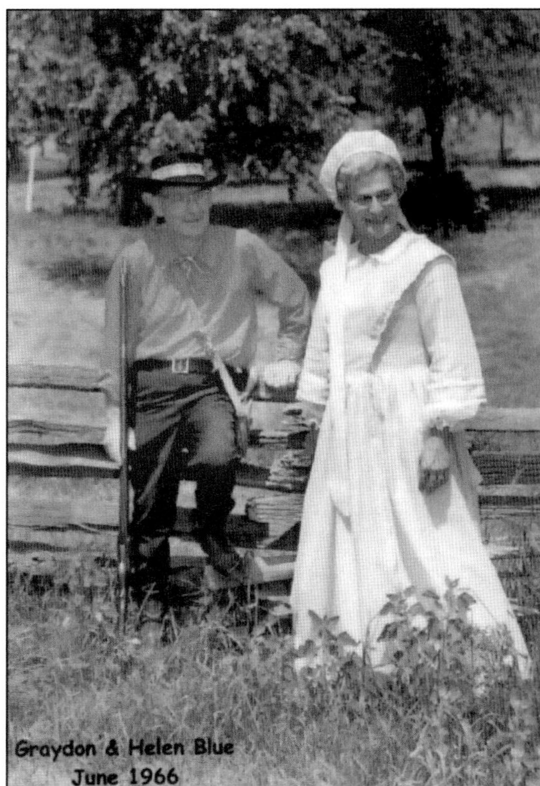

Graydon and Helen Blue dress in period costumes for the dedication of the newly restored Stone's Trace Tavern on June 26, 1966. Graydon Blue, a Ligonier pharmacist, played at the tavern as a boy, when it resembled an old barn. He approached the owner, Mary Slagle, about buying the property, which prompted her to give it to the newly organized Stone's Trace Historical Society. (STHS.)

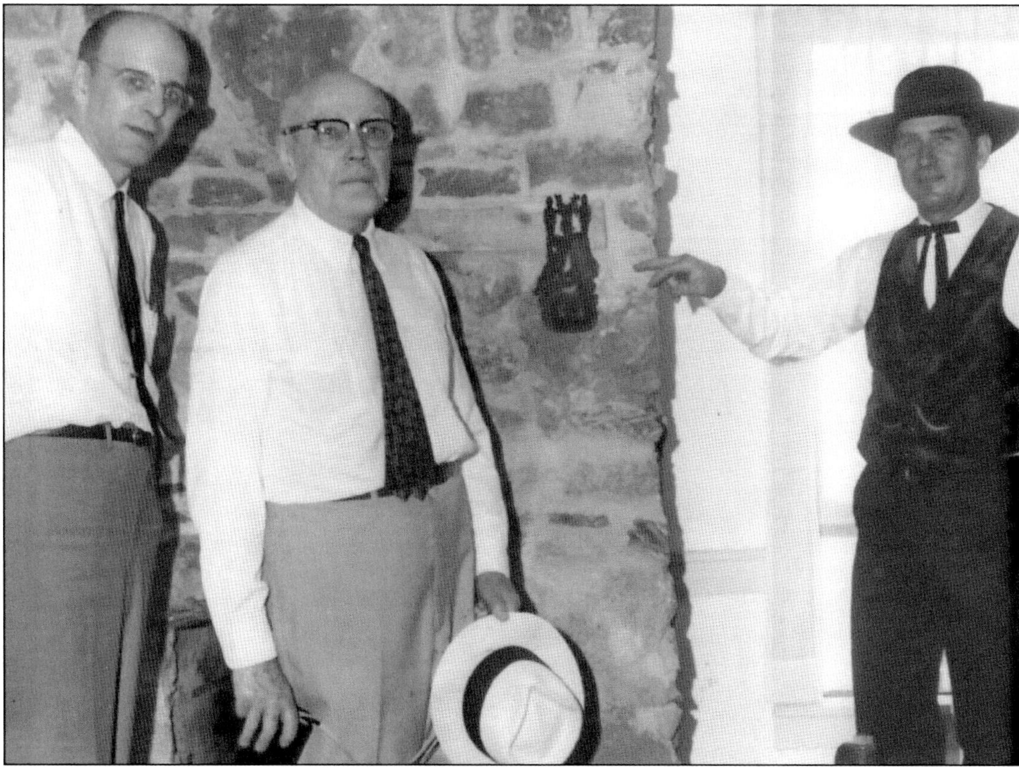

Eli Lilly, third president of the Indianapolis-based Eli Lilly and Company, stands before a fireplace inside the refurbished Stone's Tavern during its 1966 dedication. Like his grandfather, Lilly took an interest in philanthropy and history; he helped pay for the renovation. Pictured, from left to right, are Hubert Hawkins, secretary of the Indiana Historical Society; Lilly; and Dr. Floyd Warren, who helped rebuild the stone fireplace. (STHS.)

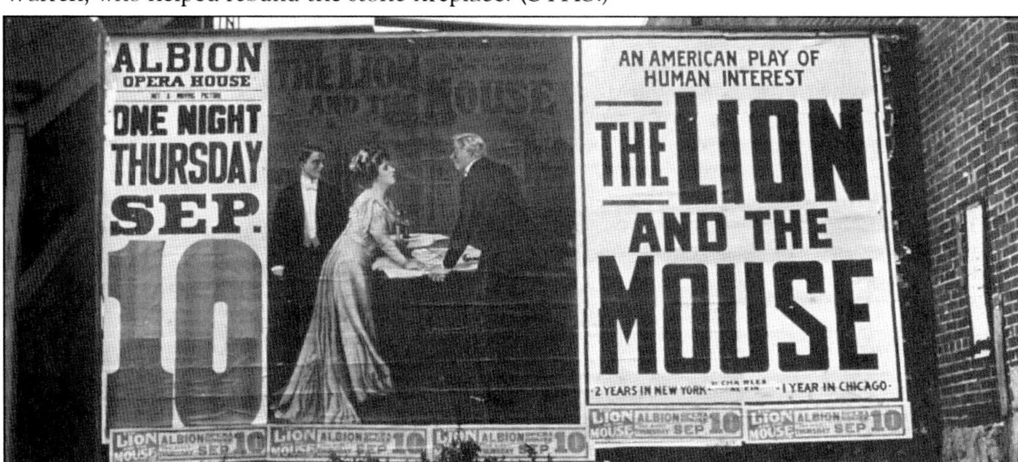

Plays often toured small towns like Albion, where a venue had been built for that purpose. This billboard was placed beside the Albion Opera House in 1907 to advertise a popular play that arrived, one can surmise, on September 10. *The Lion and the Mouse* was made into a movie three times. The last, starring Lionel Barrymore in 1928, was the third "speaking" Warner Bros. feature. (Courtesy Beth Shellman.)

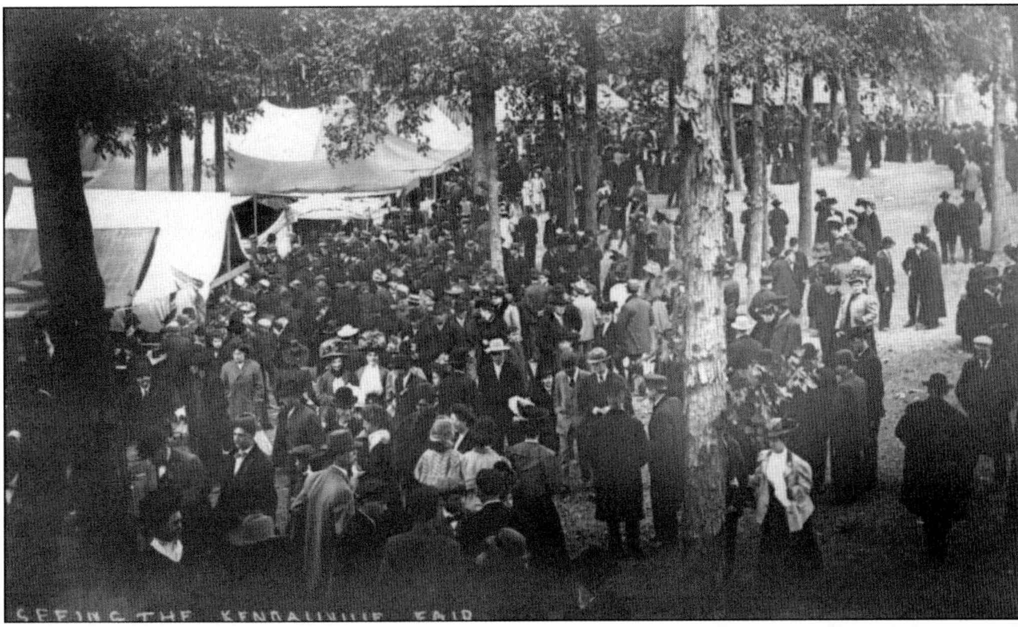

Crowds jam the Kendallville fairgrounds during the 1909 fair. The original 1883 fairgrounds included 100 horse and cattle stalls, sheep and hog buildings, a judges' stand, a floral hall, and a half-mile oval track. The first fair included exhibits of such things as a hinge from Abe Lincoln's cabin, weapons used at the Little Bighorn, and relics from the Great Chicago Fire. (Courtesy Mike Mapes.)

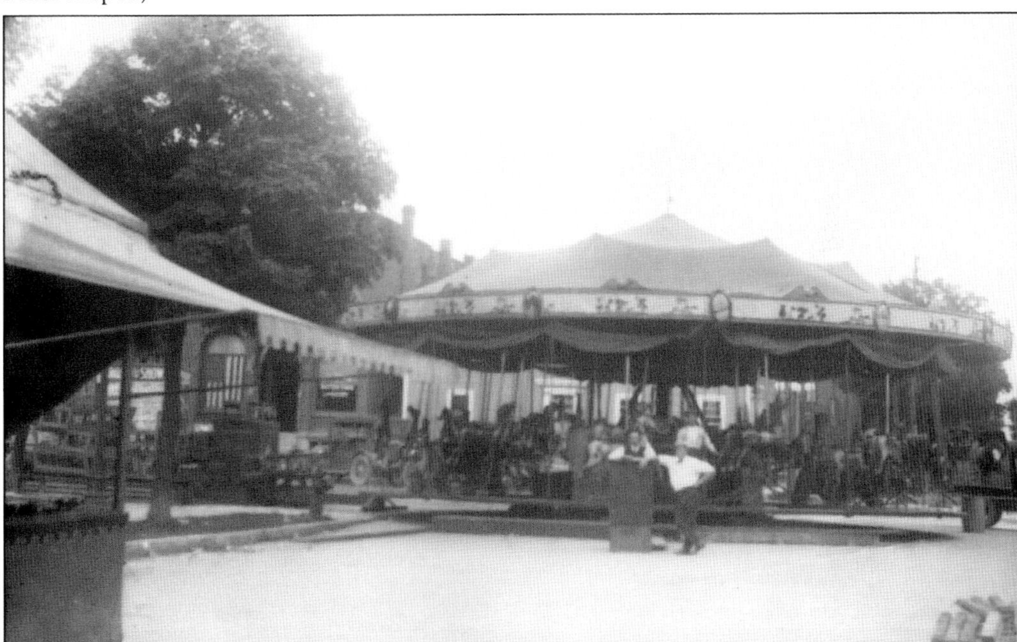

A merry-go-round waits for passengers at the Albion Street Fair. Traveling carnivals that came to small Midwest towns provided similar rides across Noble County for decades. Today, the annual celebration in Albion is called the Chain O' Lakes Festival, in honor of the nearby state park. (NCHS.)

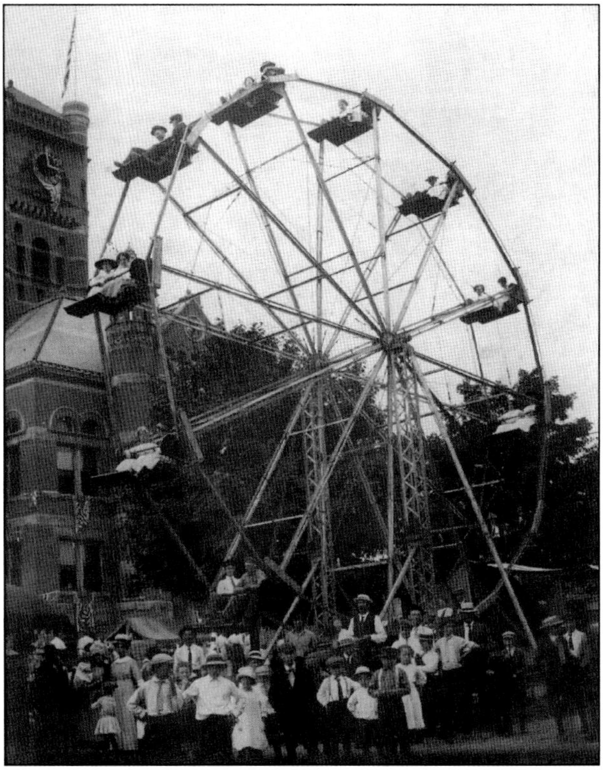

The Ferris wheel was a highlight of any fair, as in these early 1900s photographs on the Noble County Courthouse square in the center of Albion. The square was the common site for many celebrations, including an annual street fair that has come to town almost every summer for over a century. Originally, all four streets around the square would be blocked off, but since State Route 9 began running past the square on Orange Street, only the three town streets are still filled with rides, food stands, games, and other attractions. (Left, courtesy Beth Shellman; below, NCHS.)

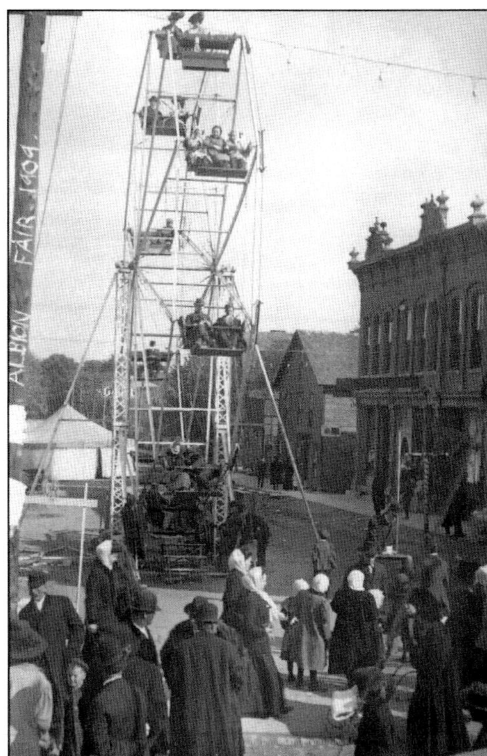

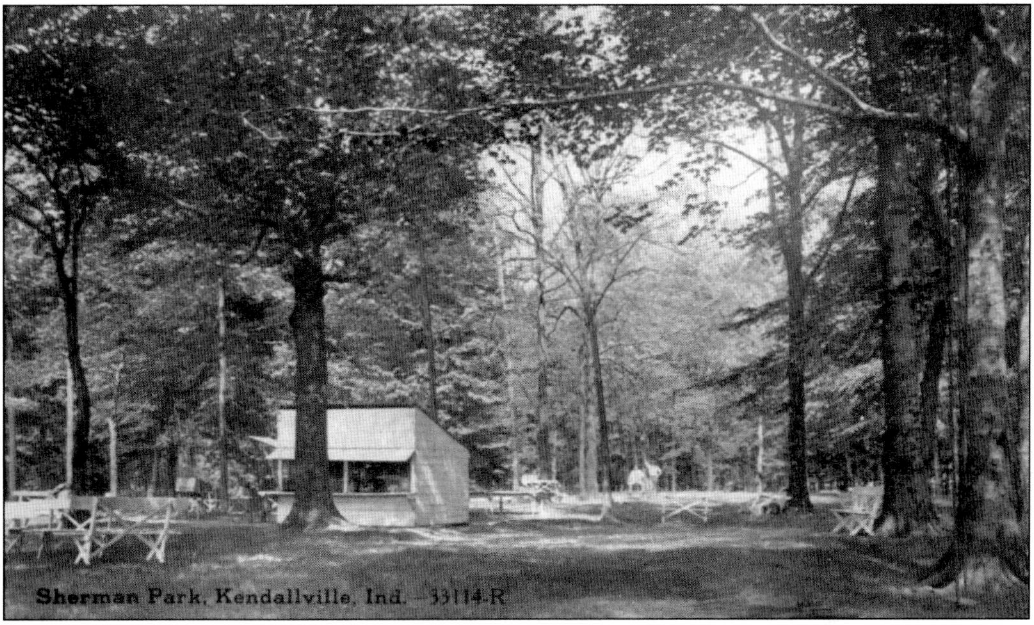

Known as Sherman Park, the east side of Bixler Lake gained popularity when boats began ferrying people across the lake from Kendallville in 1891. The Kendallville Parks Department developed the area, which today includes ball fields, camping, a swimming beach, playground, and hiking trails in a 75-acre wetlands nature area. (Courtesy Mike Mapes.)

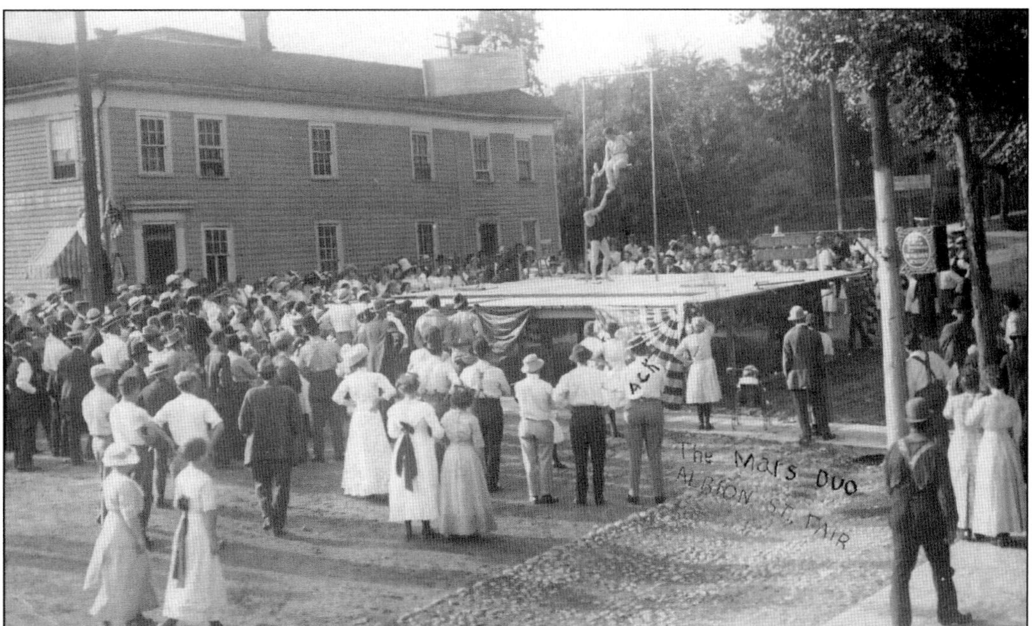

The Mars Duo, a male/female acrobat act, performs at the Albion Street Fair. The stage was set up between the Worden House Hotel and Dr. R.S. Malony's dentist office, blocking Orange Street just north of the courthouse. Since most people in town were busy attending the fair, it did not cause a major problem. (NCHS.)

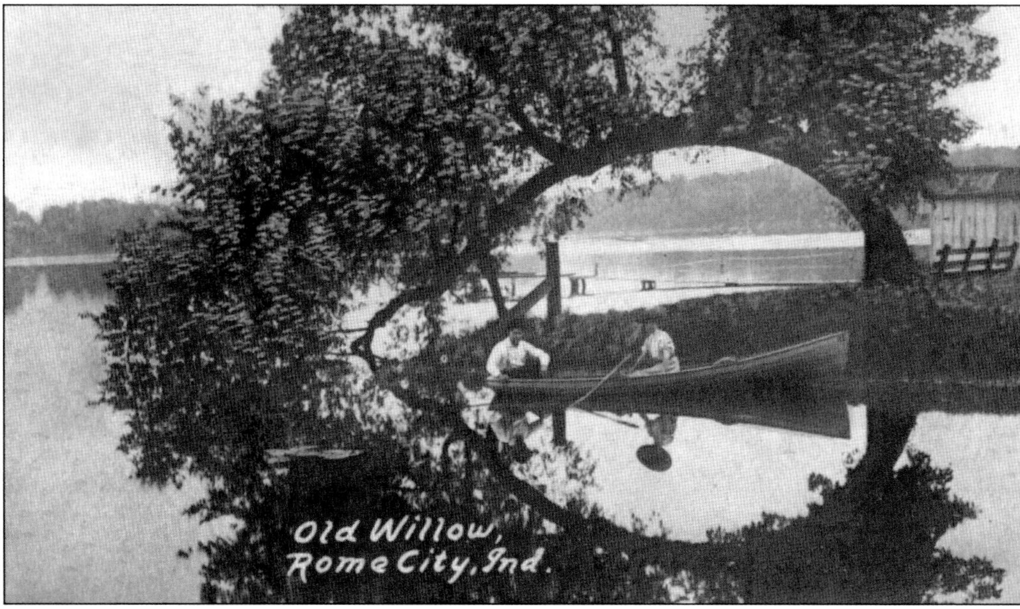

Boaters pause in 1910 under the "Old Willow," a memorable tree along the shores of Sylvan Lake near Rome City. The 669-acre lake still provides plentiful opportunity to be on the water. (Courtesy Mike Mapes.)

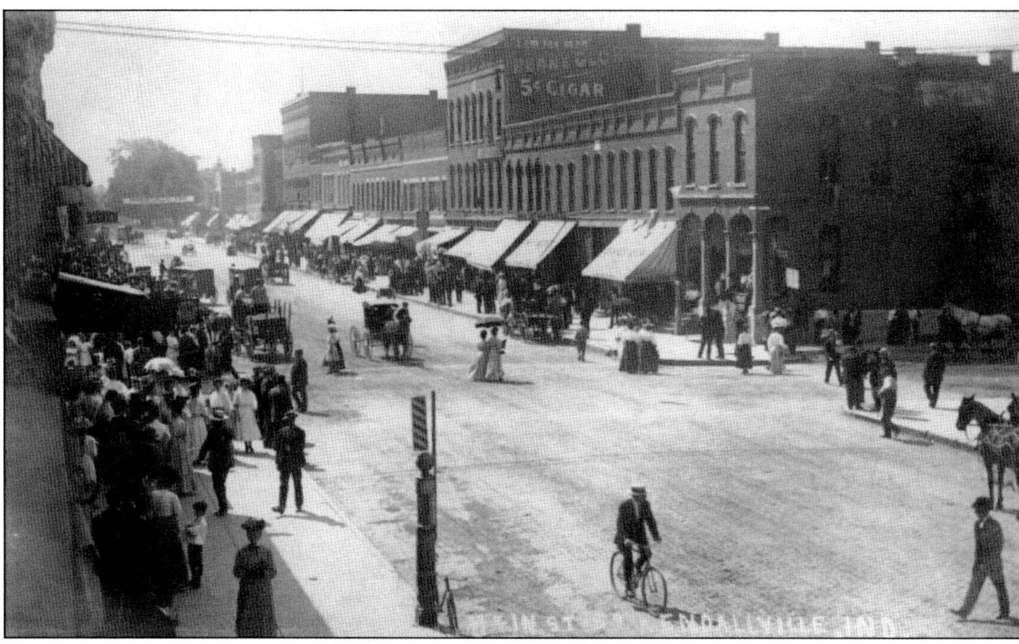

Downtown sidewalks are crowded during the Kendallville Fair. Festivals of the time were often held in the autumn, but in modern times they usually take place during summer, when students are out of school. (Courtesy Mike Mapes.)

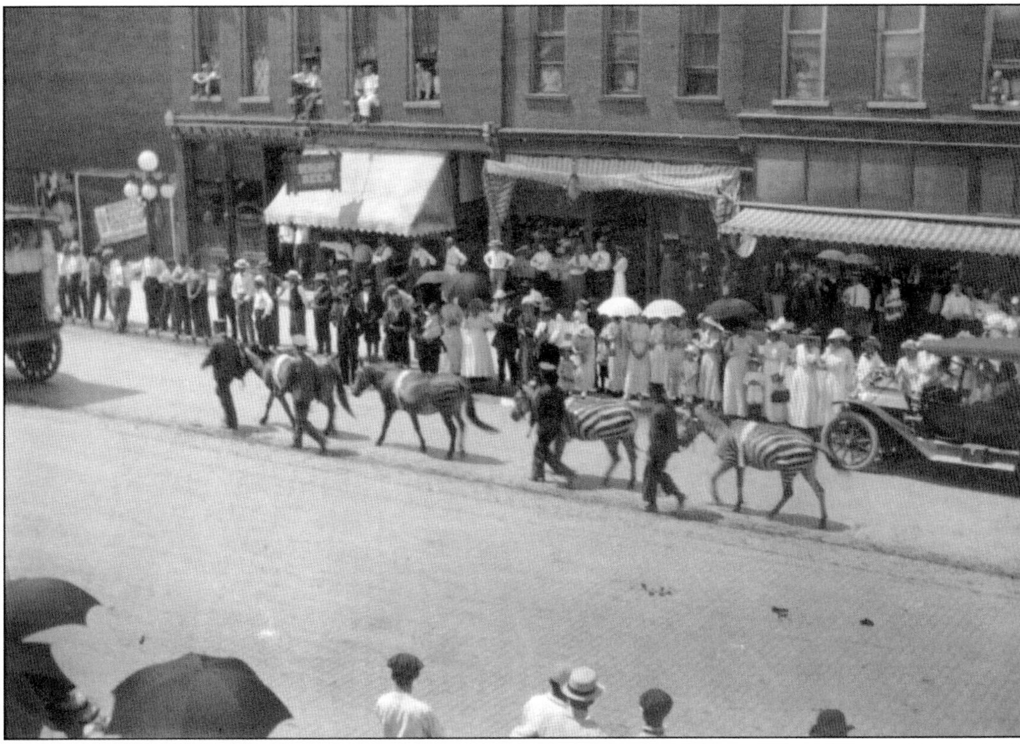

Two zebras—an unusual sight outside of zoos in Indiana—walk down Main Street during a Kendallville parade. In front of them is a zorse, a crossbred horse-zebra. (Courtesy Mike Mapes.)

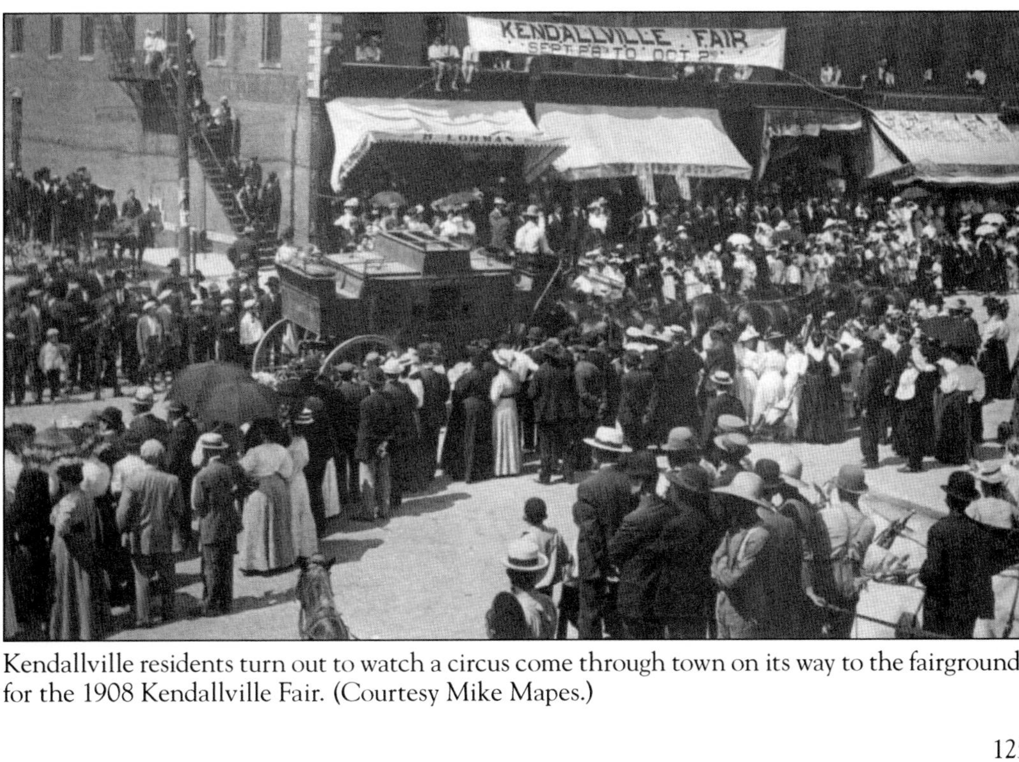

Kendallville residents turn out to watch a circus come through town on its way to the fairgrounds for the 1908 Kendallville Fair. (Courtesy Mike Mapes.)

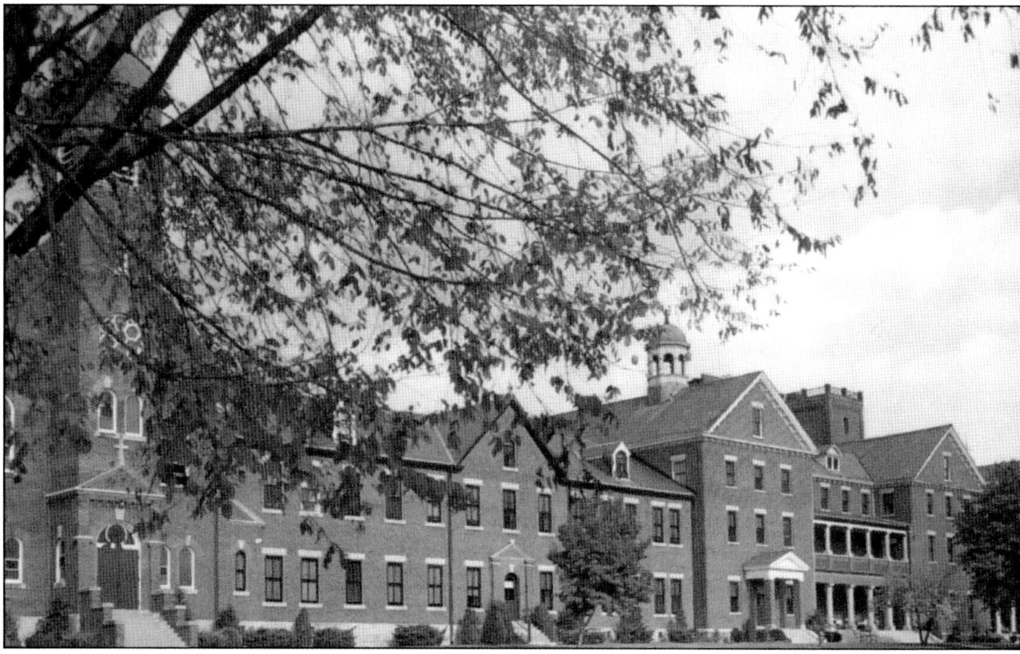

Originally called Kneipp Springs, or Kneipp Sanitarium, the site near Rome City was opened by the Precious Blood religious order of Dayton, Ohio, in 1901 as a place where people could be treated by the medicinal properties of the springwater. The order's sisters sold the property in 1976, and it was later owned by the Way religious organization. Now called Sylvan Springs, it has gone through several owners as local residents try to save it as an historical site. The main building has, among other things, a chapel and 40 individual rooms, and an underground passageway still leads to a running spring. There have been reports of spiritual experiences there, including visits by Mary, Mother of Jesus. (Both, courtesy Mike Mapes.)

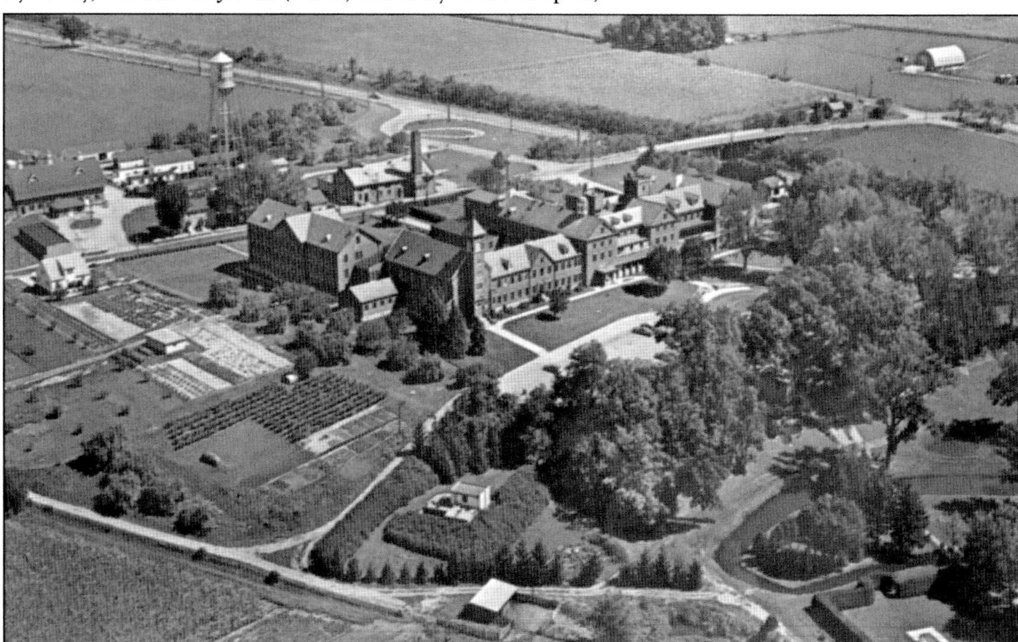

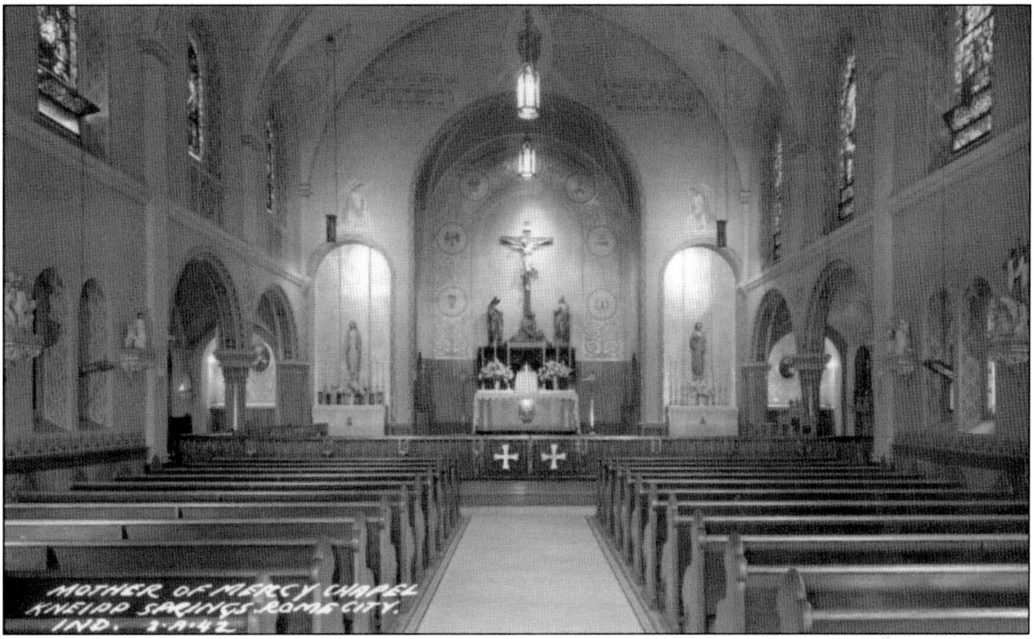

The stunning Mother of Mercy Chapel is seen inside Kneipp Springs' main building on the north side of Rome City, in 1942. A doorway in the basement of the building opened onto a tunnel, which led to an underground spring that reportedly had medicinal properties. (Courtesy Mike Mapes.)

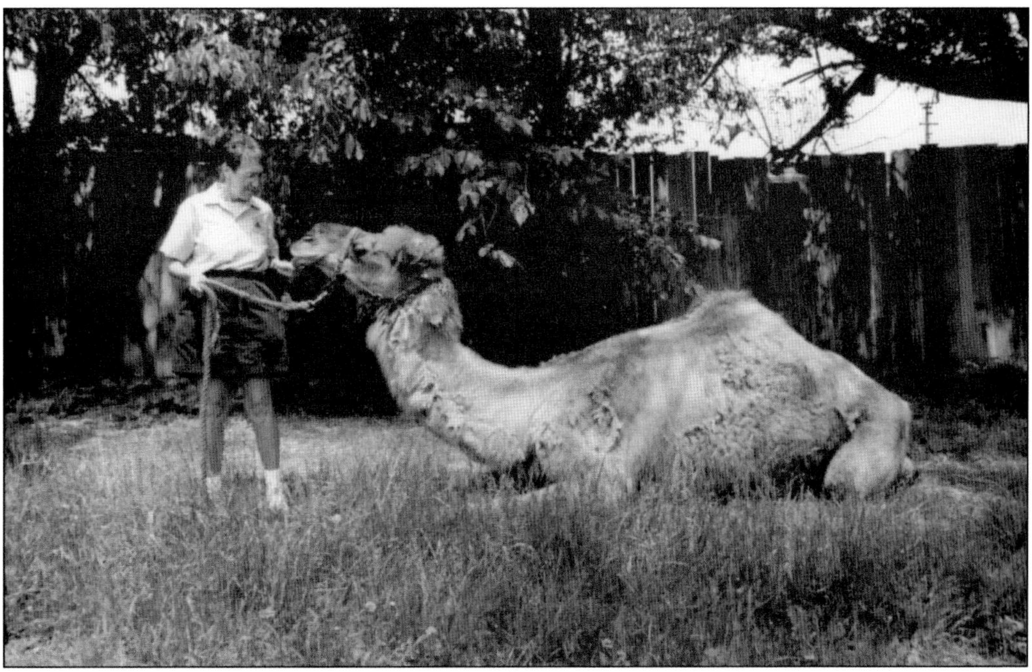

A camel poses in this 1980s photograph at the Black Pine Animal Sanctuary. From its humble origins at a home in Albion, the sanctuary moved to a more rural location just west of town, where it takes in unwanted animals from all across the country. Roughly 17,000 people come annually to visit big cats, bears, primates, reptiles, and other animals representing over 50 exotic and rare species. (Courtesy Lori Gagen.)